MONUMENTALITY IN ETRUSCAN AND EARLY ROMAN ARCHITECTURE

MONUMENTALITY IN ETRUSCAN AND EARLY ROMAN ARCHITECTURE

IDEOLOGY AND INNOVATION

Edited by Michael L. Thomas and Gretchen E. Meyers
Afterword by Ingrid E. M. Edlund-Berry

UNIVERSITY OF TEXAS PRESS AUSTIN

This book has been supported by an endowment dedicated to classics and the ancient world and funded by the Areté Foundation; the Gladys Krieble Delmas Foundation; the Dougherty Foundation; the James R. Dougherty, Jr. Foundation; the Rachael and Ben Vaughan Foundation; and the National Endowment for the Humanities.

First edition, 2012
First paperback edition, 2013

Requests for permission to reproduce material from this work should be sent to:
Permissions
University of Texas Press
P.O. Box 7819
Austin, TX 78713-7819
utpress.utexas.edu/index.php/rp-form

The paper used in this book meets the minimum requirements of ANSI/NISO Z39.48-1992 (R1997) (Permanence of Paper). ∞

Library of Congress Cataloging-in-Publication Data

Monumentality in Etruscan and early Roman architecture : ideology and innovation / edited by Michael L. Thomas and Gretchen E. Meyers.

    p   cm
    Includes bibliography and index.
    ISBN 978-0-292-75681-6
1. Architecture, Etruscan.   2. Architecture, Roman—Italy, Central.   I. Thomas, Michael L., 1966— editor of compilation.   II. Meyers, Gretchen E., 1970— author, editor of compilation.   III. Edlund-Berry, Ingrid E. M., author, honouree.
    NA300.M66 2012
    722'.7—dc23   2011048877

FOR INGRID

CONTENTS

PREFACE

ONE NEEDS ONLY TO DRIVE ITALY'S A1 *AUTOSTRADA* from Florence to Rome to experience an unrivaled combination of stunning landscape and historical place. The route takes one past ancient hill towns that have occupied the same perches for millennia. The approach to Orvieto affords one of the most stunning views of the trip. At one time an Etruscan temple occupied a conspicuous position at the edge of the town and was undoubtedly visible to those approaching from below. Today the massive Orvieto cathedral—most likely built on top of another Etruscan temple—dominates the skyline, its unmistakable silhouette punctuating the view from the A1.

As one enters Rome, especially when approaching the historical center, such scale is even more prevalent. Buildings such as the Flavian Amphitheater, Trajan's Forum, Hadrian's Temple of Venus and Rome, and the Basilica of Maxentius—to name just a few—make it clear that in imperial Rome scale, and the technical innovation required to construct such immense buildings, was a central theme in architectural design. These structures have left a mark on the city even today, and it would be hard to argue that scale was not part of their original message, a design component that added grandeur both to the patron and to Rome's cityscape. The modern viewer sees these buildings as monumental, but as my co-editor points out in the first essay of this book, there is no Latin equivalent of the word "monumental." Walking through the imperial city, ancient Romans experienced monumentality every day, even though they did not know it as such.

The concern with scale and architecture did not start in Rome; like so many other aspects of classical culture, monumental building design had its origins in the ancient Near East and in Egypt. Yet the monumentality that dominated the cityscape of imperial Rome was also very much indebted to an Italic tradition of large-scale architecture that can be traced back to the Etruscans. What factors drove the emergence of scale as a defining element of architecture in ancient Italy? At the most basic level, it seems that nearly all ancient societies—including those in Italy—utilized massive structures to create emphatic markers, markers that defined both place and patron. Often this architectural evolution toward monumentality is seen as a reflection of the changing social and political strategies of those who commissioned large-scale buildings, in most cases ruling elites. These factors, and their influence on the origins and development of Etruscan and Roman monumental architecture, are the focus of this volume.

The impetus for exploring this theme was the retirement of Ingrid Edlund-Berry, professor of classics at the University of Texas at Austin, whose career—monumental in itself—has spanned almost four decades. Gretchen Meyers and I organized a colloquium in her honor for the annual meeting of the Archaeological Institute of America in 2009. As both a professor and a mentor, Ingrid Edlund-Berry has played an integral role in our understanding of ancient Italy. A unifying theme of her work—whether it be the acroteria of Poggio Civitate, Etruscan and Republican Roman architectural mouldings, or sanctuaries in Etruria—has been the construction and message of monumental architecture. Thus the theme of monumentality made a fitting tribute. Through a variety of methodologies, six colloquium participants—Gretchen Meyers, Elizabeth Colantoni, Anthony Tuck, Nancy Winter, John Hopkins, and Penelope Davies—analyzed the ideological and technical aspects of architectural monumentality. Greg Warden, the colloquium's discussant, reassessed the themes of ideology and innovation, with particular attention to monumentality as a central characteristic in the architectural traditions of Etruria and Rome.

The overwhelming response to the colloquium led to the publication of this volume. This collection of papers makes a compelling case that within a wide chronological span, monumental architecture emerged in early Italy as a product of both technical innovation and adapted strategies for communicating power and ideology. Like the drive down the A1, the essays move through Etruria, Latium, and into Rome, the areas at the center of Ingrid Edlund-Berry's research. She offers her own reflections on monumentality in the afterword.

MICHAEL L. THOMAS

ACKNOWLEDGMENTS

THE EDITORS WISH TO BEGIN BY THANKING EACH OF the individual contributors to this volume, all of whom responded eagerly to our initial invitation to participate in an AIA colloquium on the topic of Etruscan and early Roman monumentality. It has been a privilege to work with such professional and enthusiastic colleagues. In addition we both owe a particular debt to Ingrid Edlund-Berry. We hope that this collection of insightful essays stands as a fitting tribute to such a dedicated mentor and scholar.

We have been very fortunate to work with Jim Burr at the University of Texas Press, who has been invaluable both in his support of the project and in his guidance in the publication process; we thank Leslie Tingle and Kerri Cox Sullivan for their editorial help. We are also grateful to Judith Chien and Kristen Scott for their assistance in the preparation of the final manuscript.

Finally, as always, we thank our colleagues and families for their encouragement.

NOTE ON ABBREVIATIONS

ALL ABBREVIATIONS OF MODERN JOURNALS AND books and ancient sources conform to the guidelines outlined in the *American Journal of Archaeology* 104 (2000), 10–24.

MONUMENTALITY IN ETRUSCAN AND EARLY ROMAN ARCHITECTURE

I INTRODUCTION
THE EXPERIENCE OF MONUMENTALITY IN ETRUSCAN AND EARLY ROMAN ARCHITECTURE

GRETCHEN E. MEYERS

> A monument is intended to call forth fear or wonder in the observer: to remind him of the antiquity of the dynasty, the power of the regime, the wealth of the community, the truth of its ideology, or of some event—a military victory or successful revolution—that demonstrated such wealth, power, or truth.
>
> —D. J. Olsen, *The City as a Work of Art*

EVERY SOCIETY BUILDS, AND MANY, IF NOT ALL, SOCIeties utilize architectural structures as markers to define place, patron, or experience. Often we identify these architectural markers as "monuments" or "monumental" buildings. Ancient Rome, in particular, is a society recognized for the monumentality of its buildings, with landmarks such as the Colosseum, the Pantheon, and the massive Imperial bath complexes still dominating the Eternal City's urban landscape. While few would deny that the term "monumental" is appropriate for ancient Roman architecture, the nature of this characterization is rarely considered very carefully. What is "monumental" about Roman architecture? Is it the size of the buildings? Or is it the splendor of the exterior materials? Does "monumentality" infer great expenditure of time and resources in construction? Must a monument be visible to many, or only to a few? The answers to such questions are often taken for granted in discussions of Roman architecture, and as a result the characterization of Roman architecture as "monumental" has become commonplace and somewhat diluted.

This volume reconsiders the technical and ideological components of monumental building in Etruscan and early Roman architecture. Imperial monumentality may be self-evident, but the early origins of ancient Roman monumentality are difficult to pinpoint. As with many aspects of Roman architecture, it is necessary to trace the lineage of monumental practice back through the earliest buildings in Rome to nearby Etruria. Since the first publication of Axel Böethius's work in 1970, scholars have recognized that Etruscan architecture and early Roman architecture are closely related.[1] Therefore, in order to study the emergence of monumentality as building practice in ancient Italy, one must begin in Etruria and the pre-Roman cultures of Italy. The papers of this volume focus on this crucial period before the zenith of Imperial Roman building and explore the emergence of monumentality as a product of evolving technical innovation and adapted strategies to communicate power and ideology. Much as architects do today, ancient Etruscans and Romans were able to distinguish the monumental from the ordinary through employment of the concepts of durability, visibility, and commemoration.

Monumentality in Etruscan Architecture

IT WOULD BE DIFFICULT TO ARGUE THAT A SINGLE type of building epitomizes the earliest monumental experience in ancient Italy. However, two types of structures from Etruria are often designated as "monumental" early on. The first are the monumental tumulus tombs dating to the Orientalizing period in Cerveteri,[2] and the second are the "monumental complexes," sometimes referred to as *palazzi*,[3] also originating in the Orientalizing period and in use during the Archaic period; this second architectural form does not appear to continue in central Italy beyond this time.

Although the remains of several central Italic buildings have been classified under this nomenclature,[4] the building type has largely been defined by two dominant examples: the Archaic Building at Poggio Civitate (Murlo) (fig. 1.1) and the building from the monumental area of Zone F at Acquarossa (fig. 1.2). These structures share a number of physical similarities visible in the archaeological record: first and foremost, a similar architectural form—a central courtyard bounded by

Fig. 1.1. Reconstruction of the Archaic Building complex at Poggio Civitate (Murlo) (courtesy A. Tuck).

Fig. 1.2. Reconstruction of the monumental area in Zone F at Acquarossa
(after Strandberg Olofsson 1994, fig. 26; courtesy M. Strandberg Olofsson).

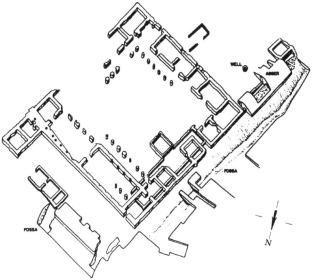

Fig. 1.3. Plan of the Archaic Building complex at Poggio Civitate (Murlo)
(original drawing by David Peck; courtesy A. Tuck).

at least two linear wings of accessible spaces; second, analogous building materials, i.e., stone foundations and tile roofs; third, their larger size in comparison to earlier building endeavors; and fourth, an elaborate decorative program of architectural terracottas. These characteristics are often used as evidence in the debate about the function and cultural significance of these buildings in Archaic Etruria; however, these are also the very factors that are used to assert their monumentality. In fact the entanglement of function and perceived monumental qualities is so dense that in English scholarship the buildings are often referred to generically as "monumental buildings" or "monumental complexes."[5]

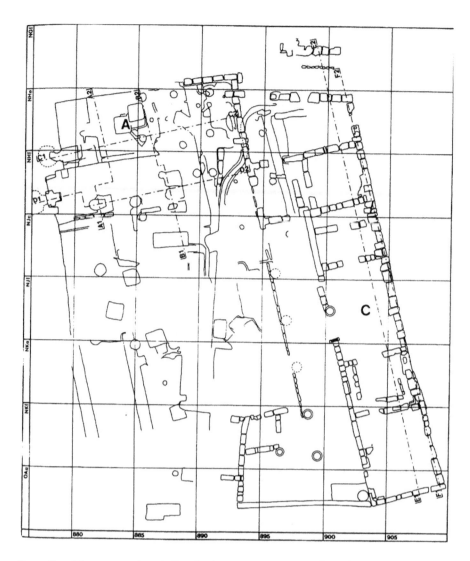

Fig. 1.4. Plan of the monumental area in Zone F at Acquarossa, orientation north–south (after Strandberg Olofsson 1989, fig. 3; courtesy M. Strandberg Olofsson).

Perhaps the most obvious way that the Etruscan *palazzi* stand out as "monumental" to modern scholars is through their size and durable materials. For example, in describing the foundations of the Archaic structure at Poggio Civitate (Murlo) (fig. 1.3), the original excavator of the site said simply, "One was immediately struck by the monumentality of the building."[6] Indeed, the Archaic Building at Murlo was remarkable for its size in the sixth century BCE, approximately 60.0 × 61.85 m. While a great deal of the enclosed area is taken up by an open-air courtyard, the four flanking wings are composed of substantial stone foundations supporting earthen walls and heavy terracotta roofs.

Although smaller in overall size than its often-cited counterpart at Murlo, Acquarossa's monumental area in Zone F (fig. 1.4) is significantly larger and more complex than surrounding contemporary buildings on the Acquarossa plateau, where small domestic structures of one or two rooms dominate. The monumental complex at Acquarossa actually comprises two main buildings arranged around a courtyard: Building A, approximately 10 m in length, and Building C, approximately 25 m in length. Other smaller structures also surround the courtyard space, although the courtyard is not completely enclosed. While formal aspects of their plans distinguish the structures at Murlo and Acquarossa from one another, much of what might be termed "monumental" remains the same: comparative size, stone foundations, and substantial terracotta roofing elements.

The large, extensive plans, utilizing stone and terracotta as support and cover, of the Archaic structure at Murlo and the monumental complex at Acquarossa differed greatly from previous constructions in Iron Age Italy, such as large huts, which did not possess lower and upper elements of such durability. In addition, the size and sturdy building materials allowed for the placement of many rich and varied terracotta decorations on the buildings' roofs. Although there is evidence for some terracotta adornment on smaller buildings in Etruria prior to these, as well as on a number of contemporary religious structures,[7] the decorative programs at Poggio Civitate and Acquarossa are remarkable in their scale, richness, and iconography. This is partly due to the enhanced size and durability of the structures themselves. For example, a foundation less substantial than the one for the massive courtyard building at Poggio Civitate would not have been able to support the vast collection of acroterial sculptures in the form of mythological creatures and seated and standing human figures, four types of frieze plaques, antefixes, and decorative simas that adorned the building and enhanced its visibility from both near and far vantage points.[8] At Acquarossa, the decorative program is somewhat less varied, but equally complex in its imagery. It includes a series of frieze plaques depicting common Etruscan visual motifs such as banqueters, dancers, and mythological creatures and characters, including Herakles.[9] These eye-catching features suggest that the visibility and readability of the *palazzi* were not an accident of monumental building practices, but an important component of monumental design itself. Clearly the *palazzi* were intended to reach beyond a small, exclusive audience of patrons, and to communicate more widely within Etruscan culture—a second characteristic that is often associated with monumental architecture.

Without a doubt, the archaeological evidence at Poggio Civitate (Murlo) and Acquarossa discussed here confirms the monumentality of the so-called Archaic Etruscan *palazzi*, which were clearly built in a manner that distinguishes them from other previous and contemporary Etruscan architectural forms. However, for many scholars their monumentality does not end there: the structures possess an ideological component as well, which might be termed "commemoration." For example, when Vedia Izzet writes about "the so-called 'monumental' complex at Acquarossa, or the elaborate courtyard building at Murlo," she notes that their very existence embodies "the increase in wealth and power" of the first half of the sixth century BCE.[10] In fact, much of the debate on the function and usage of the structures swirls around the issue of what political entity or elite individual the elaborate structures were intended to commemorate or serve, an argument that is not engaged in with regard to contemporary "non-monumental" Etruscan structures. In some cases the *palazzi* have been interpreted as elite residences; in others they are considered seats of political authority or assembly.[11] At the very least, both the Archaic complex at Murlo and the monumental area at Acquarossa were preceded by smaller constructions on the same sites, and one could thus assume that their architectural form is simply the result of evolving technical innovation.[12] However, for most the connotation of the buildings' monumentality is more than just bricks, mortar, and terracotta. Scholars generally agree that the complicated iconography of the architectural terracottas and the substantial commitment to building materials and size suggest that the Etruscan *palazzi* were intended to commemorate some source of power or influence. This third feature is less tangible in the archaeological record, but we have nevertheless come to associate it with monumental architecture.

This brief discussion of Archaic Etruscan monumental complexes exposes the tenuous nature of our actual understanding of monumentality in its earliest phases in ancient Italy. Despite a nebulous characterization of the monumental qualities of the complexes at Poggio Civitate and Acquarossa that ranges widely from scale to commemorative ideology, no one disagrees with the assertion that these structures are in fact "monumental" with respect to other buildings, particularly when they are compared with those constructed prior to this period. However, with no written sources to support an Etruscan conception of "monumentality" (if such a concept even existed), discussion of monumentality in the Etruscan archaeological record has been unavoidably merged with contemporary views of monumental architecture.

Despite the ubiquitous occurrence of the term "monumentality" and the phrase "monumental architecture" in modern archaeological and architectural literature, the establishment of a single definition of the term "monumentality" is actually much more complicated than it first appears. A close look at the term's origin and the history of its usage demonstrates that the meaning and the cultural associations of the term are far from universal; the very notion of "monumentality" is best seen as a social construct, unique and inseparable from the culture that creates, views, and experiences it.

Defining Monumentality

NEITHER THE ABSTRACT NOUN "MONUMENTALITY" nor the adjective "monumental" appears until the early modern era. According to the *Oxford English Dictionary*, the first occurrence of "monumental" dates to 1596 and the more conceptual term "monumentality" appears even later, in 1884.[13] In both these early instances the terms are descriptive of the qualities of a physical monument or memorial. The English word "monument," which appears ca. 1325, has a more distinct association with memory, and its earliest usage refers to a tomb or sepulcher.[14]

These early English references are consistent with the word's etymological origin—the Latin word *monumentum*. Itself a somewhat complicated term, *monumentum* first and foremost denotes an inherently commemorative object,[15] as illustrated by an early appearance in Latin literature in Plautus's comedy *Curculio*. In this play, Phaedromos, a comically lovesick adolescent, pleads with the female slave of a pimp to release his beloved, who happens to be a prostitute: *Tibine ego, si fidem servas mecum, vineam pro aurea statua statuam, quae tuo gutturi sit monumentum* ("You keep your word and I'll put you up a statue of vines instead of gold to commemorate your gullet") (Pl. *Cur.* 139–140).[16] Here comedic parody—a memorial made out of something as ephemeral as grapevines, honoring a female slave of a pimp—exposes the more typical associations of the term. The audience surely knows that a true *monumentum* is an austere marker, in some cases a statue, which is erected in honor of an individual of high status, probably a male, and would be more realistically constructed out of durable, even costly materials.[17] As is typical in comedy, much of the joke revolves around social status: in this case, the female slave's lack of it and her inherent undeservedness of a *monumentum* because of both her sex and her social position. It is possible to infer from this instance that to a Republican Roman audience the *monumentum*'s ideological significance is just as important as its appearance. A closer look at the term in pre-Imperial Latin literature demonstrates other meanings, and enhances our understanding of the Roman conception of the ancient *monumentum*.

Monumentum

THE NOUN *MONUMENTUM* (OR *MONIMENTUM*) DErives from the verb *moneo*, "to bring to the notice of, remind, warn."[18] Its etymological root emphasizes that the monument's primary function is to evoke a particular response through the viewer's memory. In this way the *monumentum* is interactive and we can assume that, as memories are not universal, a *monumentum* may evoke different responses for different individuals throughout time. Therefore the very nature of a *monumentum* allows for a broad range of interpretative possibilities. In one sense, the ancient *monumentum* is an object or structure with physical qualities. It can be a statue, a trophy, a building, etc. One of the term's most common meanings in Latin literature and inscriptions is "tomb,"[19] a monument that is generally intended to call to mind an individual, rather than an event or a communal group. A statue or trophy might function similarly in recalling an individual, but also could easily focus that recollection on an individual's actions or successes. In this way, *monumenta* may also recall events.

One might expect to find copious references to grand *monumenta* throughout the architectural treatise of Vitruvius. *De Architectura* was written in the early years of the Augustan principate, and it is the only surviving architectural treatise from ancient Rome. It was composed with the intention of aiding Augustus in building "public and private buildings, that will correspond to the grandeur of our history and will be a memorial to future ages" (1.pr.3)[20]—a goal surely consistent with our modern sense of "monumentality." In actuality, however, Vitruvius uses the term in only three of his ten books: in book 2 with reference to stone as a material for statues or tombs (2.7.4 and 2.8.3); in book 4 in a passage detailing Callimachus's establishment of the symmetrical proportions of the Corinthian column, derived from his imitation in stone of an acanthus root growing on top of a young girl's grave (4.1.9–10); and in book 8 to describe the placement of Euripides' stone tomb at the convergence of two streams in Macedonia (8.3.16). In general the word is used specifically for memorials for the dead, while the first passage also includes sculptures, which may have been part of funerary structures or sarcophagi.[21] Thus, these associations are much closer to the example in Plautus cited above than to modern notions of massive, imposing buildings. Noteworthy in these passages is the association of the term specifically with stone. One might suggest that for Vitruvius "monumentality" is the opposite of "ephemerality"; it encompasses something sturdy, long lasting, and durable.

A second well-documented example from the years of the late Republic and early Principate similarly emphasizes the durability of *monumenta*; however, in this case it is not stone that promotes such endurance. In the preface to his written history of Rome, *Ab Urbe Condita*, Livy uses the term twice: *Quae ante conditam condendamve urbem poeticis magis decora fabulis quam incorruptis rerum gestarum monumentis traduntur, ea nec adfirmare nec refellere in animo est* ("Such traditions as belong to the time before the city was founded, or rather was presently to be founded, and are rather adorned with poetic legends than based upon trustworthy historical proofs, I propose neither to affirm nor to refute") (pr.6);[22] and *Hoc illud est praecipue in cognitione rerum salubre ac frugiferum, omnis te exempli documenta in inlustri posita monumento intueri* ("What chiefly makes the study of history wholesome and profitable is this, that you behold the lessons of every kind of experience set forth as on a conspicuous monument") (pr.10).[23]

Scholarship on the significance of the term *monumentum* in Livy and in reference to the annalistic tradition in general is vast.[24] Livy was not the first or the last to intimate that his written work functions as an eternal *monumentum*; nor is this sort of written monumentality limited to history, as Horace's famous line describing his poetry—"a monument more lasting than bronze" (*Carm.* 3.30)—attests. Of interest here is the fact that the qualities Livy ascribes to the written monument are similar to those we have already seen attributed to physical *monumenta*. In the first instance, where Livy contrasts the fanciful legends of poets with the *incorruptis rerum gestarum monumentis*, the modifier *incorruptis* alludes to the security and permanence of historical monuments. Such histories (as Livy no doubt considers his own) are literally long lasting in their imperishability. In the second instance, it is the visual quality of the monument that receives the focus. As noted by Feldherr in reference to this passage, "the process of seeing [is] fundamental to the beneficial effects [Livy's] narrative will exert upon his readers."[25] The *inlustre monumentum* compels the viewer/reader, who, through its clarity, cannot help but witness and follow the exempla laid out within. Ultimately, as Mary Jaeger has pointed out, *monumenta* for Livy are experiential, relying on the monuments' "spatial, visual, and mnemonic" qualities to direct viewer/reader response.[26]

At this point it is interesting to consider the possibility that over time a *monumentum* might trigger a range of memories and associations—even incorrect ones.[27] An appropriate case study could be the Lapis Niger in the Forum Romanum. Although no literary reference specifically calls the black stone in the pavement in front of the Curia Iulia a *monumentum*, it appears to have functioned as one. Archaeological excavations in 1899, which uncovered an assemblage of Archaic material beneath the Lapis Niger—including an altar, an inscribed stele, and an assortment of votive bronzes, terracotta revetments, and pottery—indicated that the stone was intended to mark a location associated with some ancient event or ritual. Festus (184L) refers to the Lapis Niger as a *locus funestus* of Romulus, a term that could easily refer to a place of his death or his burial. Nonetheless, without inscriptional evidence it is impossible to know how Romans, decades or even centuries later, would have responded to the stone. They may or may not have "recalled" what event or individual the stone marked. In fact, it has been suggested that at the time of the burial of these Archaic monuments few if any Romans would have understood what the monuments themselves commemorated.[28] This example is instructive as a demonstration of the potential flexibility and limits of the Roman mind in respect to the memories evoked by a particular place or monument. One must be cautious in assuming that only one particular and finite meaning for an ancient *monumentum* is recoverable.

A final example, from a letter of Cicero dated to 54 BCE, demonstrates this uncertainty. In this letter, Cicero writes to Atticus about his role in financing a *monumentum*, believed by scholars to refer to Julius Caesar's Forum Iulium: *Itaque Caesaris amici (me dico et Oppium, dirumparis licet) in monumentum illud quod tu tollere laudibus solebas, ut forum laxeremus et usque ad atrium Libertatis explicare-*

mus, contempsimus sescenties HS *cum privatis non poterat transigi minore pecunia. Efficiemus rem gloriosissimam* ("So Caesar's friends (I mean Oppius and myself, choke on that if you must) have thought nothing of spending sixty million sesterces on the work which you used to be so enthusiastic about, to widen the Forum and extend it as far as the Hall of Liberty. We couldn't settle with the private owners for a smaller sum. We shall achieve something really glorious") (*Att.* 4.16.8).[29] We now know that this *monumentum* ultimately became the Forum Iulium (fig. 1.5). However, what Cicero actually meant by the term "*monumentum*" here is debatable; it is particularly unclear whether Cicero, Atticus, or even Caesar conceived of that space in 54 BCE as an imperial forum in the sense we now know it, and whether "*monumentum*" would have been an appropriate term for such a space at that time. Some translators have taken the term generically and translated it as "public work."[30] However, James Anderson argues, on the basis of Cicero's standard usage of the term, that in his writings "*monumentum*" is usually more concrete and that "Cicero would have been unlikely to use it in reference to a vague commission from Caesar."[31] Anderson further suggests that the terms "*laxeremus*," which stresses the act of extending or widening, and "*explicaremus*," which Cicero often uses to express disentanglement of complex issues, demonstrate that Cicero was conceptualizing Caesar's plans at this time as an extension of the Forum Romanum in order to relieve spatial pressures, not necessarily envisioning the creation of the Forum Iulium as a separate forum.[32] He concludes that the *monumentum* under discussion here must be simply the space for expanding the Forum Romanum, rather than an actual structure.

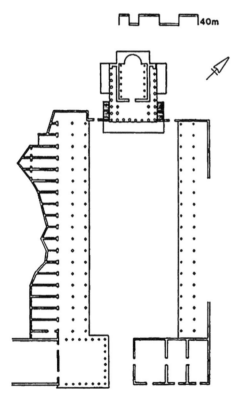

Discussion of this passage has focused principally on how much of the later Forum Iulium was conceived by Caesar or Cicero at the time of the letter, and less on the passage's role in interpreting the perception of monumentality by ancient Romans. Cicero's letter is in fact quite instructive in this respect. A closer look reveals that Cicero uses the term *monumentum* two additional times in the very same paragraph of this letter to Atticus: once immediately prior to the cited passage and again two sentences afterward. In these additional sentences Cicero discusses two other *monumenta* under construction that are more securely identified, and these references can be used to clarify his understanding of the term. The

Fig. 1.5. Plan of the Forum Iulium (after Ulrich 1993, fig. 9; original drawing by Roger B. Ulrich; courtesy R. B. Ulrich).

first is Paullus's basilica in the Forum Romanum: *Paulus in medio foro basilicam iam paene texerat isdem antiquis columnis, illam autem quam locavit facit magnificentissimam. Quid quaeris? Nihil gratius illo monumento, nihil gloriosius* ("Paullus has now almost roofed his basilica in the middle of the Forum, using the original antique pillars. The other one, which he gave out on contract, he is constructing in magnificent style. It is indeed a most admired and glorious edifice") (*Att.* 4.16.8).[33] Here the emphasis on the term "*monumentum*" rests on the sense of permanence supplied through the reused columns from the original Basilica Fulvia (one might think of them as Livy's *incorrupta monumenta*), compared with the superlative visual qualities of L. Aemilius Paullus's new additions.[34] The use of the adjective *magnificentissimam* here emphasizes the luxury and expense of these new elements of Paulus's building and looks forward to the *rem gloriosissimam* in Cicero's following remarks on the project that will become the future Forum Iulium. Clearly, building materials combining permanence and excessive display bring *gloria* to the monument's patron.

The third *monumentum* of the paragraph is the Saepta Iulia in the Campus Martius: *iam in campo Martio saepta tributis comitiis marmorea sumus et tecta facturi eaque cingemus excelsa porticu, ut mille passuum conficiatur. simul adiungetur huic operi villa etiam publica. dices "quid mihi hoc monumentum proderit?"* ("As for the Campus Martius, we are going to build covered marble booths for the Assembly of Tribes to surround them with a high colonnade, a mile of it in all. At the same time the Villa Publica will be attached to our building. You'll say, 'What good will such a structure be to me?'") (*Att.* 4.16.8).[35] Again the monument is associated with durability and expense through Cicero's reference to marble and roofing. The echo of the earlier verb *texerat* in the term "*tecta*" and the evocation of the Basilica Paulli's columns with the visual image of Saepta's mile-long portico are powerful indications of what links all three of the structures described in this letter as being "monumental." It is not size or grandiosity alone, as our modern sensibilities dictate, but rather an intriguing combination of commemoration, durability, and visual spectacle.

In all three cases the display of expenditure—in terms of either size or materials, or both—plays a central role, emphasizing a particular communicative role for a *monumentum* within the competitive, aristocratic culture of Cicero's Rome. Moreover, this passage clearly demonstrates a twist in the interpretation of the physicality of a *monumentum*. The monument need not be a specific structure— like a building, statue, or trophy—but may in fact be simply a space, as long as it is bounded and confined, as in the case of Caesar's commemorative extension of the Forum Romanum.

Together the above examples serve to establish a multivalent definition of "*monumentum*" in pre-imperial Rome, consistent in principles, if not specific details, with the nuanced characterization of the monumental complexes of Etruria. This definition recognizes the physical quality of monumental space, while also capturing a monument's communicative potential. The passages I have discussed demonstrate that by the end of the Republic many shades of meaning pertained to "monumentality," despite the lack of a specific term to describe the phenomenon. Among this variation, however, certain elements of the monumental experience dominate: commemoration, visibility, and the monument's perceived durability. Over time these experiences were destined to change, as imperial monuments in Rome and beyond became more expansive, more ornate, and more long lasting.[36] Eventually, by the late antique period, scale would become an identifying characteristic of the architecture of the Roman cityscape.[37] As the generational experience of monumentality changed to encompass each new extraordinary innovation, so did the specific associations with the term "*monumentum*." However, throughout time, the same qualities of commemoration, visibility, and durability continued to characterize the experience of monumentality.

Monumentalité

EDMUND THOMAS ASSERTS THAT THE ABSTRACT CONcept of the "monumentalization" of ancient buildings was first addressed in academic terms at a conference in 1987, when Paul Zanker defined it as "adornment with buildings and memorials intended for show."[38] While still grounded in the original sense of the term as a memorial, Zanker's statement also moves closer to the primary modern sense of architectural "monumentality," which is used to denote buildings that are grand and showy. In today's parlance, the commemorative function of a monumental building is more of an option than a necessity.

In truth the erosion of the original meaning of *monumentum* and the creation of the term "monumentality" to include generic qualities of size and ostentation began a few centuries ago. Many scholars have written about the origins of the abstract noun "monumentality," and in large part they agree that the term's genesis is connected to the late eighteenth- and early nineteenth-century interest in the ruins of ancient monuments.[39] Enlightenment debate about the relationship between ancient models and modern innovation, particularly in France and England, was fueled by a burgeoning link between archaeological exploration and tourism and architectural theory.[40] As European writers, architects, and tourists viewed the remnants of ancient Greek, Roman, and Egyptian architectural creations, they originated the modern sense of the term "monumentality" to signify the qualities that these long-standing, distinctive buildings possessed.

The French architectural historian Françoise Choay documents the linguistic shift from the original memorial-based meaning of "monument" in French dictionaries of the later seventeenth century.[41] The 1690 edition of Antoine Furetière's *Dictionnaire universel* described a "monument" as a "witness of some great power or grandeur of past centuries," and cites "the pyramids of Egypt and the Coliseum" as "beaux monuments de la grandeur."[42] This emphasis on architectural effect and quality, rather than function, led first to the adjective "monumental" and eventually to the noun "monumentality," first attested as *monumentalité* in 1845.[43] Thus, the "monumentality" of modern parlance does indeed owe much to ancient monuments, although this debt is less etymological than experiential.

Piranesi's eighteenth-century prints of decaying ancient structures, overgrown and deteriorating through the passage of time, epitomize the emotional power of these ancient monuments, which affect one through their longevity rather than through their universal architectural form.[44] In capturing their perceptions of the grandeur, size, and durability of ancient *monumenta*, eighteenth- and nineteenth-century architects and architectural theorists created the modern sense of "monumentality." "Monument" and "monumentality" essentially separate into two distinct ideas: the "monument"—more closely related to the original sense of *monumentum*—signifying a marker of the past;[45] and "monumentality" encompassing the wide range of qualities and characteristics such monuments possess.

Since the nineteenth century, monumentality has remained a topic of discussion and debate among architectural historians, anthropologists, and archaeologists. Many architects and architectural historians have grappled with issues of the architect's role in creating "monumentality" in modern architecture, the urban versus residential character of monumental buildings, and the universality of monumental experience in architecture.[46] A crisis point for modern European architects occurred after World War II, as they sought appropriate expression for the melancholy relationship of war trauma and history. Essentially as a backlash from perceived deficiencies in the International Style, architects created a "new monumentality" through the utilization of large, powerful, and emotive architectural elements, albeit without explicit reference to historical forms.[47] Ultimately, this "new monumentality" returned to ancient influences, particularly through the work of Louis Kahn, who, as a fellow at the American Academy in Rome in the 1920s, had traveled in Italy, Greece, and Egypt. Kahn's name is associated with monumentality as a result of his attention to the archaic and because of the "massive grandeur" of his creations.[48] For example, his National Assembly Building in Dacca, in present-day Bangladesh, blends a heavy concrete exterior in the shape of a citadel with wide openings throughout the interior that allow ventilation and light to burst through, creating an architectural effect not unlike the views of decaying ancient buildings in Piranesi's prints: a solid durable exterior seems able to endure for centuries, while interior space dissolves, as if eroded by time.

For archaeologists, the most influential discussions of monumentality have focused on the relationship between monumental building and the ideology of power. This relationship is at the core of an influential explanation of monumentality put forth by Bruce Trigger in 1990.[49] Trigger views monumental architecture as a universal aspect of all complex societies. He writes, "[Monumental architecture's] principal defining feature is that its scale and elaboration exceed the requirements of any practical functions that a building is intended to perform."[50] Trigger goes on to argue, however, that monumentality is not simply a feature of architecture, but rather can be useful to the archaeologist as evidence of political power embodied in the building's usage of energy. Because those in power control expenditure of energy, a monumental building epitomizes the social priorities of those who are able to marshal the time, expense, material, and labor to construct it. Trigger's view ultimately connects monumentality to power through the architectural process rather than the architectural product.

Archaeologist Jerry Moore contributes another dimension, enhancing Trigger's definition with his own: "Monuments are structures designed to be recognized, expressed by their scale or elaboration, even though their meanings may not be understood by all members of society."[51] Moore's argument is that a structure's monumentality is directly related to its visibility, both from a distance and within the structure itself. While it may have required the same amount of energy to build two distinct structures, a society's social patterns and power relationships (social, political, and ritual) become apparent when the abilities of individual monuments to control communication between patron and visitor are compared.

Later views such as these are helpful in demonstrating the complexity and continually shifting nature of a society's experience of what is monumental. Certain elements remain consistent throughout the history of the term. For example, Trigger's theoretical construct is rooted in the materiality of monumental structures, while Moore's is founded upon visual access and effect. In both cases these elements are interpreted as expressions of social power. However, it is important to remember that the generational experience of monumentality is constantly changing. We must be careful not to impose "new" monumentality on structures of the past. Rather, in investigating ancient monumental architecture, we would be wise to direct strict attention toward understanding the consistent experiential qualities of monumentality—durability, visibility, and commemoration—within the structures' original social contexts.

Conclusions and Contributions

THE EXAMPLES PRESENTED IN THIS ESSAY MAKE THE case that monumentality is best understood as an experience dictated by perspective. The Etruscan *palazzi* can be considered monumental because they made use of durability, visibility, and commemoration in a way that redefined the experience of architecture at the time. As with the Forum Iulium, social complexity demanded an unusual space for communal experience. At such moments of innovation, the ideology of monumental architecture emerges—not as a universal ideology of social power, but in a message specific to each occurrence. We need not assume that the message of the Forum Iulium is the same as the message of the *palazzi* because they are both monumental; the similarity lies instead in the means through which architecture communicates its message. Caesar's Forum signaled a change in the Republican Roman monumental experience. It looked forward to the Imperial monumentality that ultimately impressed European architects on the Grand Tour. But at the same time it looked back to the architectural traditions of Etruscan and early Roman architecture. The contributions to this volume do the same.

The essays that follow serve as a compendium of the multiplicity of monumental experiences in ancient Etruscan and early Roman architecture. While each author focuses his or her argument on a specific building or architectural perspective, their essays considered together highlight ancient monumental architecture's reliance on durability, visibility, and commemoration. Although arranged chronologically rather than according to these themes, pairs of papers are particularly relevant to each of these categories.

Monumentality as an expression of durability and the exploitation of building materials is at the center of the arguments of Colantoni and Davies. In "Straw to Stone, Huts to Houses: Transitions in Building Practices and Society in Protohistoric Latium," Elizabeth Colantoni uses ethnographic data to explore the movement from small, ephemeral huts to larger, more sturdy houses in the seventh and sixth centuries BCE. She argues that this change in size and material is as much the result of technical innovation as of societal structure and strengthened political authority. Penelope Davies, discussing architecture that appeared several centuries later in "On the Introduction of Stone Entablatures in Republican Temples in Rome," similarly confronts monumentality in terms of evolving building materials—this time, the replacement of wooden temple entablatures with entablatures of stone on Roman temples. By examining this phenomenon not simply as a product of the increased availability of building materials, but also from the ideological perspective of Rome's political climate, Davies argues that this architectural development belongs to an earlier period than previously thought, namely, to the beginning of the third century BCE.

Visual cues and their role in enhancing the visibility of monumental architecture are discussed in the papers of Winter and Hopkins. Nancy Winter turns her attention to the distinctive Etruscan round moulding—an easily recognizable feature in Etruscan temple architecture. In "Monumentalization of the Etruscan Round Moulding in Sixth-Century BCE Central Italy," she documents the occurrence of this visual marker of transitions in architectural terracottas in central Italy, based on its similar role in temple architecture. She further demonstrates that after the monumental construction of the Temple of Jupiter Optimus Maximus in Rome, a corresponding monumentalization of the Etruscan round moulding occurred on architectural terracottas. The impact of the Capitoline temple and its features on the perception of monumentality in the Republican Roman world is the subject of John Hopkins's essay, "The Capitoline Temple and the Effects of Monumentality on Roman Temple Design." Through an extensive survey of Republican Roman temples, Hopkins demonstrates that the Capitoline temple became a paradigm for the concept of monumentality in later temple architecture. He argues that the implementation of certain of its visual features, such as colonnades, deep foundations, and architectural decoration, allowed even smaller buildings to claim monumental status through their association with the definitive monumental temple on Rome's Capitoline Hill.

Finally, the papers of Tuck and Warden consider monumentality broadly, in terms of not only the physical qualities of monumental architecture, but also the commemorative and performative aspects that are at the core of the original *monumentum*'s role as a reminder of burial and death ritual. Anthony Tuck's "The Performance of Death: Monumentality, Burial Practice, and Community Identity in Central Italy's Urbanizing Period" looks at changing communal identity in Etruscan burial practices. By examining the evolution of the Etruscan funerary marker (*monumentum*?) from small, individual forms to opulent monumental tombs of the seventh–sixth centuries BCE, Tuck documents the role of monumental architecture in reflecting social ideology and cultural priorities. Shifting attention to religious architecture, Gregory Warden considers the mingled relationship between monumental architecture and culture in physical terms in "Monumental Embodiment: Somatic Symbolism and the Tuscan Temple." In his discussion of the metaphorical "burial" of a monumental temple from the Etruscan site of Poggio Colla, Warden connects the rituals of death to architecture itself, challenging further our conception of ancient monumentality and our own limited ability to perceive its parameters in ancient Italy.

Notes

I owe an immeasurable debt of gratitude to Ingrid Edlund-Berry, who introduced me to the monumental architecture of the Etruscans and has continued to encourage me to pursue my scholarship in this area. I also wish to thank my colleagues, Alexis Castor and Kostis Kourellis, for their comments on early drafts of this essay; as well as Ily Nagy and the anonymous reader for suggestions.

1. Böethius 1978.
2. Riva 2010, 108–140, and Tuck (essay 3) in this volume.
3. I use the term "*palazzo*" here in the general Italian sense of a large edifice, not necessarily

a palace. A *palazzo* is usually residential in character, serving as home to a ruling family or aristocrat, but it can also be public, as in the *palazzo comunale* or *palazzo pubblico*, which serves as a municipal or civic administrative center.

4. For example, the catalog of the 1985 exhibition, *Case e palazzi d'Etruria* (Stopponi 1985) includes a number of other examples.

5. For example, Haynes (2000, 118): "[At Poggio Civitate] the new residence, or Upper Building, is perhaps better referred to as the Archaic Building Complex. . . . On the leveled site after the fire, the complex formed a monumental square." Or Barker and Rasmussen (1998, 161), about Acquarossa: "In the northwestern part of the hill, a road some 7 m wide brought the visitor up from the valley into a public space demarcated by two monumental buildings at right-angles to one another, each consisting of a series of rooms fronted by a portico." Or more generally, Barker and Rasmussen (1998, 153): "There were probably public spaces at the centre of the [Etruscan] towns, with other areas reserved for the monumental buildings. Such buildings differed radically from developed Greek architecture because the soft tufo rock of the region was ill-suited to sculpture in the round. . . . [This] stone was often employed only for the footings of the walls, the rest of the structures making extensive use of less durable materials."

6. Phillips 1993, 7.

7. Winter 2009.

8. For a summary of the Archaic architectural terracottas see Phillips (1985; 1993).

9. For a summary see Strandberg Olofsson 1994.

10. Izzet 2007, 232.

11. The scholarly literature on this debate is vast and covers many years. For particularly noteworthy early discussions of the elite residential qualities of the buildings, see Cristofani 1975, Staccioli 1976, and Torelli 1983. More recently, de Grummond (1997) and Turfa and Steinmayer (2002) have provided valuable reassessments of the archaeological and architectural evidence.

12. For Poggio Civitate see Nielsen and Tuck 2001; for Acquarossa, Wikander and Wikander 1990.

13. *OED*, s.v. *monumental, monumentality*.

14. *OED*, s.v. *monument*.

15. *OED*, s.v. *monumentum*.

16. Loeb translation (Nixon 1965).

17. Plautus uses the term *monumentum/monimentum* in three other plays: *Mil*. 704, *St*. 63, and *Rud*. 935. In *Miles Gloriosus* he refers ironically to children as a tribute (*monumentum*) for elite families. In *Stichus* the phrase *bubulis monimentis* is used to characterize the marks of disobedience on a slave; in *Rudens* a slave facetiously uses the term while grandly musing about founding a town in his name should he be set free. In all cases the term is used playfully and heightens jokes about social status and class.

18. Varro *Ling* 6.49; *OED* s.v. *moneo, monere*.

19. *OED*, s.v. *monumentum*.

20. Loeb translation (Granger 1983).

21. Granger 1983, 109 n. 6.

22. Loeb translation (Foster 1925).

23. Loeb translation (Foster 1925). Foster (p. 6, n. 2) notes the comparison between "history" and a monument of stone.

24. For example, Wiseman 1994, Jaeger 1997, and Bonfante 1998.

25. Feldherr 1998, 1.

26. Jaeger 1997, 24.

27. T. P. Wiseman (1994) uses literary examples as evidence to argue that Roman historians were aware of, and perhaps even manipulated, the misinterpretation of monuments, particularly those from early Rome.

28. Richardson 1992, s.v. *Niger Lapis*. The stone has also been associated with the shepherd Faustulus and the ancestor of Tullus Hostilius. Based on literary evidence, Coarelli (1983, 161–178) argues for yet another interpretation of the stone: that it is the Volcanal (a further indication that the original intent of the monument was lost in antiquity).

29. Loeb translation (Shackleton Bailey 1999).

30. Winstedt (1962) translates the term as "public work," while Shackleton Bailey opts for simply "work." In his earlier commentary on this letter, Shackleton Bailey (1965, 205) emphasizes that for Cicero a *monumentum* need not be a positive reference, as at *Mil.* 17.

31. Anderson 1984, 40.

32. Anderson (1984, 39–44) concludes that the Forum began taking shape soon after 54 BCE, while Ulrich 1993 suggests 48 BCE after the Battle of Pharsalus.

33. Loeb translation (Shackleton Bailey 1999). Bailey's translation treats Paullus's work on the already existing Basilica Fulvia and the new Basilica Paulli as two separate projects. Previous translations, for example that of Winstedt (1962), had considered them as a single building project of renovation and addition. In either case, it is clear from Cicero's text that they are part of the same building initiative. For a discussion of the architecture see Richardson 1992, s.v. *Basilica Paulli*.

34. The rebuilt Basilica Paulli of 54 BCE maintained the axis and north–south dimensions of the earlier Basilica Fulvia; however, its east–west extension was shortened. See Haselberger et al. (2002, s.v. *Basilica Paulli*). Coarelli (1985, 205–207) suggests that the *antiquis columnis* might in fact refer to marble columns erected in the building ca. 80 BCE, due to the unlikelihood that Paullus would have used simple tufa columns in his elaborate restructuring of the monument.

35. Loeb translation (Shackleton Bailey 1999).

36. For a thorough study of Imperial monumentality see Thomas 2007.

37. See, for example, Ammianus Marcellinus 16.10.14.

38. Thomas 2007, 2.

39. For example, see R. Wesley 1984 (with comprehensive bibliography), Choay 2001, Thomas 2007, 1–14.

40. Bergdoll 2000, 9–41.

41. Choay 2001, 7–8.

42. *Dictionnaire universel de Furetière*, s.v. *monument*.

43. See Thomas 2007, 2.

44. I am grateful to Kostis Kourellis for this insight and for his guidance in my discussion of this period and modern architecture.

45. Choay (2001, 17) places the birth of the concept of the "historic monument" in fifteenth-century Rome, with the terminology to follow. The definition of "monument" in these terms has wide implications for discussions of cultural patrimony and theories of cultural memory. For example, see Alcock 2002, Nelson and Olin 2003, and Loukaki 2008.

46. See especially vol. 4 of the *Harvard Architecture Review* (1984) and vol. 22.2 of *World Archaeology* (1990), both dedicated to the concept of monumentality.

47. In many ways the position statement of Sert, Giedion, and Léger (1984), originally published in 1944, serves as a clear articulation of the movement.

48. Curtis 1996, 513–527.
49. Trigger 1990.
50. Trigger 1990, 119.
51. Moore 1996, 92.

Bibliography

Alcock, S. 2002. *Archaeologies of the Greek Past: Landscape, Monuments, and Memories*. Cambridge: Cambridge University Press.

Anderson, J. C., Jr. 1984. *The Historical Topography of the Imperial Fora*. CollLatomus 182. Brussels: Latomus.

Barker, G., and T. Rasmussen. 1998. *The Etruscans*. Oxford: Blackwell.

Bergdoll, B. 2000. *European Architecture, 1750–1890*. New York: Oxford University Press.

Böethius, A. 1978. *Etruscan and Early Roman Architecture*. Reprint. New York: Penguin.

Bonfante, L. 1998. "Livy and the Monuments." In *Boundaries of the Ancient Near Eastern World. A Tribute to Cyrus H. Gordon*, ed. M. Lubetski, C. Gottlieb, and S. R. Keller, 480–492. *Journal for the Study of the Old Testament* Suppl. 273. Sheffield: Sheffield Academic Press.

Choay, F. 2001. *The Invention of the Historic Monument*. Trans. L. M. O'Connell. New York: Cambridge University Press.

Coarelli, F. 1983. *Il foro romano: Periodo arcaico*. Rome: Quasar.

———. 1985. *Il foro romano: Periodo repubblicano e augusteo*. Rome: Quasar.

Cristofani, M. 1975. "Considerazioni su Poggio Civitate (Murlo, Siena)." *Prospettiva* 1:9–17.

Curtis, W. J. R. 1996. *Modern Architecture since 1900*. London: Phaidon.

de Grummond, N. T. 1997. "Poggio Civitate: A Turning Point." *EtrStud* 4:23–40.

Feldherr, A. 1998. *Spectacle and Society in Livy's History*. Berkeley: University of California Press.

Foster, B. O. 1925. *Livy Books I and II*. Loeb Classical Library. London: William Heinemann.

Granger, F. 1983. *Vitruvius: De Architectura*, vols. 1 and 2. Loeb Classical Library. Cambridge, Mass.: Harvard University Press.

Haselberger, L., D. G. Romano, E. A. Dumser, and D. Borbonus. 2002. *Mapping Augustan Rome*. *JRA* Suppl. 50. Portsmouth, R.I.: Journal of Roman Archaeology.

Haynes, S. 2000. *Etruscan Civilization: A Cultural History*. Los Angeles: J. Paul Getty Museum.

Izzet, V. 2007. *The Archaeology of Etruscan Society*. Cambridge: Cambridge University Press.

Jaeger, M. 1997. *Livy's Written Rome*. Ann Arbor: University of Michigan Press.

Loukaki, A. 2008. *Living Ruins, Value Conflicts*. Aldershot: Ashgate.

Moore, J. D. 1996. *Architecture and Power in the Ancient Andes: The Archaeology of Public Buildings*. New York: Cambridge University Press.

Nelson, R. S., and M. Olin, eds. 2003. *Monuments and Memory, Made and Unmade*. Chicago: University of Chicago Press.

Nielsen, E. O., and A. S. Tuck. 2001. "An Orientalizing Period Complex at Poggio Civitate (Murlo): A Preliminary View." *EtrStud* 11:35–63.

Nixon, P. 1965. *Plautus*, vol. 2. Loeb Classical Library. Cambridge, Mass.: Harvard University Press.

Olsen, D. J. 1986. *The City as a Work of Art: Paris, London, Vienna*. New Haven: Yale University Press.

Phillips, K. M. Jr. 1985. "Poggio Civitate (Murlo)." In *Case e palazzi d'Etruria*, ed. S. Stopponi, 98–127. Milan: Electa.

———. 1993. *In the Hills of Tuscany: Recent Excavations at the Etruscan Site of Poggio Civitate (Murlo, Siena)*. Philadelphia: University Museum, University of Pennsylvania.

Richardson, L., Jr. 1992. *A New Topographical Dictionary of Rome*. Baltimore: Johns Hopkins University Press.

Riva, C. 2010. *The Urbanisation of Etruria: Funerary Practice and Social Change, 700–600 B.C.* Cambridge: Cambridge University Press.

Sert, J. L., S. Giedion, and F. Léger. 1984. "Nine Points on Monumentality." In *Monumentality and the City*, 62–63. *Harvard Architecture Review* 4. Cambridge, Mass.: MIT Press.

Shackleton Bailey, D. R. 1965. *Cicero's Letters to Atticus*, vol. 2. Loeb Classical Library. Cambridge: Cambridge University Press.

———. 1999. *Cicero. Letters to Atticus*, vol. 1. Loeb Classical Library. Cambridge, Mass.: Harvard University Press.

Staccioli, R. A. 1976. "Considerazioni sui complessi monumentali di Murlo e di Acquarossa." In *Mélanges offerts à Jacques Heurgon: L'Italie préromaine et la Rome républicaine*, 471–492. *CÉFR* 27. Rome: École française de Rome.

Stopponi, S., ed. 1985. *Case e palazzi d'Etruria*. Milan: Electa.

Strandberg Olofsson, M. 1989. "On the Reconstruction of the Monumental Area at Acquarossa." *OpRom* 17(12):163–183.

———. 1994. "Some Interpretational Aspects of the Acquarossa/Tuscania Mould-Made Terracottas and Their Architectural Context." In *Opus Mixtum: Essays in Ancient Art and Society*, 135–147. Stockholm: Paul Åströms Förlag.

Thomas, E. 2007. *Monumentality and the Roman Empire: Architecture in the Antonine Age*. Oxford: Oxford University Press.

Torelli, M. 1983. "*Polis* et 'palazzo': Architettura, ideologia e artigianato greco in Etruria tra VII e VI sec. a.C." In *Architecture et société de l'archaïsme grec à la fin de la république romaine*, 471–492. *CÉFR* 66. Rome: École française de Rome.

Trigger, B. G. 1990. "Monumental Architecture: A Thermodynamic Explanation of Symbolic Behaviour." *WorldArch* 22:119–132.

Turfa, J. M., and A. G. Steinmayer, Jr. 2002. "Interpreting Etruscan Structures: The Question of Murlo." *PBSR* 70:1–28.

Ulrich, R. B. 1993. "Julius Caesar and the Creation of the Forum Iulium." *AJA* 97:49–80.

Wesley, R. 1984. "Monumentality and the Triumph of the Treatises." In *Monumentality and the City*, 185–205. *Harvard Architecture Review* 4. Cambridge, Mass.: MIT Press.

Wikander, C., and Ö Wikander. 1990. "The Early Monumental Complex at Acquarossa: A Preliminary Report." *OpRom* 18:189–205.

Winstedt, E. O. 1962. *Cicero. Letters to Atticus*, vols. 1–3. Loeb Classical Library. Cambridge, Mass.: Harvard University Press.

Winter, N. A. 2009. *Symbols of Wealth and Power: Architectural Terracotta Decoration in Etruria and Central Italy, 640–510 B.C. MAAR* Suppl. 9. Ann Arbor: University of Michigan Press.

Wiseman, T. P. 1994. "Monuments and the Roman Annalists." In *Historiography and Imagination: Eight Essays on Roman Culture*, 37–48. *Exeter Studies in History* 33. Exeter: University of Exeter Press.

II STRAW TO STONE, HUTS TO HOUSES
TRANSITIONS IN BUILDING PRACTICES AND SOCIETY IN PROTOHISTORIC LATIUM

ELIZABETH COLANTONI

RECONSTRUCTIONS OF THE PROTOHISTORIC OR IRON Age huts uncovered on the Palatine Hill in Rome in the 1940s are well known to scholars of the Roman world, as images of these iconic reconstructions are commonplace in books surveying ancient Roman history, culture, and architecture (fig. 2.1). A typical scholarly discussion of the huts includes details about the structures' measurements and number of posts, perhaps followed by a quotation of the assertion of Dionysius of Halicarnassus (*Ant. Rom.* 1.79.11) that such a building, the so-called Hut of Romulus, still existed on the Palatine Hill in his own day, the first century BCE, as a reminder of the bucolic life of herdsmen in the eighth century BCE.[1] In this context, the huts are presented as the residences of nuclear families, such as that of Romulus and his adoptive father, Faustulus. According to F. E. Brown, for instance, "Each was the dwelling of a single family—*pater* and *mater familias* with their offspring—in a close and necessarily strictly ordered bond of kinship and space."[2]

Archaeological evidence shows that there was a transition in Rome and Latium over the course of the seventh and sixth centuries BCE, from small huts made of relatively impermanent materials to orthogonal stone architecture and houses with multiple rooms, often identified as the dwellings of people of locally elite status.[3] Many scholars have seen this change as directly attributable to the arrival in Italy of influences and ideas from the eastern Mediterranean, whether brought in by Greeks specifically or by other less well identified groups from the East more

Fig. 2.1. Partial reconstruction of a hut on the Palatine Hill (courtesy Antiquarium Palatino, by concession of the Ministero per i Beni e le Attività Culturali—Soprintendenza Speciale per i Beni Archeologici di Roma).

generally.[4] For instance, Carmine Ampolo has proposed that the Regia, one of the earliest stone structures in Rome, was intended to replicate, in function as well as form, the Archaic *prytaneion* building in the agora in Athens.[5] More recently, Gabriele Cifani has argued that the stone-based structures built in Latium in the seventh and sixth centuries BCE were modeled on palaces in Syria, as members of local aristocracies in central Italy looked to Eastern (but not Greek) artisans and technicians for new means of expressing their power and identity.[6] The ramifications of such arguments are twofold, as their proponents imply or even state explicitly that people in Italy were directly influenced by foreign ideas, both in technical matters of construction and also in the ways in which such buildings were actually used.

In the present essay, this period of transition from simple huts to monumental houses is examined from a different perspective, with a focus on the configuration and evolution of social space rather than on structural characteristics; questions of foreign influence and technical knowledge as they pertain to building practices are addressed in relation to this focus. In particular, consideration is given to a source of information that has not previously been used in any depth in analyses of housing in early Italy, namely modern ethnographic data. Certainly, passing reference to shepherds' huts of the nineteenth-century Roman countryside as modern counterparts to the ancient structures is a commonplace in the scholarly literature on early

Italian architecture, but, as Cifani has recently suggested, a closer examination of this comparison shows that it is not necessarily an apt or helpful one.[7] The nineteenth-century huts were temporary structures made from lower-quality materials, without, for instance, plastered walls, and these huts were never intended as long-term, primary residences in the way that the ancient structures seem to have been.

A more appropriate source of ethnographic data is relatively recent, so-called traditional societies in which members live in a fixed way in houses and villages not unlike those that the archaeological evidence records from protohistoric Latium. Ethnographic studies of these societies provide interesting statistics, parallels, and possible alternative explanations for the nature of the material remains of early housing in Latium, although it should be emphasized that such ethnographic information is helpful as a source of ideas for understanding the archaeological evidence rather than for use in direct analogies.[8] Iron Age huts and villages are, of course, known from throughout central Italy and beyond; the focus here, however, is the evidence from Latium, and in particular Rome and Satricum, as these two sites provide useful examples that, in the case of Rome, can be extended profitably into the Classical period.

First, a brief review of the evidence for early huts and the subsequent transition to stone architecture in central Italy is in order. Remains of huts have been found at a number of sites in Latium, and they tend to share several recurring features, including: holes for posts that would have supported the structure and that also mark a doorway and sometimes a porch; a small trench in the ground for the base of the hut walls; bits of clay packing that suggest wattle-and-daub walls; and, sometimes, a patch of carbon and ashes on the floor that indicates a hearth.[9] The small trenches outlining the walls show that the huts were circular, oval, square, or rectangular in shape, generally with no clear and consistent difference in chronology between the various forms.[10] The superstructure, and in particular the presence of a testudinate roof with a small smoke hole, can be further surmised on the basis of the hut-shaped burial urns that people in Italy favored in this time period.[11] Indeed, the urns, fashioned from terracotta or metal, seem to be accurately detailed, small-scale replicas of real-life if not particular huts. Overall, some less common variations of huts do occur, but the general characteristics described here pertain to most examples.

At the site of Rome, the evidence for early huts is widespread, but also relatively fragmentary.[12] The best-known instances are, of course, those on the Palatine Hill, where one complete floor surface and an indeterminate number of other huts were found in the first half of the twentieth century. The remains of some ten or eleven huts have likewise been identified in various explorations in the area of the Regia on the edge of the future Roman Forum, with further evidence of huts here also in the places where the Temple of Julius Caesar, the probable Arch of Augustus, and the Temple of Antoninus Pius and Faustina were erected many centuries later. Some of the post holes in the Forum area have been identified as marking animal pens and cook sheds, so the number of actual habitations may be relatively few.[13] It has also been suggested that there were huts in other areas of Rome—on the Velia, on the Quirinal, and in the S. Omobono sacred area—but the evidence in these cases is thin.[14] With the exception of the most famous example uncovered on the Palatine, the data concerning early huts in Rome are fairly elusive. The only sure statements that can be made about them beyond the basic details of their construction are that at least some of the huts were habitations—with domestic debris such as weaving implements and broken cooking pots found in them—and that the huts tended to be clustered together in groups. The huts are generally thought to have been in use in the eighth and into the seventh century BCE, at which point the huts on the Palatine were destroyed and those in the Forum area were superseded by the Regia building, the supposed home of a king or priest, with stone foundations and a more orthogonal floor plan.

Indeed, this is the time period when there is a shift from huts to more solid stone architecture in central Italy in general. Several buildings were constructed during the seventh century BCE—for instance, at the sites of Poggio Civitate (Murlo) and Acquarossa—that consist of strips of small, rectilinear rooms grouped around a central court or an open area (figs. 1.1 and 1.2).[15] Such buildings had foundations of stone, earthen walls, and wooden roof-supports covered by terracotta roof tiles. Monumental in contrast to the huts of the eighth century BCE, these structures are generally thought to have been the houses of the elite members of Italian society at the time.[16] In Rome, some of the earliest signs of the change to this style of architecture are found in association with the Regia and the recently excavated large building near the Regia on the north slope of the Palatine Hill, also identified by the excavator, Andrea Carandini, as a royal house of Rome's legendary kings.[17] In both cases, remains of stone foundations indicate that the structures consisted of a series of small rooms that opened onto a courtyard. In other words, the Roman examples have a configuration consistent with the floor plans of the early stone buildings hypothesized to have belonged to members of the ruling classes at other sites in central Italy as well.

Such was the situation at Rome. Evidence for huts has also been identified at a number of other sites in Latium, but the remains at Satricum are particularly substantial and instructive.[18] Here, some 60 kilometers south of Rome, evidence of at least forty-seven huts of varying sizes and dates has been found on the acropolis, grouped in an area around a water basin, perhaps sacred, and near the future Archaic Temple of Mater Matuta, Satricum's most famous monument in antiquity.[19] Many of the huts were uncovered at the turn of the twentieth century in an excavation campaign that was not well documented by modern standards. More recently, in the 1970s and 1980s, approximately twenty huts have been explored by archaeological teams from the University of Groningen and the Dutch Institute in Rome.

Three main phases of early habitation have been discerned, with perhaps some overlap in the use of the various structures among the phases.[20] In the first period, in the eighth century BCE, the site featured smaller oval huts alongside round depressions that one of the site's excavators, Marianne Maaskant-Kleibrink, interprets as cook sheds, or small structures used solely for heating and cooking food (fig. 2.2). Subsequently, during the late eighth and the seventh century BCE, larger oval huts, square huts, and more small, round cook sheds occupied the site (fig. 2.3). Finally, in the sixth century BCE, large courtyard-houses with stone foundations and regular plans were laid out on Satricum's acropolis (fig. 2.4).[21] These seem to have had walls composed of clay packing and roofs covered with terracotta tiles. In plan, the structures consisted of two long, narrow strips of small square and rectangular rooms that flank a central open space. The buildings are therefore similar in component materials and layout to the elite houses seen elsewhere in central Italy at this time. Alongside the courtyard-houses at Satricum were smaller orthogonal structures that Maaskant-Kleibrink argues had religious significance, although these may simply have been houses.[22] By this time a temple building recognizable as such—the Temple of Mater Matuta—had likewise been erected on the acropolis very close to the courtyard-houses. Thus, at Satricum there appear to have been two hut phases, followed by the development of stone-based constructions that resemble the well-known early monumental buildings at Rome and other sites of similar date in central Italy. Finds from the huts as well as the courtyard-houses are domestic in nature, including, for instance, pottery for cooking, serving, and storage as well as weaving implements.[23]

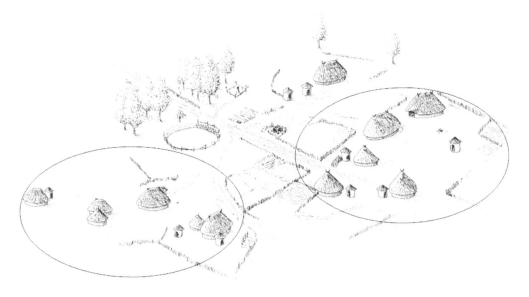

Fig. 2.2. Reconstructive drawing of the settlement on the acropolis at Satricum in the eighth century BCE. Circles indicate clusters of huts (after Maaskant-Kleibrink 1991, 73; original drawing by H. J. Waterbolk).

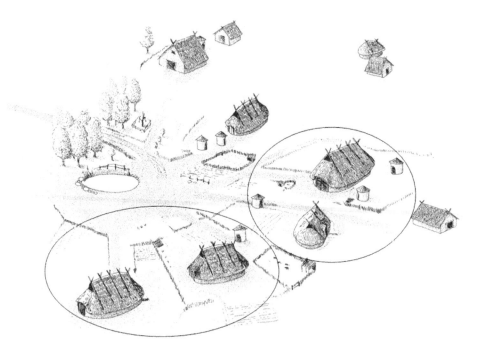

Fig. 2.3. Reconstructive drawing of the settlement on the acropolis at Satricum in the late eighth and seventh centuries BCE. Circles indicate clusters of huts (after Maaskant-Kleibrink 1991, 79; original drawing by H. J. Waterbolk).

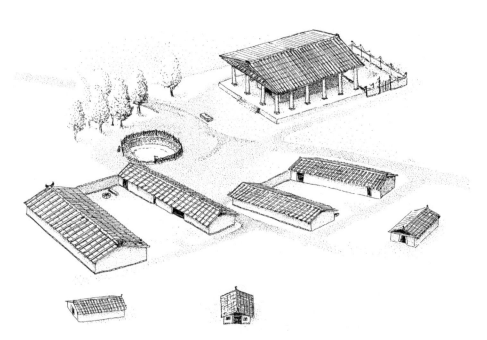

Fig. 2.4. Reconstructive drawing of the settlement on the acropolis at Satricum in the sixth century BCE (Maaskant-Kleibrink 1991, 93; original drawing by H. J. Waterbolk).

These basic facts about the early huts at Rome and Satricum provide a context for the introduction of ethnographic data. In 1962, at a time when it was becoming fashionable in American archaeology to seek scientific and almost mathematical explanations for human behavior, anthropologist Raoul Naroll gathered statistics on the amount of living space that was generally used by one person in a wide range of traditional towns and villages from around the world (table 2.1).[24] He reached the conclusion that in such societies one person occupied approximately 10 m^2 of space, and he therefore argued that archaeologists could estimate the population of a site by dividing the area of its living surfaces by ten.

Table 2.1: Naroll's Data: Floor Area and Settlement Population

Society	Largest Settlement	Estimated Population of Largest Settlement	Estimated Floor Area of Largest Settlement
Vanua Levu	Nakaroka	75	412.8
Eyak	Algonik	120	836
Kapauku	Botekubo	181	362
Wintun		200	900
Klallam	Port Angeles	200	2,420
Hupa	Tsewenalding?	200	2,490
Ifaluk	Ifaluk	252	3,024
Ramkokamekra	Ponto	298	6,075
Bella Coola	Bella Coola	400	16,320
Kiwai	Oromosapua	400	1,432.2
Tikopia	Tikopia	1,260	8,570
Cuna	Ustupu	1,800	5,460
Iroquois		3,000	13,370
Kazak		3,000	63,000
Ila	Kasenga	3,000	47,000
Tonga	Nukualofa	5,000	111,500
Zulu		15,000	65,612
Inca	Cuzco	200,000	167,220

Source: Naroll 1962, 588 (reproduced by permission of the Society for American Archaeology from *American Antiquity* 27 [1962]).

Since Naroll published his study, many scholars have sought to refine his formula, while others have debated its usefulness. For instance, Charles C. Kolb proposes that a more accurate calculation of the space needed per person at archaeological sites in Mesoamerica is 6.12 m², while Daniel Shea argues that an "average" person would live in a far smaller area—he suggests 4.57 m²—than an elite member of any society, for whom Shea predicts a use of 19.39 m² of space.[25] Certainly, there are many factors, whether cultural, social, economic, political, or psychological, that could cause local variations in the conception and use of dwelling space, and it is clear that Naroll's constant (as it has come to be called) and other similar calculations offer dangerously deceptive statistics. Even a quick glance at Naroll's figures (table 2.1) reveals that some populations used a good bit more space than 10 m² per person, while others used less. The formula is likely not particularly useful for establishing the population size of villages in ancient Latium, but it does at least offer a point of departure for thinking, in a concrete way, about how many people might have lived in an early Italian hut.

Naroll's constant suggests that the most famous of the Palatine huts, with a floor area of approximately 17 m², might have housed one to two people, while one of the smaller oval huts at Satricum, which seem to have had slightly less than 10 m² of living space, would theoretically have provided shelter for only one person.[26] One of the larger oval huts at Satricum has an area of just over 30 m², room for three or perhaps four people in Naroll's formulation. Let me be clear that I believe that these statistics are to be treated with great skepticism. They do, however, suggest that we should at least consider the possibility that one early Italian hut might not have sufficed for a full family, even one composed only of parents and children. Given this possibility, it seems worthwhile to consider how a larger family might have been housed, if not in a single hut.

A second set of ethnographic data—this time from the twentieth-century settlements of the Bamangwato, a tribe of the Tswana people in Botswana, in southern Africa—will be helpful in generating possible answers to this question.[27] The Bamangwato, who live in sprawling towns and villages, have a hierarchical political structure, with a tribal chief at the top and local headmen beneath him. The position of headman is a hereditary one, handed down from father to eldest son, and each headman presides over a ward, typically populated by one to two hundred members who are related by lineage or marriage. The settlement patterns within these wards are of particular interest here. In architectural terms, a ward consists of a horseshoe-

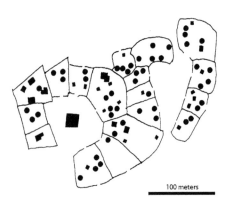

100 meters

Fig. 2.5. Bamangwato wards (after Fewster 1999, 182, fig. 11.3).

shaped string of connected hut compounds that enclose the ward's central meeting area (fig. 2.5). The headman and his family live in the compound at the apex of the horseshoe, and other families are situated within the ward complex on the basis of their relationship to the headman. For instance, the closest male relative of the headman, his brother, might inhabit the compound adjacent to the headman, although if the brother is perceived to be a rival and a threat to the headman's position of authority, he might instead live at the end of the horseshoe.

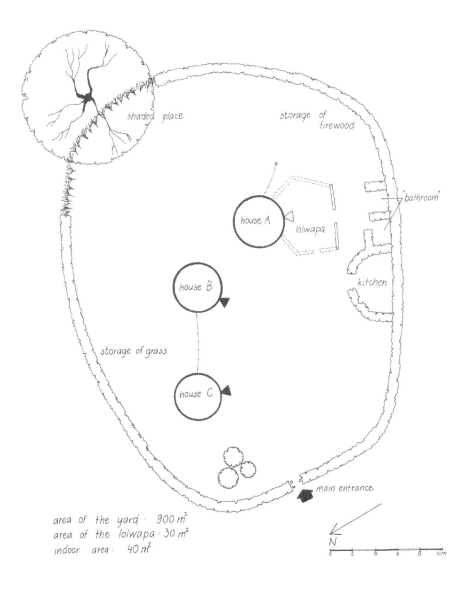

shaded place

storage of firewood

bathroom

house A

lolwapa

kitchen

house B

storage of grass

house C

main entrance

area of the yard : 900 m²
area of the lolwapa : 30 m²
indoor area : 40 m²

N

0 2 4 6 8 10m

Fig. 2.6. A Tswana hut compound (Larsson and Larsson 1984, 205; original drawing by Viera Larsson).

Fig. 2.7. A traditional Tswana hut (Larsson and Larsson 1984, 99).

Each hut compound in turn consists of multiple structures that house a nuclear family and possibly several extended family members, with up to about ten people living in the compound (fig. 2.6). There is a hut for the father and mother, and there are often separate huts for older children—one for the girls and one for the boys—and for other unmarried or widowed adults of the extended family who might also live there. Traditionally, the huts are round structures with mud walls and a thatched roof with wooden supports (fig. 2.7).[28] On average, they have 10 to 20 m^2 of floor space, and they are used primarily for sleeping and for storage. The compound as a whole is usually enclosed or fenced in by a hedge of the cactus-like plant Euphorbia. The focus of family life is the outdoor hearth, and Kathryn Jane Fewster, who has conducted ethnographic fieldwork among the Bamangwato, emphasizes that "cooking and chatting takes place at outside hearths and not, according to Western expectation, inside houses or huts."[29]

A number of points can be drawn from this look at settlement patterns among the Bamangwato in Botswana. First, it provides a clear example of nuclear families who live spread out across more than one hut. Furthermore, the space occupied by these families is conceived of as including the area around the huts, and, in fact, most familial interaction actually takes place outside rather than within the huts. The effect here is that the multiple huts are really elemental parts of a larger unit; in fact, for an ethnographer or archaeologist, studying a single hut in isolation would provide a rather distorted image of Bamangwato society. Finally, it should be clear from the case of the Bamangwato that, as with many other traditional societies, social and especially family relationships are key factors in determining the placement of structures, and the configuration of huts and compounds therefore reflects social arrangements.[30]

How do all of these ideas pertain to the ancient Italian structures? Naroll's statistics suggest that we should at least consider the possibility that one Iron Age hut was not enough for an entire family; the Bamangwato data offer one model of how a family could live spread out among several huts that have slightly differing functions but nonetheless operate together as a single domestic unit. Archaeological data about the specific uses of floor space within individual early Italian huts are, unfortunately, limited. A relatively large (30 m^2) well-preserved and well-studied hut at the site of Fidene, on the outskirts of modern Rome, seems to have been used both for storage (along the north wall, where the remains of large ceramic jars were found) and for what the excavators term "normal" activities—cooking, eating, and perhaps sleeping.[31] Space inside one of the huts at Satricum, which yielded a notable number of weaving implements alongside cooking equipment, has been interpreted as belonging to the female realm. However only part of the hut was preserved, and it is not clear if the entire floor area of the structure should be characterized in this way.[32] Maaskant-Kleibrink makes a convincing argument that the smallest, round huts at Satricum were cook sheds, as the very small structures have yielded carbon layers with animal bones and fragments of cooking stands and other food preparation equipment.[33] Although the evidence is limited, on the whole it does not seem unreasonable to posit that functionally differentiated huts existed. At the least, the separate cook sheds show that life in Iron Age Satricum was not confined to the interior of a single hut: some domestic activities did take place elsewhere.

Despite the difficulties in identifying specific functions for individual early Italian huts or for discrete areas within these, the hut remains at Satricum in particular do at the least seem, intuitively, to form groups or compounds. Thus, as can be seen in the reconstructive drawing of the village in the eighth century BCE, two clusters of huts stand out on the south side of the central water basin (these are circled in fig. 2.2). This pattern of two clusters of huts is repeated in the seventh century BCE as well (fig. 2.3). Finally, in the sixth century BCE, the two groups of huts were replaced by two imposing courtyard-style houses with orthogonal plans (fig. 2.4). In other words, over time each cluster of small huts at Satricum was effectively replaced by a single monumental structure with stone foundations.

In his classic article "Of Huts and Houses," Frank Brown suggests in passing that the strings of small rooms in the new, orthogonal stone architecture in Italy of the seventh century BCE were little more than "so many hut-spaces, single, set end to end or side by side."[34] In terms of the layout of space in the new buildings, this theory makes perfect sense. The little rooms in these structures often do not communicate; instead they open onto a shared courtyard, not unlike individual huts that give out onto communal space between them. Brown, however, states explicitly that he considers each Iron Age hut to be the dwelling place of a complete nuclear family, and he does not discuss why multiple single-family hut spaces would ultimately morph into one large structure.[35] This difficulty can be explained if we accept that families in early Latium lived not in one hut, but in a compound or collection of huts.[36] With the transition to stone architecture, the different functional spaces in the various huts were each replicated by a small square or rectangular room. The living space outside of the huts, so important in traditional village societies such as that of the Bamangwato, was, in the early Italian example, transformed into an enclosed courtyard, sometimes framed by a colonnade, perhaps the conceptual successor of the small porches clearly present on some hut urns and in the archaeological remains of actual Iron Age huts. Later, as Andrew Wallace-Hadrill, among others, has suggested, the courtyard was compressed considerably and appears in the typical Roman *domus* of the Republican period as the *atrium*.[37] In other words, the *atrium* was a vestigial courtyard that represented the open space between the Iron Age huts. If this is the case, it is then easier to understand how the *atrium* in a private house in Rome was later considered essentially public,[38] for it would have been an elaborated version of what was in origin simply open space, albeit open space that had social meaning in connection with the structures around it. If it is true that individual huts were not occupied by entire families, it is also easier to understand how an Iron Age hut urn might in some way represent a single deceased person, or at least serve as an appropriate resting place for that person, as the urns seem to have done.[39]

Finally, there is the question of the extent to which the new, more monumental houses represent a change brought about by the arrival of foreign influence and, in particular, more advanced technology and building know-how. One interesting implication of the trajectory of architectural development in Latium that I have sketched is that the change from small hut to monumental house is not as dramatic as it might otherwise seem, especially in social terms.[40] Although the later buildings have a markedly different and more imposing appearance, the space they shelter seems to reflect the same social configuration as that of the earlier groups of huts, housing the same range of inhabitants, possibly a nuclear family with some extended family members, around a communal open area.[41] Indeed, there is perhaps more social continuity than not; any foreign influence exerted in the change is relatively superficial, inasmuch as it would involve a switch from less permanent foundations to stone ones but not, contrary to what others have argued in the past, a complete rearrangement of social space.[42] Furthermore, to judge from the presence of monumental tombs with architectural features, people living in central Italy already knew how to work stone and create monumental architecture early in the seventh century BCE, at least half a century before buildings for the living were constructed with stone foundations.[43] For instance, the Regolini-Galassi Tomb at Cerveteri included a *dromos* and chamber built of large, regular stone blocks forming walls and a corbelled covering, while Tomb II at Satricum featured a series of pillars made of half-meter-high blocks of stone with dressed surfaces on the interior of the tomb chamber.[44] If the new house floor plan was a local development and knowledge of stone-working was already present for some time when orthogonal stone foundations were first used for houses, there is neither much room nor much need to suppose direct foreign influence, whether from Greece or elsewhere in the eastern Mediterranean, in the architectural changes. Other explanations should be sought.

A final pair of ethnographic examples offers some insight. Among the Bamangwato, there has been a gradual transition over the course of the last century from the traditional round huts to rectilinear houses made with European-style materials, which were introduced in the 1800s by foreign traders and missionaries who built their own European-style houses in Tswana territory.[45] The reasons for this transition include a desire to emulate the politically dominant Europeans, a desire for modernization, and, in more direct terms, government mandates. One motivation for and also consequence of the change in housing styles has been a developing perception of houses as financial assets and symbols of power. Mud huts, as Anita Larsson points out, require no capital expenditure: the component materials are readily available to anyone who has the time to gather them, and the structures can be built by the same people who live in them.[46] Therefore, unlike European-style houses, they do not require special economic means, nor do they allow inhabitants to display a financial status greater than that of their neighbors. Conversely, wealth and, in turn, power can be accumulated in modern structures built from relatively expensive materials and specialized labor. The transition to European-style houses was therefore desirable to those who wished to display their economic and social power to their neighbors, not necessarily because the houses were European-style per se, but because the new structures could function as symbols of accumulated wealth.[47] A similar change in building materials and style was observed by anthropologist Friedrich Schwerdtfeger in Hausaland in northern Nigeria, where traditional round thatched mud huts gave way in the 1950s to European-inspired rectilinear concrete structures with corrugated tin roofs, well after the time when these materials first became known in Nigeria.[48] Schwerdtfeger concluded that the direct impetus for these changes was, more than anything else, rising income, both because greater income meant that families could afford the relatively expensive new materials, and because it allowed larger families to divide into smaller groups more suitable to the compact newer structures. Clearly in the case of both the Hausa and Bamangwato, direct emulation of practices of the politically dominant, colonialist Europeans living in Africa was a motivating factor for the transition in building styles, but in both cases, economic means and changes tied to local values and considerations were also paramount.[49]

As in Hausaland in the 1950s, the period in which monumental tombs and then houses were first built in central Italy was a time of increased economic prosperity, at least for some, as we know from the rich grave goods found in the so-called princely tombs at many sites in central Italy in the late eighth and early seventh centuries BCE.[50] To give but one example, the Barberini Tomb at Palestrina yielded an impressive array of high-quality gold, silver, ivory, and bronze items.[51] Curiously, there is no evidence for equally regal housing during the time period in which these notably rich tombs were most common.[52] The so-called princely tombs then disappear at roughly the same time that more elaborate dwellings become a standard feature at a number of central Italian settlements. These two concurrent changes may thus indicate a shift in economic strategy on the part of some members of the upper classes over the course of the seventh century BCE, with wealth now in some cases being diverted from tombs and funerals to housing. As with the traditional structures of the Bamangwato, early Italian huts were made of readily available materials that involved no capital expenditure (or whatever the equivalent might be in protohistoric terms), whereas the stone-based structures would have required extra economic resources both for specialized materials and for labor. The new houses could therefore serve as symbols of accumulated wealth and status in a way that the traditional huts by their very nature could not.

Notably, if the huts were the conceptual ancestors of the courtyard-houses, this situation does suggest that the earlier structures were, despite their simple appearance, the homes of the elite members of central Italian society.[53] Certainly their placement on the Palatine Hill in Rome and on the acropolis near the site of the future Temple of Mater Matuta in Satricum suggests an elite status as well. At any rate, if the change from huts made wholly of perishable materials to houses with stone foundations was, on the one hand, a reworking of traditional architectural forms and space and, on the other hand, the result at least in part of local economic developments and choices, it is difficult to argue that the transition from impermanent to monumental architecture was simply an imitation of Greek or other foreign models or the result of new technical knowledge. Central Italy was clearly developing a wider international outlook in the eighth and seventh centuries BCE—as evidenced, for instance, by the more exotic items found in the princely tombs—and there is no question that the inhabitants of Latium were aware of and on some level interacting with people from other parts of the Mediterranean world at this time. Indeed, it seems probable that, as in colonial Africa, the changing economic circumstances in central Italy were directly related to the new international horizons. But the inhabitants of Latium—who, unlike the Bamangwato or Hausa, do not seem to have been directly colonized by or subject to outsiders—were not simply looking to foreign models and copying them, and the ideas of Greeks or others cannot be mapped onto the practices of people living in Latium simply because of superficial formal similarities in architecture. The context in which orthogonal stone architecture came to be used in places such as Rome and Satricum should be seen as a local one, connected primarily with local history and local concerns.

In this essay, I have tried to demonstrate how ethnographic studies can provide new ways of looking at old data. In the case of the Iron Age huts of Latium, the possibility that these structures were not intended to house an entire family has opened up different lines of inquiry and allowed us to look at the huts in their larger context in a new way. This examination has led in turn to the conclusion that the simple huts of protohistoric Latium were both the homes of elite members of society and the direct conceptual predecessors of later monumental, courtyard-centered houses, as well as of the Classical period Roman *domus*. Moreover, the transition from hut to house was most likely the result of intentional, locally motivated economic choices on the part of the people living in central Italy in the Iron Age, rather than the wholesale adoption of strictly foreign practices. In other words, by drawing on ideas from a completely different time and place, I have been able to argue that the transition from straw to stone and from small huts to monumental houses in protohistoric Latium was a largely local phenomenon, very much rooted in its own time and place.

Notes

It is a pleasure to offer my thanks to Ingrid Edlund-Berry, to whom this volume is dedicated: her scholarship has provided me with much inspiration on the present topic as well as on many others pertaining to ancient Italy. I would also like to thank the editors of the volume for inviting me to participate in both the original conference session and the subsequent publication; I have very much appreciated their organized and professional approach, and the success of the endeavor as a whole is certainly owed to them. I am also grateful to Ily Nagy and to the volume's anonymous reviewer for their helpful comments. Finally, I wish to thank Elaine K. Gazda, who provided guidance for me in the initial stages of my research on early Italian huts, and Kent Flannery, who, although he will likely not remember me, years ago generously suggested invaluable bibliographical sources to me on the topic of round huts and orthogonal houses in areas outside of Italy.

1. Boëthius 1978, 23, 28; see also Brown 1976.
2. Brown 1976, 6. See also De Albentiis 1990, 18.
3. Cifani 2008, 265–278; see also Stopponi 1985.
4. See, for example: Ampolo 1971; Boëthius 1978, 27–31; Torelli 1985, 27, and Stopponi 1985 more generally; De Albentiis 1990, 33–36; Scheffer 1990; Torelli 2000; Cifani 2008, 265–278, esp. 271.
5. Ampolo 1971; see also Scheffer 1990 and now cf. Losehand 2007.
6. Cifani 2008, 269–272. See also Torelli 1985, 31–32; Torelli 2000; Prayon 2001.
7. Holloway 1994, 51; cf. Cifani 2008, 267.
8. See the discussion on this topic by Ucko (1969, 262–264).
9. Bartoloni, Beijer, and De Santis 1985; Bartoloni et al. 1987, 135–143; De Santis, Merlo, and De Grossi Mazzorin 1998, 31–35.

10. But cf. Bartoloni, Beijer, and De Santis 1985.

11. Bartoloni et al. 1987.

12. Gjerstad 1960, passim; Brown 1976; Holloway 1994, 51–55; Angelelli and Falzone 1999.

13. Ammerman (1990) argues that there were no huts at all.

14. Gjerstad 1960, 132, 165, 460.

15. Poggio Civitate: Stopponi 1985, 64–154; Phillips 1993; Tuck and Nielsen 2001. Acquarossa: Östenberg 1975; Stopponi 1985, 41–58; Wikander and Roos 1986. Cf. the overview of the transition to more complex stone buildings in Etruria by Torelli (2000, esp. 71–72). See also the discussion of monumental structures in general by Meyers in this volume.

16. Stopponi 1985.

17. Carandini 2006, 240–243. See Cifani 2008, 123–130 for a summary of the evidence and previous bibliography for both sites.

18. For further information on the site of Satricum, see Holloway 1994, 52, 142–155; Heldring 1998; Gnade 2007.

19. Maaskant-Kleibrink 1991, 61–68; Stobbe 2007a.

20. Maaskant-Kleibrink 1991, 68–100.

21. Maaskant-Kleibrink 1991, 91–100. See also Stobbe 2007b for information on other stone structures in the vicinity.

22. Maaskant-Kleibrink 1991, 88–90. See also Stobbe 2007b, 49–50.

23. Maaskant-Kleibrink 1987; Stobbe 2007a, 22–24; Stobbe 2007b, 49–50; Gnade 2007, 102–104, 123–124.

24. Naroll 1962.

25. Kolb 1985. Shea's remarks appear in the comments on Kolb's article: Kolb 1985, 594. On this topic, see also: LeBlanc 1971; Casselberry 1974; Wiessner 1974; Brown 1987; Gracia et al. 1996; Chamberlain 2006, 126–127.

26. Area calculations are based on the formula length × width and are therefore quite approximate.

27. Schapera 1935; Fewster 1999.

28. On the construction of these huts and also many social considerations connected with their use, see Hardie 1981; Larsson and Larsson 1984; and Larsson 1988, 1989, 1990.

29. Fewster 1999, 185.

30. Fraser 1968, esp. 47. See also Hardie 1985.

31. Bietti Sestieri and De Santis 2001, 219. Bietti Sestieri and De Santis propose that the hut would have been inhabited by a nuclear family, but they also suggest that it would have functioned as part of a larger complex of domestic structures.

32. Gnade 2007, 104.

33. Maaskant-Kleibrink 1991, 69–72.

34. Brown 1976, 10.

35. Brown 1976, 6.

36. Of course, there is the question of what constituted a family in this time period. It is generally assumed (for example, by Fayer [1982, 147–150]) that the nuclear family was the core of society in early Latium, as it was in later times, but there is no clear evidence either for or against this hypothesis. Remains of domestic architecture would seem to be one of the best sources of information relative to the question, but an argument based on the remains of huts or houses would be circular in the present context.

37. Wallace-Hadrill 1997, 226; see also Holloway 1994, 63–64. *Nihil novi sub sole*: In researching this paper, I found that the argument I wanted to make had already been proposed by Amedeo Maiuri as early as 1946, albeit in a more summary version and published only in a limited-circulation study guide for his students: "La casa di città ad atrio, chiusa

all'esterno, aperta verso l'interno, in netto contrasto con la casa moderna, non è che la continuazione della casa di campagna a cortile centrale, quale ancor oggi sopravvive in Italia nel tipo dell'abitazione rurale. La disposizione delle stanze riproduce la dispozione della capanna del *pater familias* e delle minori capanne degli altri componenti la famiglia, cinte per comune difesa da una palizzata in legno e raccolte intorno ad uno spazio centrale d'aria e di luce. Dall'aggregato di più capanne, affiancate l'una all'altra, si passò ad una più organica fusione degli ambienti mediante pareti e tetti comuni. Le due *alae* mantengono il distacco tra l'abitazione del capofamiglia e quelle dei suoi figli o dei servi. Quando s'incomincia a costruire in materiale più solido, prima in tavolato e poi in muratura, la fusione tra capanna e capanna è già avvenuta, e l'organismo pluricellulare della casa è già costituito" (Maiuri 1946, 127 = Maiuri 2000, 89). Leaving aside the question of an Iron Age *pater familias*, my only objection to Maiuri's formulation is that he sees it as applicable only to a rural environment. Certainly the evidence from Satricum suggests that such a transition could take place in a village or proto-urban setting as well.

38. Vitr. *De arch.* 6.5.2.
39. See the discussion by Bartoloni et al. (1987, 14–15) and also their interesting compilation of data about the human remains from hut urns from several different sites in Etruria and Latium (pp. 229–246). Each of the urns apparently held a single individual, although that person could be male or female, child or adult. Practices seem to have been local in nature: at Osteria dell'Osa, for instance, all of the individuals buried in hut urns were male.
40. Cf., most recently, Cifani 2008, 273.
41. But see supra n. 36.
42. E.g., Ampolo 1971; Scheffer 1990; Torelli 2000; Cifani 2008, 271–272, etc.
43. See Waarsenburg 2001, 180.
44. Prayon 1975, 15–17, 53–58; Waarsenburg 1995, 187–194.
45. Larsson 1988, 1989, 1990.
46. Larsson 1989, 507.
47. Not everyone, however, saw a display of one's wealth as appropriate or desirable behavior: Larsson 1990, 90–91.
48. Schwerdtfeger 1972, 553.
49. For a similar argument, see Lyons 1996.
50. Most recently, see Fulminante 2003, with previous bibliography.
51. Curtis 1925.
52. Waarsenburg 2001.
53. See also the converging argument of Waarsenburg 2001; cf. Maaskant-Kleibrink 1987, 95.

Bibliography

Ammerman, A. J. 1990. "On the Origins of the Forum Romanum." *AJA* 94:627–645.
Ampolo, C. 1971. "Analogie e rapporti fra Atene e Roma arcaica: Osservazioni sulla *Regia*, sul *rex sacrorum* e sul culto di Vesta." *PP* 26:443–460.
Angelelli, C., and S. Falzone. 1999. "Considerazioni sull'occupazione protostorica nell'area sud-occidentale del Palatino." *JRA* 12:5–32.
Bartoloni, G., A. J. Beijer, and A. De Santis. 1985. "Huts in the Central Tyrrhenian Area of Italy during the Protohistoric Age." In *Papers in Italian Archaeology IV. The Cambridge Conference*, ed. C. Malone and S. Stoddart. *BAR-IS* 246:175–202.
Bartoloni, G., F. Buranelli, V. D'Atri, and A. De Santis. 1987. *Le urne a capanna rinvenute in Italia*. Rome: Giorgio Bretschneider.
Bietti Sestieri, A. M., and A. De Santis. 2001. "L'edificio della I età del ferro di Fidene (Roma):

Posizione nell'abitato, tecnica costruttiva, funzionalità in base alla distribuzione spaziale dei materiali e degli arredi." In *From Huts to Houses: Transformations of Ancient Societies. Proceedings of an International Seminar Organized by the Norwegian and Swedish Institutes of Rome, 21–24 September 1997*, ed. J. R. Brandt and L. Karlsson, 211–221. Stockholm: Paul Åströms Förlag.

Boëthius, A. 1978. *Etruscan and Early Roman Architecture*. London: Penguin.

Brown, B. M. 1987. "Population Estimation from Floor Area: A Restudy of Naroll's Constant." *Behavior Science Research* 21:1–49.

Brown, F. E. 1976. "Of Huts and Houses." In *In Memoriam Otto J. Brendel: Essays in Archaeology and the Humanities*, ed. L. Bonfante and H. von Heintze, 5–12. Mainz: von Zabern.

Carandini, A. 2006. *Remo e Romolo: Dai rioni dei Quiriti alla città dei Romani (775/750–700/675 a.C.)*. Turin: Einaudi.

Casselberry, S. E. 1974. "Further Refinement of Formulae for Determining Population from Floor Area." *WorldArch* 6:117–122.

Chamberlain, A. T. 2006. *Demography in Archaeology*. Cambridge: Cambridge University Press.

Cifani, G. 2008. *Architettura romana arcaica: Edilizia e società tra Monarchia e Repubblica*. Rome: L'Erma di Bretschneider.

Curtis, C. D. 1925. "The Barberini Tomb." *MAAR* 5:9–52.

De Albentiis, E. 1990. *La casa dei Romani*. Milan: Longanesi.

De Santis, A., R. Merlo, and J. De Grossi Mazzorin. 1998. *Fidene: Una casa dell'età del ferro*. Milan: Electa.

Fayer, C. 1982. *Aspetti di vita quotidiana nella Roma arcaica*. Rome: L'Erma di Bretschneider.

Fewster, K. J. 1999. "The Uses of Ethnoarchaeology in Settlement Studies: The Case of the Bamangwato and Basarwa of Serowe, Botswana." In *Making Places in the Prehistoric World: Themes in Settlement Archaeology*, ed. J. Brück and M. Goodman, 178–197. London: UCL Press.

Fraser, D. 1968. *Village Planning in the Primitive World*. New York: George Braziller.

Fulminante, F. 2003. *Le sepolture principesche nel Latium Vetus*. Rome: L'Erma di Bretschneider.

Gjerstad, E. 1960. *Early Rome, III: Fortifications, Domestic Architecture, Sanctuaries, Stratigraphic Excavations*. Lund: C. W. K. Gleerup.

Gnade, M., ed. 2007. *Satricum: Trenta anni di scavi olandesi*. Amsterdam: Amsterdams Archeologisch Centrum.

Gracia, F., G. Munilla, E. García, R. M. Playà, and S. Muriel. 1996. "Demografía y superficie de poblamiento en los asentamientos ibéricos del NE. peninsular." *Complutum Extra* 6:177–191.

Hardie, G. J. 1981. "Tswana Design of House and Settlement. Continuity and Change in Expressive Space." PhD diss., Boston University.

———. 1985. "Continuity and Change in the Tswana's House and Settlement Form." In *Home Environments*, ed. I. Altman and C. M. Werner, 213–236. New York: Plenum Press.

Heldring, B. 1998. *Satricum: A Town in Latium*. Tonden, Netherlands: Foundation Dutch Centre for Latium Studies.

Holloway, R. R. 1994. *The Archaeology of Early Rome and Latium*. London: Routledge.

Kolb, C. C. 1985. "Demographic Estimates in Archaeology: Contributions from Ethnoarchaeology on Mesoamerican Peasants." *CurrAnthr* 26:581–599.

Larsson, A. 1988. *From Outdoor to Indoor Living: The Transition from Traditional to Modern Low-Cost Housing in Botswana*. Lund: Wallin och Dahlholm Boktryckeri AB.

———. 1989. "Traditional versus Modern Housing in Botswana—An Analysis from the User's Perspective." In *Dwellings, Settlements, and Tradition: Cross-Cultural Perspectives*, ed. J.-P. Bourdier and N. AlSayyad, 503–525. Lanham, Md.: University Press of America.

———. 1990. *Modern Houses for Modern Life: The Transformation of Housing in Botswana.* Lund: Wallin och Dahlholm Boktryckeri AB.

Larsson, A., and V. Larsson. 1984. *Traditional Tswana Housing: A Study in Four Villages in Eastern Botswana.* Stockholm: Spångbergs Tryckerier AB.

LeBlanc, S. 1971. "An Addition to Naroll's Suggested Floor Area and Settlement Population Relationship." *AmerAnt* 36:210–211.

Losehand, J. 2007. *Häuser für die Herrscher Roms und Athens?* Hamburg: Verlag Dr. Kovač.

Lyons, D. 1996. "The Politics of House Shape: Round *vs.* Rectilinear Domestic Structures in Déla Compounds, Northern Cameroon." *Antiquity* 70:351–367.

Maaskant-Kleibrink, M. 1987. *Settlement Excavations at Borgo Le Ferriere "Satricum", 1: The Campaigns 1979, 1980, 1981.* Groningen: Egbert Forsten.

———. 1991. "Early Latin Settlement-Plans at Borgo Le Ferriere (*Satricum*): Reading Mengarelli's Maps." *BABesch* 66:51–114.

Maiuri, A. 1946. *Lezioni sulla casa romana e pompeiana.* Raffaele Pironti & Figli.

———. 2000. *La casa pompeiana: Struttura, ambienti, storia nella magistrale descrizione d'un grande archeologo.* Ed. A. M. Ragozzino. Naples: Generoso Procaccini. (Reprint edition of Maiuri 1946.)

Naroll, R. 1962. "Floor Area and Settlement Population." *AmerAnt* 27:587–589.

Östenberg, C. E. 1975. *Case etrusche di Acquarossa.* Rome: Multigrafica Editrice.

Phillips, K. M., Jr. 1993. *In the Hills of Tuscany: Recent Excavations at the Etruscan Site of Poggio Civitate (Murlo, Siena).* Philadelphia: University Museum, University of Pennsylvania.

Prayon, F. 1975. *Frühetruskische Grab- und Hausarchitektur.* RM-EH 22. Heidelberg: F. H. Kerle.

———. 2001. "Near Eastern Influences in Early Etruscan Architecture?" In *Italy and Cyprus in Antiquity, 1500–450 B.C. Proceedings of an International Symposium Held at the Italian Academy for Advanced Studies in America at Columbia University, November 16–18 2000*, ed. L. Bonfante and V. Karageorghis, 335–350. Nicosia: Costakis and Leto Severis Foundation.

Schapera, I. 1935. "The Social Structure of the Tswana Ward." *Bantu Studies* 9:203–224.

Scheffer, C. 1990. "'Domus Regiae'—A Greek Tradition?" *OpAth* 18:185–191.

Schwerdtfeger, F. W. 1972. "Urban Settlement Patterns in Northern Nigeria (Hausaland)." In *Man, Settlement, and Urbanism*, ed. P. J. Ucko, R. Tringham, and G. W. Dimbleby, 547–556. London: Duckworth.

Stobbe, J. 2007a. "L'inizio di una comunità sull'acropoli." In *Satricum: Trenta anni di scavi olandesi*, ed. M. Gnade, 20–28. Amsterdam: Amsterdams Archeologisch Centrum.

———. 2007b. "L'architettura intorno ai templi." In *Satricum: Trenta anni di scavi olandesi*, ed. M. Gnade, 43–50. Amsterdam: Amsterdams Archeologisch Centrum.

Stopponi, S., ed. 1985. *Case e palazzi d'Etruria.* Milan: Electa.

Torelli, M. 1985. "Introduzione." In *Case e palazzi d'Etruria*, ed. S. Stopponi, 21–32. Milan: Electa.

———. 2000. "Le *regiae* etrusche e laziali tra orientalizzante e arcaismo." In *Principi etruschi tra Mediterraneo ed Europa*, ed. G. Bartoloni, F. Delpino, C. Morigi Govi, and G. Sassatelli, 67–78. Venice: Marsilio.

Tuck, A., and E. O. Nielsen. 2001. "An Orientalizing Period Complex at Poggio Civitate (Murlo): A Preliminary View." *EtrStud* 8:35–63.

Ucko, P. J. 1969. "Ethnography and Archaeological Interpretation of Funerary Remains." *World-Arch* 1:262–280.

Waarsenburg, D. J. 1995. *The Northwest Necropolis of Satricum: An Iron Age Cemetery in Latium Vetus. Scrinium VIII Satricum III.* Amsterdam: Thesis.

———. 2001. "Living Like a Prince: The Habitation Counterpart of *tombe principesche*, as Represented at Satricum." In *From Huts to Houses: Transformations of Ancient Societies. Pro-*

ceedings of an International Seminar Organized by the Norwegian and Swedish Institutes of Rome, 21–24 September 1997, ed. J. R. Brandt and L. Karlsson, 179–188. Stockholm: Paul Åströms Förlag.

Wallace-Hadrill, A. 1997. "Rethinking the Roman *atrium* House." In *Domestic Space in the Roman World: Pompeii and Beyond*, ed. R. Laurence and A. Wallace-Hadrill. *JRA* Suppl. 22:219–240.

Wiessner, P. 1974. "A Functional Estimator of Population from Floor Area." *AmerAnt* 39:343–350.

Wikander, Ö., and P. Roos, eds. 1986. *Architettura etrusca nel viterbese: Ricerche svedesi a San Giovenale e Acquarossa, 1956–1986*. Rome: De Luca.

III THE PERFORMANCE OF DEATH
MONUMENTALITY, BURIAL PRACTICE, AND COMMUNITY IDENTITY IN CENTRAL ITALY'S URBANIZING PERIOD

ANTHONY TUCK

THE DISCOVERY OF PREVIOUSLY UNKNOWN ETRUSCAN tombs, especially those from the wealthy urban centers along the southern stretches of the Tuscan coast and the opulent burials of the "Orientalizing" period, is often attended by considerable public fanfare. And yet, no matter how remarkable the surviving material environment of such a burial may be, the physical space of a tomb and the assemblage it contains represent merely the final stages of a ritual process that surrounds and defines the events that follow the death of a member of a community. During the socially and politically dynamic period of the late eighth through seventh centuries BCE, these ritual formulae emerged as key mechanisms whereby citizens of Etruria's developing city-states declared not only selected aspects of their own individual and familial identity, but also the broader expression of affiliation with their given communities. The rituals were accompanied by changes to the physical form of burial spaces themselves, changes often involving a significant and monumental modification of the existing landscape.

When considering evidence of ancient monumentality, archaeologists and art historians are normally and quite naturally drawn to expressions of such behavior within the realm of architecture. Yet for the purposes of this brief study, we might also consider how social conditions inform and direct the emergence of behaviors that result in such material amplification. Within the evolving social fabric of the central Italic Iron Age, it is useful to note that the audience for monumentalized behavior is immediate and present at the creation of a given archaeological context.

As such, the resulting monumentalized contexts are expressions of motivations that seize upon preexisting quotidian behaviors and seek to impress an audience through a radical rescaling of otherwise normative actions. In this way, any social action that amplifies and magnifies behaviors beyond the expectations of the commonplace might be viewed as a necessary precursor to subsequent, more readily apparent forms of monumentalized archaeological contexts. From this perspective, we may see suggestions of the impetus for monumentalized behavior in any number of social actions: banqueting, festival events, religious processions, ostentatious clothing, and many other behaviors that might be used as arenas wherein the immediate sociopolitical benefits of impressive, amplified actions can be realized. In considering the evolution of these kinds of behaviors as expressed in burial forms from the Iron Age into the Archaic period, we can trace not only their evolution, but also the underlying social motivations that guide them. In so doing, we may be able to see an evolution in central Italy from expressions of monumentality arising exclusively from familial interests into ones whereby familial interests are balanced against those of more broadly defined urban communities.

Prior to the political and social changes that mark the clear emergence of Etruscan city-states, Iron Age burial form at sites throughout the region of ancient central Italy is remarkably consistent. By far, the most common type of burial is one utilizing the rite of cremation, with the collected bone and ash placed in a distinctive form of biconical urn.[1] Such urns are often ornamented with incised or applied decoration and covered with a similarly distinctive bowl and, in infrequent cases, a bronze helmet or a ceramic imitation of such a head covering (fig. 3.1). Biconical urns used as cineraria display other notably consistent features. Urns typically are manufactured by hand using a simple coiling method. Horizontal loop handles are placed at the widest point of the vessel. While some variation in specific forms of vessels or their ornamentation appears from site to site, the widespread use of this type of cinerary urn is one of the defining characteristics of Iron Age burial throughout the region of central Italy.

In fact, some remarkably specific and consistent details concerning the treatment of such urns suggest the existence of a collectively held set of coded ritual behaviors reflecting this Iron Age Etruscan population's underlying beliefs regarding the nature and meaning of these vessels when used to contain the remains of the dead. While many such urns are manufactured asymmetrically with only one handle, numerous examples are created and fired with two. How-

Fig. 3.1. Volterra, Tomba di Badia (photo A. Tuck).

ever, with biconical urns made with two handles, one of the handles is typically removed at some point prior to the vessel's final deposition in the grave. In fact, the ubiquity of the practice of removing one handle is evident even in rare specimens of biconical urns made from bronze sheets and also in an unusual example from Tarquinia of an eighth-century Rhodian transport amphora used as a cinerary urn.[2] The consistency of the practice appears to suggest an underlying ritual motivation associated with the action, albeit one with a specific meaning that remains obscure.[3] Moreover, the fact that this action is archaeologically visible at virtually all central Italic burial grounds of the period implies that the ritual meaning, whatever its precise significance, is one that is shared among various Iron Age Etruscan communities of the region.

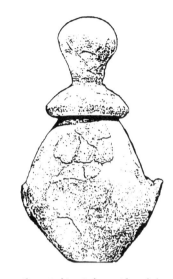

Fig. 3.2. Saturnia, biconical urn with cephalomorphic cover (drawing by Michael Thomas).

Other common treatments of biconical urns from numerous sites indicate that the custodians of this form of ritual burial understood the vessel to be a conceptualization of the deceased individual whose remains were contained inside.[4] This idea is reflected in numerous distinctive treatments of these biconical urns, such as those that are adorned with jewelry and decorative bronze belts. Fibulae—often found outside the urn but within the grave and sometimes actually adhering to the urn's surface—indicate that the vessel was covered in cloth, as if dressed or shrouded.[5] Similarly, outside the cinerary urn itself, bronze "razors" are often recovered. These objects, thought to be included exclusively in male burials, are sometimes found with fibulae threaded through the eyelets of their exceptionally small handles, suggesting they may be better understood as ornamental bangles originally worn on the shoulder rather than as shaving instruments. The head, suggested by the occasional use of metallic or ceramic helmets used as covering elements, is sometimes even more explicitly represented by covers displaying rounded, headlike projections (fig. 3.2).[6]

To be sure, variations on this Iron Age ritual form are also well documented. At Tarquinia during the earliest period of such Iron Age burials, Phase I, a small number, five in total, utilize ceramic urns in the shape of huts.[7] All appear to be male burials and are surrounded by notably complex assemblages of funerary material. Hut urns are also known from other Iron Age Etruscan cemeteries in similarly small numbers from site to site, their relative infrequency and greater materiality again suggesting they were usually associated with elite males, perhaps the leaders of *gens* groups. The opposite end of the social spectrum may be reflected in the use of inhumation to dispose of the dead, a rite often employed for marginal members of ancient communities such as children, and appearing almost as infrequently in Iron Age Tarquinia as the hut urn phenomenon.[8]

Recent studies considering the evidence of incrementally greater complexity reflected throughout the burial record of the Iron Age have significantly advanced our understanding of the social processes at work throughout this formative period.[9] However, one characteristic of the burials of this period that appears to be largely accepted and passed over without further comment concerns the remarkable similarity of the material expression of this ritual behavior at sites throughout the region of Iron Age Etruria, for example the idea of the cinerarium as a conceptualization of the body of the deceased, as well as habitual idiosyncrasies expressed in Iron Age forms of burial, such as the removal of one handle on urns originally manufactured with two. Despite minor variations in the types of equipment used from site to site, the ritual constituencies suggest that the cultural assumptions implicit in such acts were communicated through these material forms and were thus shared among the population of central Italy throughout the Iron Age. On the strength of this observation we might confidently assume that other factors of cultural identity (linguistic, social, technological, etc.) were likely also shared among this Iron Age Etruscan population.

By the late eighth and into the seventh century BCE, especially in Latium and in the southernmost Etruscan communities, there is a visible tendency to limit the use of cremation to a selected subset of a given community. By the later stages of the Iron Age, it appears that the ritual of cremation was reserved for extraordinary, elite members of a given community.[10] Shortly thereafter, inhumation generally appears to replace cremation almost entirely, with the important exception of a few communities, such as that of Chiusi.

We might ask what kinds of ritual advantages cremation provides to the population that survives the deceased. Specific evidence addressing this issue is not likely to be extant archaeologically, but one effect we can assume is that the act of cremation allows the population to significantly attenuate the period of time between the ritual action of cremation and the actual event of burial. As the material assemblages associated with the burial ritual grow increasingly focused on the presentation of specific social roles, the corruptible body, destroyed by fire, is symbolically reconstituted by the more permanent ceramic or bronze urn, which can then serve as an effigy of the dead. This can easily be transported, carried in procession along with other implements chosen for inclusion in burial to mark the social position of the deceased, or made to symbolically complete the iconography of burial, as is the case with slightly later elite burials from near Chiusi, where the urn is enthroned at a ritual meal.[11]

Moreover, the lengthening of the time period available for the comprehensive expression of all ritual actions associated with burial would also allow for a much broader participation in those rituals by members of the surviving community—

or even beyond the immediate community to parties from other communities that share some political or social relationship to the deceased. However, we have no specific evidence to indicate what these customs might have been, nor is it very likely that the archaeological record can provide direct evidence for such events. Even so, the logistical advantages afforded by cremation may have informed the development of this restriction of ritual form to a specific subset of some communities.

Such a concern for a funerary display of social distinction and position, especially among the sociopolitical elite, grows even more acute in the period immediately following the transition from the Iron Age into the Etruscan "Orientalizing" period, ca. 725–600, with some degree of chronological variation from region to region.[12] High-status burials of this period are primarily notable for the remarkable degree of invested material wealth they contain.[13] These "princely" graves appear to be the final form of a gradually escalating process of the representation of gentility in Iron Age burials. Cemeteries from the latest stages of the Iron Age have produced a very small number of burials that contain an exceptional number of metal objects, especially weapons in male graves and objects of personal adornment in female burials. However, these intrinsically valuable objects usually conform to the typological standards of materials manufactured in the region of central Italy. With the advent of "princely" burials during the transitional period from the eighth to the seventh century BCE, we see a similar deposition of metal goods—some local products, some versions of traditional indigenous forms produced in valuable metals—all of which is joined by an array of imported materials of a decidedly nonlocal character.

Such objects—acquired from Eastern sources or local products inspired by them generally—tend to display decorative features emphasizing specific types of iconography. Within this body of material, images of the Eastern fertility divinity Astarte and motifs related to this goddess dominate to such an extent that the general nature of virtually all such imports appears prescribed by a desire to present this specific iconographic theme. Indeed, among elite families of central Italy during the "Orientalizing" period, the incorporation of these Eastern images associated with fertility appears to be not an accident of commerce, but instead the conscious selection of a package of alien iconographies that are particularly well suited to emphasize the fundamental and overriding concern of aristocratic groups: fertility and the divine blessing of it.[14]

The fact that the "princely" burials of this brief period all display such similar iconographies through remarkably similar material assemblages suggests that the purveyors of these status objects understood the social and political subtleties of their market, and that their consumers fully grasped the narrative nuances of the iconographies they adopted and adapted.[15] Thus, it is also possible that, in addition to providing a material template upon which the access to and disposal of exclusive types of goods may be presented to the broader community, such assemblages were consciously designed to communicate an implicit message that announced and re-inforced the political intentions of an emergent aristocratic class that was increasingly interested in the concerns of political succession created by the event of the death of one of its members.

In addition, some elements of these burials appear to reflect increased attention not only to the iconography and equipment of burial, but also to the elaborate performance of funerary ritual. For example, the shockingly opulent Regolini-Galassi Tomb from the Sorbo cemetery of Caere, a rare example of an archaeologically intact elite burial of this period, contained not only imported ceramic and metal wares, indigenous versions of the same (including some of the earliest known specimens of Etruscan bucchero), a range of bronze furniture, and impressive quantities of gold jewelry, but also a large cart decorated with bronze fittings. Three burials were found within the tomb, two of cremated men and one of an inhumed woman.[16] Much of the gold jewelry included in the burial assemblage appears to be associated with the woman's burial, and, while we cannot know with any certainty how her body was conveyed to the cemetery, it is inviting to imagine that the cart was used as a bier, allowing the surviving family the opportunity to proceed from the domestic sphere of the household to the funerary sphere of the tomb, thereby creating a monumental spectacle witnessed by the surrounding community.

The "princely" burial phenomenon and the often stunning degree of material excess invested in these unusual graves should not necessarily be construed as representing a meaningful or immediate increase in the economic sophistication of the region. The mere fact that the surviving family members created such opulent burial groups, investing in them large quantities of precious metals and exotic goods, suggests that such materials were of greater value to the family as the equipment of social display than as objects of intrinsic value in their own right. Burial events associated with members of this period's elite families parade such goods before the witnessing population of a community in the context of funerary rites to emphasize both the divine sanction of elite familial lineage and the material environment thereof. Whatever the intrinsic value of such items may be, it is eclipsed by the social value the items convey when they are displayed in the context of burial and thenceforth removed from socioeconomic interaction when sealed in a grave.

The subsequent diminution of visible wealth invested in elite burials toward the end of this period may in fact reflect not a contraction in the availability of such status goods, but rather a more robust and mature economic environment wherein surviving family members are loathe to dispose of goods that have come to have a fungible socioeconomic value that outstrips their value as props in the context of the politically performative rites of burial. This is not to suggest that the expense associated with burial is necessarily less, but rather that the expression of such expense takes a different form. For example, at some sites such expression of the significant investment of this social energy can be found in the radical reformation of the existing landscape of the cemetery itself, as at Caere, where massive earthworks forming tumuli surmounting rock-carved burial chambers emerge as visible landmarks.

It is also possible that, in the period after the "princely" burials, the lesser degree of intrinsically valuable materiality invested in graves reflects a more mature political environment. The event of a death among the members of an elite family triggers not only the rituals associated with death, but also those of social and political succession. Upon the death of a member of a given community's socially powerful elite class, the relationship of that deceased person to an heir is further accentuated by the adopted iconographies of fertility mentioned above. While the iconography of fertility and its implicit relationship to familial lineage remains ubiquitous in subsequent periods of Etruscan Italy, the environment within which that iconography is displayed reflects important compromises in the political dynamic that balance the interests of family groups against those of the collective environment of the city.[17]

It is also in the period immediately following that of the "princely" burial phenomenon that another curious evolution in Etruscan burial practice becomes evident. The previously marked and broad similarity of burial types characteristic of Iron Age burials visible at sites throughout the region gives way to site-specific forms of monumentalizing burial practices associated with particular urban centers. For the purposes of the somewhat limited scope of this study, three major urban settlements of the Archaic period that typify this phenomenon are considered: Tarquinia, Caere, and Chiusi.

Tarquinia

IRON AGE BURIALS OF TARQUINIA ARE FOUND IN NUmerous concentrations on hills around the main settlement plateau. However, through the later stages of the Iron Age, the overall number of burials significantly declines at all cemeteries except for that of Monterozzi. Spatial organization at the individual cemeteries varies to some degree, with those of Le Rose burial ground found in small groups suggesting areas dedicated to nuclear families. This pattern is rather different from that at the Arcatelle burying ground, where much denser clusters of cremation burials are connected by enigmatic channels cut into the bedrock. The density of the grave clusters of Arcatelle suggests that burial areas were in use for a longer period of time, and the graves found there are often more complex and display a greater material investment than their Le Rose counterparts. The different pattern may relate to variation in spatially defined behavior, with the burials of Le Rose representing small, distinct families and those of Arcatelle consisting

Fig. 3.3. Tarquinia, Tomb of the Panthers (photo A. Tuck).

of groups concerned with using the spatial relationships of burial to emphasize lineage and descent.[18] From the seventh century onward, burial activity focuses almost exclusively on the Monterozzi hill, to the exclusion of all others.[19] This phenomenon of coalescence of most funerary activity onto a specific area is seen at the nearby urban centers of Caere and Veii as well, apparently indicating that peripheral burial grounds, perhaps associated with specific *gens* groups, were abandoned in favor of cemeteries used in common by an entire community.[20]

During the period in which Monterozzi emerges as Tarquinia's primary cemetery area, the practice of cremation is largely abandoned in favor of inhumation, and elite funerary architecture at the cemetery takes the form of subterranean chambers ornamented with painted frescoes.[21] The chronology associated with the earliest examples of such painted tombs is not well established, but graves such as the Tomb of the Panthers, probably constructed during the second half of the seventh century BCE, is among the earliest to make use of figural painted decoration (fig. 3.3).[22] The central motif of the fresco depicts a pair of panthers heraldically posed over a masklike representation of another feline face, apparently festooned with garlands. The panther on the viewer's right is depicted in profile while that on the left turns to present its face frontally.[23]

Similar burial chambers with figural painted decoration become more common by the second quarter of the sixth century BCE, although the form remains a type limited to Tarquinia's social elite. The Tomb of the Bulls, with its vague suggestion of blood sacrifice implicit in the mythological representation of the murder of Troilus, is among the earliest of the Archaic period series of such burials.[24]

However, with those burials that appear to follow shortly thereafter, we see the representation of a general theme among several tombs of this period that suggests that both funerary architecture and funerary iconography had become codified. Images of banqueting, dancing, athletic competitions, and similar activities appear to represent the events of funerals themselves.[25] Indeed, some such representations do so in a manner that is quite explicit: at the Tomb of the Juggler, for example, the scene on the back wall of the chamber depicts a young girl balancing vessels on her head as she prepares to juggle balls handed to her by a youthful attendant.[26] Elsewhere in the scene, a piper stands behind the juggler as two additional figures look on from the side. In other painted chamber tombs of the period, such as the Tomb of the Hunter, the fresco ornamentation is used to represent the patterns of cloth tents beneath which events of the funeral would have occurred.[27] The Tomb of the Dead Man, with its central image of a body placed on a couch attended by a young woman, suggests that the *ekphora*—the public display of the body during the events of the funeral—may have been one such function of these tents.[28]

The relative scarcity of such opulent painted burial chambers at Tarquinia would seem to indicate that such ornamented tombs were reserved for a limited, elite class. And yet, nothing in the way of externally visible, monumental modification of the surrounding landscape survives. To judge from the available evidence, it would seem that the elite families of Tarquinia directed their investment of energy inward, into the space of the tomb. However, as noted above, the types of scenes represented point to a significant degree of public display, impermanent though these might have been. It appears that the banqueting, public spectacle, sponsored athletic competition, and other such events recorded upon the walls of the tomb occurred outside the tomb within the ritual framework of the funeral and were performed in honor of the dead by the deceased's surviving family and for the benefit of the surviving population of the community. As such, the monumental spectacle of such events, especially when rendered on a presumably amplified scale, would have served to reinforce the status of the family responsible for them while also providing a forum wherein participation in the event reinforced the social dynamics of the community.

Caere

ALTHOUGH THE DISTANCE BETWEEN TARQUINIA AND Caere is less than 50 kilometers, a distance potentially able to be traversed in a single day, the architecture associated with elite burial at Caere is notably different. Much like the phenomenon seen at Tarquinia, the use of a number of peripheral burying grounds active throughout the Iron Age fades, and funerary activity concentrates on the Banditaccia cemetery.

The social elite who utilized this justifiably famous cemetery constructed massive tumuli that surmounted subterranean chambers carved from the underlying

Fig. 3.4. Caere, Tomb of the Thatched Hut
(photo A. Tuck).

tufa bedrock. Beginning around the middle of the seventh century, these chambers are typically carved into the form of the interior of houses, a phenomenon very likely connected to the use of cinerary urns in the shape of huts witnessed in the earlier period of the Iron Age. Among the early examples of this phenomenon is the Tomb of the Thatched Hut. This sepulcher consists of two chambers. The roof of the first chamber is pitched, and its apex is carved to suggest the form of a ridge pole, while the gently convex sides are slightly striated, recalling the reed thatching that would have been used to cover curvilinear huts (fig. 3.4).[29] It is difficult to determine whether the Tomb of the Thatched Hut reflects the technological form of domestic architecture with which it is contemporary or whether it instead represents some form of intentional archaism. It is thought to date to roughly the point when the technology of tiled, terracotta roofs was developed, along with the rectilinear foundations that such buildings normally employ.[30] The chamber tombs constructed throughout the remainder of the seventh century and onward through the Hellenistic period are carved with the representation of columns, rafters, and numerous other architectural details representing the interior domestic space of Etruscan houses. Some of these sepulchers are quite baroque. The Tomb of the Reliefs, datable to the Late Classical or Early Hellenistic period, employs stucco suspended from the chamber walls to represent the trappings of an elite household. Banqueting equipment, armor, parade equipment, even household pets are represented on the walls of the tomb (fig. 3.5).[31]

Thus, the general trajectory of funerary architecture at Caere amplified a pre-existing Iron Age idea—already manifest in the hut urn tradition—and translated the definitional sociopolitical architectural space of the subsequent periods, the *domus*, into sculpted funerary sepulchers within which a given generation of an elite family was interred.[32] For the members of the highest social echelons of the Caere community, such chambers were placed beneath earthen tumuli that served to modify the existing landscape in a monumental manner that remains dramatically visible even today, as reflected in just one such example, Banditaccia Tumulus II (fig. 3.6). The interplay between symbolic environments—the internal, symbolic representation of the elite household and the enduring, extrinsic modified landscape—appears to have served as an arena for the performance of a variety of ritual events beyond that of mere burial, suggesting a physical space wherein, in the presence of the remains of one's familial ancestry, the possible worship of that ancestry is enacted through competitively monumentalized forms of architecture.[33]

Fig. 3.5. Caere, Tomb of the Reliefs (photo A. Tuck).

Fig. 3.6. Caere, Tumulus II (photo A. Tuck).

The externally visible form of elite burial behavior at Caere's Banditaccia cemetery, notably distinct from that of Tarquinia's Monterozzi, lends itself to a significant amplification of scale that preserves some elements of the earlier, familially driven motivations associated with the "princely" tomb phenomenon. With the Banditaccia complex familial interests are reflected in the representation of the *domus* and externally escalated through the creation of dominant, massive tumuli that are placed among subordinate, smaller familial sepulchers. Over time, the cemetery evolves into a parallel representation of the living city of Caere itself, reflecting the social and political conditions of the city while offering an architectural means of both reinforcing those conditions and promoting competition within them. However, Caere's emerging political maturity is apparent in the fact that this competition occurs within a monumentalized architectural and ritual form specific to Caere.

Chiusi

THE NORTHERN INLAND COMMUNITY OF CHIUSI CONtinued to utilize the rite of cremation well after the practice was largely abandoned by the cities of Tarquinia and Caere. Unlike these sites, the traditional burial practice at Chiusi, the so-called canopic urn tradition, represents a somewhat more explicit and direct evolution of the Iron Age tradition of conceptualizing the dead through the biconical cinerary urn.[34] Bodies were cremated and the remains placed in vessels covered with modeled images of human heads. In many cases, arms are represented on the vessel's body and various other attributes are included to further conceptualize the deceased (fig. 3.7). Many examples of such canopic burials represent the face of the deceased in a manner that is clearly intended to suggest the idea of a mask. This may explain the occasional example of a burial from this region that employs a cinerary urn without an explicit representation of the deceased. The head or face may in fact have been originally present in a material, such as cloth or leather, that does not survive.

Another feature visible on many examples of canopic urns are perforations on the lower edge of the canopus that correspond to perforations on the upper neck of the cinerary urn. The likely function of these perforations was to keep the lid joined to the urn.[35] This feature seems to imply that the events surrounding a Chiusine funeral involved activities that might cause the lid to move or fall off were it not so secured. Although direct archaeological evidence of such activities is inevitably wanting, one probable scenario is that the container, used to symbolically represent and conceptualize the body of the dead, functions as an effigy. The Republican writer Polybius provides a description of a somewhat later Roman variation of this phenomenon, wherein effigies are carried in procession and eulogized both for the purposes of honoring the dead, and to politically and socially valorize the family and its surviving members.[36] It is inviting to imagine similar events taking place in the communities of Chiusi in the days and hours immediately prior to the actual ritual of burial, with the anthropomorphic urn serving as both effigy and cinerarium.

The social performance implied in this treatment of the cinerary urn as effigy is again employed in customs designed to reflect social status within the fabric of the community of the region. In 1994, at the locality of Morelli, near Chianciano Terme, excavation revealed the presence of a large tumulus containing a roughly bicameral internal space (fig. 3.8). The chamber contained multiple burials, but the tumulus appears to have been constructed for and around a primary deposition consisting of a cremated individual whose remains were placed before a table and surrounded by an impressive array of banqueting equipment and military equipment. Preserved traces of gold foil and a pair of bone and amber eyes indicate that the urn originally displayed a mask akin to those seen elsewhere in the region, although made in this instance from an intrinsically valuable material.[37] Similar tumuli, such as the Pania Tumulus and another from Poggio alla Sala, containing equally impressive burial assemblages, are known throughout the region around Chiusi.[38] By constructing monumental tombs, the region's dominant families distinguished themselves not by deviation from the common ritual practices of the area, but rather by the increase and amplification of the traditional framework in which those common behaviors were expressed. In this sense, the burial practices of the region of Chiusi appear motivated by sociopolitical concerns similar to those seen at Caere, albeit in a more geographically dispersed form.

Fig. 3.7. Tolle (region of Chiusi), canopic burial (photo A. Tuck).

Fig. 3.8. Morelli (region of Chiusi), tumulus interior (photo A. Tuck).

Certainly, the pattern and distribution of burial practice characteristic of the region around Chiusi differs to some degree from that of Caere and Tarquinia, in that burials utilizing such canopic effigies are not limited to the settlement of Chiusi alone, and neither does the settlement experience the phenomenon of the emergence of a single, dominant burying ground that is apparent at the southern, coastal centers. This may be an effect of the topography of the inland region where Chiusi is located. The plateaus of Tarquinia and Caere are many times the size of the hilltop of Chiusi.[39] For the Roman tradition of Chiusi's emergence as a major urban entity of the Archaic and Classical period to be valid, the settlement would likely have required the benefit and allegiance of a citizenry far more numerous than could occupy the hill of Chiusi alone. Therefore, the wider geographic distribution of the ritual use of the canopic urn form, if we are correct in seeing its use as a mechanism reflecting participation in the sociopolitical sphere of a dominant center located at Chiusi, may be a sign of that community's need to extend social control and community allegiance to a more topographically dispersed population.[40] The use of a shared burial ritual, especially one that employed significant public performance, could conceivably have been one of the means by which social and political allegiance to a central authority was represented. At the same time, as seen in the architectural evidence, variation in social status within that geographically dispersed community was reflected in the amplification of scale and permanence of certain traditional contexts.

Conclusions

THROUGHOUT THE IRON AGE, BURIALS AT TARQUINIA, Caere, and Chiusi followed a similar ritual trajectory. Biconical urns were most commonly used to conceptualize the deceased, although variations in equipment or ritual such as hut urns and inhumation were also sometimes used. The similarity of minor ritual behaviors involving the treatment of biconical urns demonstrates that the underlying assumptions and beliefs concerning the symbolic meaning of such burial equipment were shared at all three sites. Throughout the middle to later stages of the period, the assemblages included in some burials appear to reflect an incremental increase in the use of materiality to indicate variation in social status. By the end of the Iron Age, a small number of graves within preexisting cemeteries came to include dense concentrations of both locally manufactured and imported goods, much of which is ornamented with the adopted iconography of fertility divinities, reflecting an increased concern with the politics of family lineage.

With the transition into the late eighth and seventh centuries, the separate family burying grounds of the Iron Age ceased to be used and funerary activity focused on particular cemeteries, just as the material similarity of Iron Age burials at Tarquinia, Caere, and Chiusi gave way to a series of architectural and ritual forms distinct to each of these communities. In spite of the abundant evidence for common linguistic, religious, and social practices at the three sites, the performance of funerary ritual stands out as peculiarly site-specific in its form. To be sure, variations and exceptions to this general pattern of site-specific burial form are present at all three sites, but such outliers are not so common as to undermine the conclusion that the site-specific burial forms described above are consciously selected and maintained by their given communities.

Although evidence for constitutionally defined citizenship does not exist in Etruria at this time as it does at the Greek *poleis* with which they are contemporary, the particularity of burial form may reflect ideas of membership in and allegiance to the emerging city-state. Among the various transitional rituals of social groups—the events surrounding birth, rites of maturation, marriage, and death—only death is likely to produce a material record readily visible to archaeologists. The examples of Tarquinia, Caere, and Chiusi demonstrate that the visible behaviors associated with death diverge from a common Iron Age form into a series of site-specific types at precisely the same time as other indications of the urban process (fortifications, industrial development, craft specialization) become discernible.[41] The tradition of segregated, smaller burial plots is replaced by a single cemetery space shared by an entire community's elite class, thus emphasizing the participation of that family within the corporate political landscape of the city.

In some instances, amplifications of the architectural scale of such burials are visible within the cemeteries, as with Caere's massive Tumulus II or other examples of Banditaccia's large tumuli, but such monumentality occurs within the framework of the site's preferred form of ritual architecture, perhaps reflecting internal sociopolitical tensions and conditions that remain as permanently visible expressions of familial status within their communities. Ostentatious expense at other sites that do not preserve such evidence of monumental funerary architecture—whether accomplished through lavish funerary events or opulent, impermanent structures such as those suggested by the painted tombs of Tarquinia—may simply be an effect of an investment of social energy in community-specific directions no less monumental but without enduring archaeological visibility. As Warden rightly states in this volume, monumentality need not be understood simply in terms of amplification of architectural scale. The perception by the intended audience of monumentality, whether of structure or event, relates more to the degree of observable energy and expense invested in it. It is nevertheless within and outside of these social dynamics that the more readily observable aspects of monumentality arise; these result from the need to further distinguish personal or familial roles within the complex matrices of these emergent Etruscan urban centers.

Finally, it bears noting that similar evidence for public display of ritual behavior associated with burial and continued veneration of the dead is visible at other Etruscan communities. For example, the funerary altars associated with the Melone del Sodo Tumulus II at Cortona (fig. 5.6)[42] and the S. Iacopo Tumulus near Pisa (fig. 5.8)[43] preserve evidence of highly visible, monumentalized spaces upon which ritual behaviors associated with the veneration of familial ancestry would have occurred.[44] Yet here again, even as such sites reflect common motivations for similar behaviors that trend toward monumentalism, the specific means of expression of those interests remains notably site specific.

Archaeologists investigating the urban development of Etruscan Italy lack the ability to reference the political and historical texts so often useful in reconstructing early Greek political and civic identity. However, in the visible markers of the burial traditions of Etruria's communities, the highly distinctive forms suggest that the performative rituals associated with death served not only to facilitate generational transition but also to announce a family's place among other groups of the same city. The divergent and site-specific expressions of funerary practice that emerge out of the commonly held Iron Age traditions of the region monumentalize not only communal identity, but also what the body politic of an Etruscan city felt it was to be a member of that community.

Notes

I am deeply honored to contribute this essay to a volume dedicated to a scholar as inspiring as Ingrid Edlund-Berry. The guidance, insight, and wisdom she has shared with me through the years is appreciated far beyond the capacity of mere words. I would also like to thank the editors of this volume, Michael Thomas and Gretchen Meyers, for their vision in conceiving the book and their patience and dedication in shepherding it through to its conclusion.

1. Bartoloni 1992, 118–128.
2. Hencken 1968, 141.
3. Iaia 1999, 141.
4. Tuck 1994, 626–627.
5. Gleba 2008, 89.
6. Donati 1989, 34–39.
7. Iaia 1999, 22–23. For a recent treatment of this type of cinerary urn, see Leighton 2005.
8. Iaia 1999, 62.
9. Riva 2010; Iaia 1999; Bartoloni 1992; Bietti Sestieri 1992.
10. Bietti Sestieri 1992, 242.
11. Tuck 1994, 622. An example of one such burial was recently recovered intact from the area of Morelli, near Chianciano Terme. See Paolucci and Rastrelli 2006.
12. Riva 2010. Riva's survey of evidence associated with the urbanization process in Etruria rightly places an emphasis on indigenous social factors to explain the rapid movement from village structures to urban centers, one effect of which is the rapid development of use of the funerary environment to communicate emergent social roles within communities.
13. Winther 1999.
14. Tuck 2010.
15. For a consideration of various types of objects often deposited in such "princely" burials that reflects the common materiality of such graves, see Winther 1999, 426.
16. Pareti 1947.
17. Tuck 2010, 219.
18. Iaia 1999, 138.
19. Steingräber 1985, 23.
20. Berardinetti, De Santis, and Drago 1997, 331.
21. Steingräber 1985, 24. The high status of family groups interred in such painted tombs is reflected by the fact that of the more than 6,000 chamber tombs known from the area of the Monterozzi cemetery, only 2–3 percent are ornamented with this type of decoration.
22. Steingräber 1985, 333.
23. Curiously, the arrangement of one animal depicted frontally and another in profile is seen in the pedimental animal compositions of many subsequent Monterozzi tombs, including the mid-sixth-century Tomb of the Bulls. The representation of the bulls has been viewed by some (e.g., Holloway [1986]) as related to the phallic symbol and its implied notion of fertility, suggested by the horns of the frontally depicted bull. Oddly, for another such example, the pedimental painting of the Tomb of the Juggler, the felines are depicted in a similar fashion, but a close inspection of the feline on the viewer's right indicates that

the original cartoon of the image depicted the animal in profile and the arrangement was not corrected until the final rendering of the fresco. Not all images of such pedimental animals display this arrangement, but a large number do. It remains unclear whether some deeper symbolic meaning is at work here, one perhaps associated with the broader traditional significance of masks suggested by the frontal depictions of animal faces.

24. The puzzling combination of images from this tomb have intrigued many scholars. While many of the images appear related to a general concern with apotropaism, the underlying relationship to the unusual central image drawn from Greek myth is not readily apparent. See Holloway 1986.

25. Holloway 1965, 347.

26. Steingräber 1985, 310.

27. Steingräber 1985, 295.

28. Steingräber 1985, 325–326.

29. Prayon 1975, 98, pl. 28.

30. The seventh-century BCE settlement at Poggio Civitate preserves evidence of a curvilinear domestic space that appears to be contemporary with elements of an architectural complex on the plateau of Piano del Tesoro. This suggests that for a brief period of time, the use of terracotta roofing systems (and the monumental, extremely attenuated architectural forms they more easily allow) remains another element of aristocratic prerogative available to the nonelite members of such communities. However, the excavation of the curvilinear domestic architecture at Poggio Civitate remains in progress, and any conclusions drawn from this evidence must be considered preliminary. See Carroll, Rodriguez, and Tuck 2009.

31. Blanck and Proietti 1986.

32. Leighton 2005.

33. Prayon 2010.

34. Gempeler 1974, 251–252.

35. E.g., Gempeler 1974, 34, pl. 6.4. Several more recently discovered examples of canopic urn burials displaying this characteristic have been recovered from excavations in the village of Tolle, near Chianciano Terme, and are on display at the Museo Civico of Chianciano Terme. See Paolucci 2001, 73–79.

36. Shuckburgh 2002, 383.

37. Paolucci and Rastrelli 2006, 21.

38. Minetti 1998, 31; Rastrelli 2000, 159.

39. Rasmussen 2005, 73–74; Steingräber 2001, 14.

40. Riva (2010, 19) sees a process of urban development in the northern, inland region of central Italy akin to that of southern and coastal communities, despite the region's significantly different geomorphology. However, the wider regional distribution of the "Chiusine" form of burial marks it as rather different from the significantly more regionally restricted funerary architectural forms seen at Etruscan coastal centers. Another example of such community development is arguably visible at the site of Poggio Civitate, where a central aristocratic community complex appears to have been surrounded by a series of affiliated towns and hamlets. Unlike Chiusi (and perhaps because of Chiusi's success), Poggio Civitate was obliterated in the mid- to late sixth century and never reinhabited, although occupation of the surrounding, nonelite communities continued. See Tuck et al. 2009.

41. Damgaard Andersen 1997.

42. Zamarchi Grassi 1992.

43. Floriani and Bruni 2006.

44. Warden 2011, 62–63.

Bibliography

Bartoloni, G. 1992. *La cultura villanoviana*. Rome: La Nouva Italia scientifica.

Berardinetti, A., A. De Santis, and L. Drago. 1997. "Burials as Evidence for Proto-Urban Development in Southern Etruria: The Case of Veii." *Acta Hyperborea* 7:317–342.

Bietti Sestieri, A. M. 1992. *The Iron Age Community of Osteria dell'Osa: A Study of the Socio-Political Development of Central Italy*. Cambridge: Cambridge University Press.

Blanck, H., and G. Proietti. 1986. *La Tomba dei Rilievi di Cerveteri*. Rome: De Luca.

Carroll, A., A. Rodriguez, and A. Tuck. 2009. "Light Framed Architecture at Poggio Civitate: A Comparison of Elite and Non-Elite Domiciles." *Rasenna: Journal of the Center for Etruscan Studies* 2.1. http://scholarworks.umass.edu/rasenna/vol2/iss1/4/.

Damgaard Andersen, H. 1997. "The Archaeological Evidence for the Origin and Development of the Etruscan City in the 7th and 6th Centuries B.C." *Acta Hyperborea* 7:343–382.

Donati, L. 1989. *La Tomba da Saturnia*. Florence: Olschki.

Floriani, P., and S. Bruni. 2006. *La Tomba del Principe: Il tumulo etrusco di via San Iacopo*. Pisa: ETS.

Gempeler, R. 1974. *Die etruskischen Kanopen: Herstellung, Typologie, Entwicklungsgeschichte*. Einsiedeln: Benziger.

Gleba, M. 2008. *Textile Production in Pre-Roman Italy*. Oxford: Oxbow Books.

Hencken, H. 1968. *Tarquinia, Villanovans, and Early Etruscans*. Cambridge, Mass.: Peabody Museum.

Holloway, R. R. 1965. "Conventions of Etruscan Painting in the Tomb of Hunting and Fishing at Tarquinii." *AJA* 69:341–347.

———. 1986. "The Bulls in the 'Tomb of the Bulls' at Tarquinia." *AJA* 90:447–452.

Iaia, C. 1999. *Simbolismo funerario e ideologia alle origini di una civiltà urbana: Forme rituali nelle sepulture 'villanoviane' a Tarquinia e Vulci, e nel loro entroterra*. Florence: All'insegna del giglio.

Leighton, R. 2005. "House Urns and Etruscan Tomb Painting: Tradition versus Innovation in the Ninth–Seventh Centuries B.C." *OJA* 24:363–380.

Minetti, A. 1998. "La tomba della Pania: Corredo e rituale funerario." *Annali di archeologia e storia antica* 5:27–56.

Paolucci, G. 2001. *Antiche genti di Castelluccio la Foce e Tolle*. Siena: Amministrazione provinciale di Siena.

Paolucci, G., and A. Rastrelli. 2006. *La Tomba 'Principesca' di Chianciano Terme*. Pisa: Pacini.

Pareti, L. 1947. *La Tomba Regolini-Galassi*. Rome: Vatican City.

Prayon, F. 1975. *Frühetruskische Grab- und Hausarchitektur*. Heidelberg: F. H. Kerle.

———. 2010. "Tomb as Altar." In *Material Aspects of Etruscan Religion: Proceedings of the International Colloquium Leiden, May 29 and 30, 2008*, ed. L. Bouke van der Meer, 75–82. *BABesch* Suppl. 16. Leuven: Peeters.

Rasmussen, T. 2005. "Urbanization in Etruria." In *Mediterranean Urbanization, 800–600 B.C.*, ed. R. Osborne and B. W. Cunliffe, 91–113. Proceedings of the British Academy 126. Oxford: Oxford University Press for the British Academy.

Rastrelli, A. 2000. "La tomba a Tramezzo di Poggio alla Sala nel quadro dell'Orientalizzante recente di Chiusi." In *Atti del convegno di Orvieto-Chianciano (7:1999)*, 159–164. Annali della Fondazione per il Museo Claudio Faina VII. Rome: Edizioni Quasar.

Riva, C. 2010. *The Urbanization of Etruria: Funerary Practices and Social Change, 700–600 B.C.* Cambridge: Cambridge University Press.

Shuckburgh, E., trans. 2002. *The Histories of Polybius*. Cambridge, Ont.: In Parentheses.

Steingräber, S., ed. 1985. *Etruscan Painting*. New York: Harcourt Brace Jovanovich.

———. 2001. "The Process of Urbanization of Etruscan Settlements from the Late Villanovan Period to the Late Archaic Period." *EtrStud* 8:7–34.

Tuck, A. 1994. "The Etruscan Seated Banquet: Villanova Ritual and Etruscan Iconography." *AJA* 98:617–628.

———. 2010. "Mistress and Master: The Politics of Iconography in Pre-Roman Central Italy." In *The Master of Animals in Old World Iconography*, ed. D. B. Counts and B. Arnold, 211–222. Budapest: Archaeolingua.

Tuck, A., J. Bauer, K. Kreindler, T. Huntsman, S. Miller, S. Pancaldo, and C. Powell. 2009. "Center and Periphery in Inland Etruria: Poggio Civitate and the Etruscan Settlement in Vescovado di Murlo." *EtrStud* 12:215–237.

Warden, G. 2011. "The Temple Is a Living Thing: Fragmentation, Enchainment, and Reversal of Ritual at the Acropolis Sanctuary of Poggio Colla." In *The Archaeology of Sanctuaries and Ritual in Etruria*, ed. N. T. de Grummond and I. Edlund-Berry. *JRA* Suppl. 81. Portsmouth, R.I.: Journal of Roman Archaeology.

Winther, H. 1997. "Princely Tombs of the Orientalizing Period in Etruria and *Latium Vetus*." *Acta Hyperborea* 7:423–446.

Zamarchi Grassi, P. 1992. *La Cortona dei principes*. Cortona: Banca popolare di Cortona.

IV MONUMENTALIZATION OF THE ETRUSCAN ROUND MOULDING IN SIXTH-CENTURY BCE CENTRAL ITALY

NANCY A. WINTER

A LARGE HALF-ROUND MOULDING IS ONE OF THE hallmarks of Etruscan architecture. Regularly appearing as a base moulding and/or crowning moulding on altars, on columns, and on the stone podia and terracotta roofs that characterize temples of Vitruvius's Tuscan order (*Tuscanicae dispositiones*), it is so typical that it was given the name "Etruscan round" by Lucy Shoe Meritt.[1] Many more examples of the Etruscan round have been excavated since her original publication in 1965, confirming the strength of her association of the moulding with Etruscan architecture. Her prediction that its presence on architectural terracottas may have been more common than evidence suggested at the time has been amply confirmed,[2] and it is the primary focus of this essay.

A survey of its occurrence in the architecture of sixth-century BCE Etruria and central Italy demonstrates that the Etruscan round, often with a painted scale pattern, marks visual transition points in architecture and in architectural decoration: as a crowning moulding separating the stone podium from the mudbrick walls of early temples, as a base moulding for the raking sima that sits above the rafters on the pedimental slopes, and/or as the crowning moulding for the revetment plaques that protect the rafters of the pedimental slopes and sit directly below the raking sima. Where the type of building carrying an Etruscan round with a painted scale pattern can be determined, it is generally a temple or sacred building, often of modest size. With the enlargement of the scale of temple architecture in the later sixth century BCE, the Etruscan round became a standard element of the roof, as its visibility could be assured, even at a distance high up on a tall building. At the same time, the decoration of the terracotta roof changes from figural scenes to floral patterns, probably also at least in part because the latter were more visually discernible to the viewer at ground level than figural scenes would be.

Late Seventh-Century BCE Use of Half-Round Elements on Terracotta Roofs

ALREADY IN THE LATE SEVENTH CENTURY BCE ON terracotta roofs in Rome and Etruria, a convex half-round element appears as a cap between two adjacent ridge tiles, themselves in the form of large half rounds. Because these half rounds play a role that is more functional than decorative, protecting the roof from rainwater damage to the woodwork below, they may better be considered predecessors of the Etruscan round moulding, which is primarily decorative in function, and they may have been a source of inspiration for the round moulding; in some respects they provide visual markers for points of transition on the roof, at the apex of the ridge and at the transition from one ridge tile to the next, a feature that becomes characteristic for the standard Etruscan round.

The earliest datable example is a separately made convex ridge tile cover joint carrying two horn-shaped acroteria, from the roof of the first building on the site of the later Regia in the Roman Forum, dated stratigraphically 620 BCE.[3] This cover joint would have shielded the gap between two adjacent ridge tiles of semicylindrical shape; it may have inspired the form of a later type of ridge tile which has a half-round element at one short end, first documented at Rome on an example from the Capitoline Hill, tentatively dated 620–600 BCE, but present throughout the sixth century BCE at several sites in southern Etruria.[4] No traces of paint have been preserved on the earliest examples, but plain pan and cover tiles of the late seventh century BCE often were colored dark red. At Acquarossa, however, some examples of this type of ridge tile, dated 550–530 BCE, are painted red, with the half-round capping element set off not only by its contour but also by white paint.

The Etruscan Round on Buildings with Decorated Terracotta Roofs of the So-Called First Phase, 580–510/500 BCE

THE ETRUSCAN ROUND MOULDING DECORATED WITH a painted upright scale pattern can be documented on several sixth-century BCE terracotta roofs employing revetment plaques with figured friezes in relief, known as the First Phase style of Etruscan terracotta roofs.[5]

An Etruscan round moulding occurs in several positions on the earliest known temple of the Tuscan order of architecture, the first temple of Mater Matuta at S. Omobono in Rome (table 4.1), generally dated between 580 BCE and 560 BCE.[6] On this small temple, the stone podium consists of seven courses, with an Etruscan round moulding just below the uppermost ashlar course supporting the mudbrick walls.[7] Nothing remains of the superstructure except for parts of the terracotta roof. Along the top of the pedimental slopes sat an S-shaped raking sima (fig. 4.1),[8] documented by one large section preserving part of a deep cavetto upper moulding with widely spaced, flat strigils in low relief, above an Etruscan round moulding with a painted upright scale pattern. Also preserved are fragments of revetment plaques[9] that protected the rafters of the pedimental slopes on which the raking sima sat, a placement indicated by the outer side edges of the corner plaques, which were set at an obtuse angle to the top edge so that the outer edges would sit vertically at the bottom of the left and right slopes. These have a crowning moulding of an Etruscan round with a painted upright scale pattern, above a cavetto with a painted tongue pattern; the main frieze is decorated with felines in relief, moving toward the apex on both slopes. Thus, the pedimental slopes were accentuated with what appeared as a double Etruscan round, consisting of the lower element of the raking sima sitting directly above the crowning element of the revetment plaque, both with painted upright scale patterns. A second revetment plaque, which should belong to the right slope of the back pediment, as indicated by the finished right side edge set at an obtuse angle to the top edge, has instead a crowning moulding of a cavetto with painted tongues above an intermediary flat half round; the preserved part of the plaque below the half round has no visible decoration, painted or relief.[10]

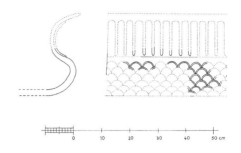

Fig. 4.1. Raking sima of the first temple of Mater Matuta at S. Omobono in Rome, 580 BCE (drawing by Renate Sponer-Za).

Table 4.1. First temple at S. Omobono in Rome, 580 BCE

L/W foundations	10.30 m/side
H podium	1.70 m
H podium moulding	ca. 30 cm
RH raking sima	28 cm
H raking sima half-round base moulding	13.5 cm
H revetment plaque half-round crowning moulding	11 cm
H revetment plaque intermediary half-round moulding	7.2 cm

Table 4.2. Caere double Etruscan round moulding, 550–540 BCE

H	18.5–18.8 cm
H upper round	9–9.5 cm
H lower round	8.5–9.6 cm

Table 4.3. Satricum, temple of Mater Matuta with Etrusco-Ionian roof, 540–530 BCE

W foundations	6 m
L foundations	10.40 m
H podium moulding	29.2 cm
H column quarter-round base moulding	10.1 cm
RH revetment plaques	39.5 cm
H revetment plaques quarter-round crowning moulding	8.3 cm

The visual effect of the two separate Etruscan rounds as the base moulding of the raking sima and the crowning element of the revetment plaques placed below the sima on the first temple at S. Omobono may have inspired the impressive double Etruscan round moulding from Caere (table 4.2), which probably belongs with a roof of 550–540 BCE.[11] It may have formed a separate course between the raking sima, of unknown type, and figural revetment plaques of the pedimental slope depicting a departing warrior scene moving to right and armed riders moving to left (fig. 4.2).[12]

At Satricum on the small temple of Mater Matuta (table 4.3) dated 540–530 BCE, an Etruscan round moulding of tuff stone has been restored on the podium;[13] a column base of red tuff with a quarter-round moulding has also been associated with this temple.[14] The pedimental slopes of the terracotta roof had a raking sima with a painted meander, above revetment plaques with a deep quarter round with a painted upright scale pattern over a hawk's beak with a painted tongue pattern crowning figured friezes with a possible chariot scene to right and armed riders to left (fig. 4.3).[15] This Etrusco-Ionian style roof has been shown by petrographic analyses, as well as by style, to have been made at Caere,[16] where comparable roof elements have been excavated.

A very similar deep quarter round with a painted upright scale pattern above a cavetto with concave tongues crowns the figured friezes of revetment plaques from the pedimental slopes of a roof of unknown provenience (table 4.4) that shares many common elements with the Satricum roof, discussed above, and with other roofs at Caere.[17] The figured friezes depict a chariot race to right and armed riders moving to left.[18] Probably belonging with this roof is an L-shaped raking sima with a painted meander similar to the one on the Satricum roof. The roof might be dated

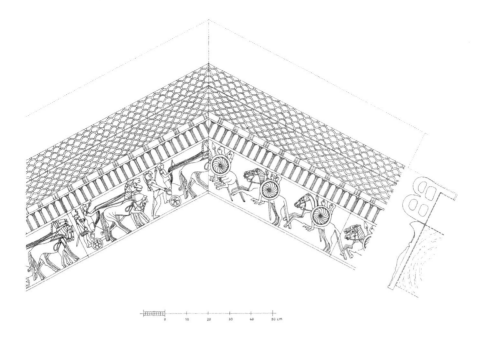

Fig. 4.2. Reconstruction of the pediment for an unknown building at Caere, 550–540 BCE (drawing by Renate Sponer-Za).

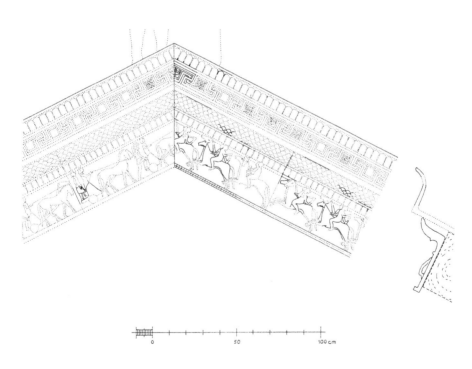

Fig. 4.3. Reconstruction of the pediment of the Etrusco-Ionian roof of the temple of Mater Matuta at Satricum, 540–530 BCE (drawing by Renate Sponer-Za).

ca. 530 BCE based on stylistic comparisons and fits well with the Etrusco-Ionian style first documented at Satricum. A fragmentary crowning moulding with a similar quarter round has been excavated at Pyrgi in the sanctuary of Leukothea,[19] the Greek counterpart to Mater Matuta.

The positioning of the Etruscan round between the raking sima and the revetment plaque is confirmed both by the evidence of revetment plaques preserving the Etruscan round crowning moulding, as at Rome, Caere, and Satricum, and by at least one raking sima from Caere,[20] where an Etruscan round (H 12.9 cm) is attached to the bottom of an L-shaped raking sima with a painted meander, set back slightly from the front of the sima. The moulding is a full half round with a painted upright scale pattern, and the piece may date 530 or 530–520 BCE.

The first temple of Mater Matuta at S. Omobono in Rome was destroyed and rebuilt ca. 530 BCE. The rebuilt temple (table 4.5) is also modest in size, with a podium.[21] Here too the Etruscan round is a prominent element of both the podium and the roof. The podium has an ashlar base course, above which is a typical quarter-round base moulding crowned by a large half round below the upper ashlar course that supported mudbrick walls.[22] The terracotta roof (fig. 4.4) employs a half round in several prominent positions. A half-round crowning element with a painted upright scale pattern occurs on the revetment plaques that decorated the slopes of the pediment, above a row of concave tongues and figured friezes with scenes of chariot processions moving toward the apex.[23] The morphology and placement of these revetment plaques may be an intentional copying of the revetment plaques on the slopes of the temple it replaced. A second crowning moulding for revetment

Table 4.4. Roof of unknown provenience, 530 BCE

RH revetment plaque	ca. 38 cm
H revetment plaque quarter-round crowning moulding	8 cm

Table 4.5. Second temple at S. Omobono in Rome, 530 BCE

W foundations	11.54 m
L foundations	13.20 m
H podium	1.61 m
H podium moulding	ca. 40 cm
H revetment plaque	37.5 cm
H revetment plaque half-round crowning moulding	10.7 cm
H revetment plaque intermediary half-round moulding	7.9 cm
H half-round crowning moulding on acroterion bases	13.4 cm

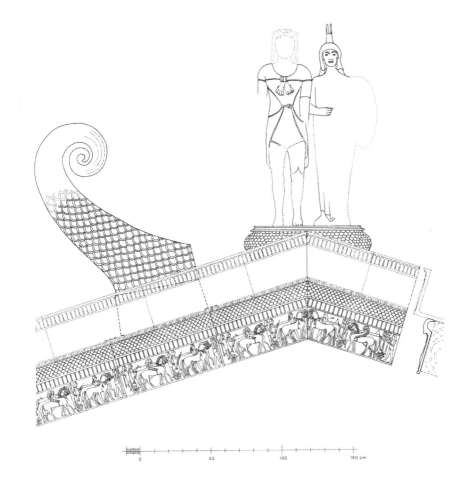

Fig. 4.4. Reconstruction of the pediment of the second temple of Mater Matuta at S. Omobono in Rome, 530 BCE (drawing by Renate Sponer-Za).

plaques with a figured frieze of a chariot procession moving to left has an intermediary flat half-round moulding immediately above the frieze;[24] there may have been a cavetto with a band of concave tongues above the half round, if this type is also copying the morphology of the revetment plaque assigned to the back pediment of the first roof, discussed above. On the ridge of the roof, the central acroterion of Herakles and Athena stands on a base[25] with a large Etruscan round with a painted upright scale pattern, while a second acroterion base,[26] with a half-round moulding decorated with painted crescents (the single documented exception to the use of a painted upright scale pattern on Etruscan round mouldings of sixth-century BCE roofs), can be assigned to a second acroterial group of which several fragments remain.

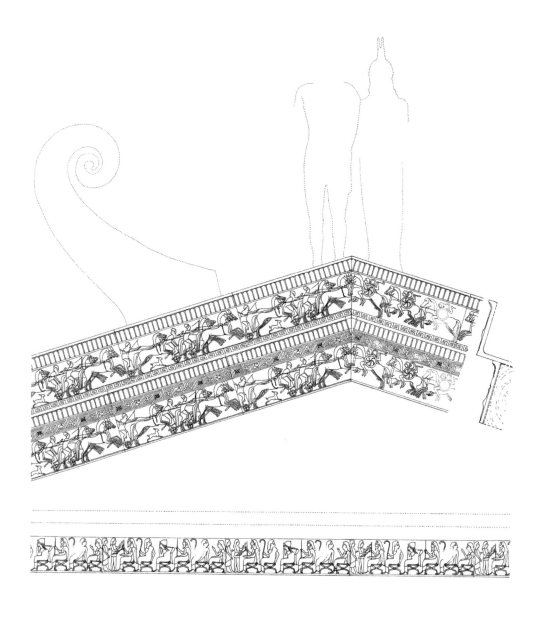

Fig. 4.5. Reconstruction of the pediment of the temple at Velletri, 530 BCE (drawing by Renate Sponer-Za).

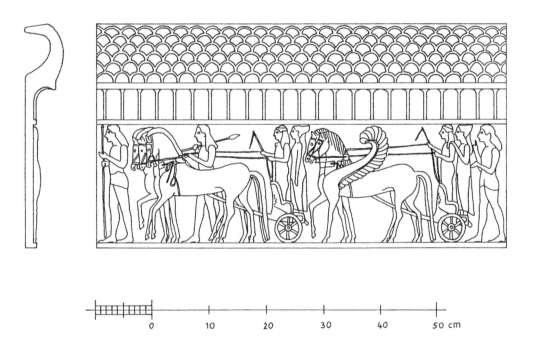

Fig. 4.6. Reconstruction of Veii-Rome-Velletri revetment plaques with chariot processions, 530 BCE (drawings by Renate Sponer-Za).

The terracotta roof of the second S. Omobono temple forms part of a decorative system of roofs used on temples at Veii, Rome, and Velletri, all dated around 530 BCE and all using roof elements made from the same series of moulds.[27] The home of the workshop has still not been determined. Recent petrographic analyses of elements of the Veii, Rome, and Velletri roofs have shown, however, that, while all roofs share the same formula or recipe for mixing clays and inclusions, the Rome and Velletri roofs are close enough in fabric to have been made in the same place.[28] That place is more likely to have been Rome than Velletri, as a number of different roofs of this decorative system are documented by the evidence at Rome. The terracottas of the same types from Veii employ local clays and inclusions but use the same formula, reinforcing the close association with Rome suggested by the shared moulds.

Use of combination moulds for the manufacture of the Veii-Rome-Velletri roofs enabled the creation of a range of revetment plaques mixing diverse figured scenes with different crowning mouldings. Modifying the placement of the figured scenes on the roof could also create a totally varied appearance for the different buildings, as can be demonstrated by comparing the façade of the second S. Omobono roof (fig. 4.4) with that of the Velletri roof (fig. 4.5).[29] On these roofs, figured friezes with chariot processions, for example, were combined with two different crowning mouldings, both using a half-round moulding with a painted upright scale pattern but differently positioned. The S. Omobono revetment plaques (figs. 4.4 and 4.6, bottom), as well as another from the Esquiline Hill in Rome and examples from Velletri,[30] have the half round (its full height preserved only at S. Omobono) with a painted scale pattern as the crowning element above a band of concave tongues, visually forming a transition from the separately made raking sima above, of unknown type. A second crowning moulding (fig. 4.6, top), documented at Rome and at Velletri for the same type of figured frieze with chariot processions,[31] places an intermediary, flat half round with a painted scale pattern between an upper band of concave tongues and the figured frieze below. This crowning moulding is also used for revetment plaques with a banquet scene, fully documented only at Velletri.[32]

The existence of a possible contemporary local version of the Veii-Rome-Velletri decorative system at Tarquinia is suggested by a fragmentary crowning moulding of a revetment plaque with an Etruscan round (table 4.6) above a cavetto with concave tongues; the figured frieze is not preserved.[33] Another crowning moulding typical of the Veii-Rome-Velletri decorative system, with a relief meander below concave tongues, has also been documented at Tarquinia.[34]

The workshop that created the Veii-Rome-Velletri decorative system may also have produced a slightly later series of roofs made with a shared set of moulds found in Rome and Caprifico, datable 520 BCE, to judge from the similarity in the morphology of the different roof elements and the similar but more complex scenes of chariot races, armed riders, and chariot processions. Documented in Rome only

Table 4.6. Various half-round mouldings, 530–520 BCE

Tarquinia half-round crowning moulding, 530 BCE	H 7.7 cm
S. Omobono intermediary half-round moulding, 520 BCE	H 7.3 cm
Caprifico half-round crowning moulding, 520 BCE	RH 7.8 cm

Table 4.7. Vetulonia, Basse degli Olmi roof, 510–500 BCE

H revetment plaque half-round crowning moulding	7.5 cm
R diam disk acroterion	ca. 56 cm
W disk acroterion outer half-round moulding	4.8 cm

at S. Omobono is one type of revetment plaque with a crowning moulding of a band of concave tongues over an intermediary flat half-round moulding (table 4.6), similar to the second type of crowning moulding for revetment plaques of the Veii-Rome-Velletri type with chariot procession (fig. 4.6, top) and banquet scene, discussed above; the figured frieze here is a chariot procession moving to left.[35] Given the sparse representation of the Rome fragments among the roof elements at S. Omobono, it might be suggested that they represent repairs to the original roof of the Veii-Rome-Velletri type at S. Omobono and that they copied the morphology of the plaques they were replacing. At Caprifico itself, the roof reportedly included a half-round moulding (table 4.6) that had been reconstructed above a row of concave tongues over a figured frieze with a chariot procession scene in relief.[36]

A late roof from Basse degli Olmi at Vetulonia (table 4.7) that represents a local imitation of roofs of the Veii-Rome-Velletri decorative system—but with a mixture of Campanian roof elements that are perhaps datable 510–500 BCE—has revetment plaques with figured friezes of unarmed riders moving to right and to left; the crowning moulding with a half round probably belongs with these friezes, but it is so fragmentary that it is impossible to determine whether there was a band of concave tongues separating the half round from the frieze.[37] The disk acroterion of this roof has an outer round moulding framing a band of concave tongues.[38]

The Etruscan Round on Buildings with Decorated Terracotta Roofs of the So-Called Second Phase, after 510 BCE

BEGINNING AROUND 510 BCE, PROBABLY FOLLOWING the construction of the Temple of Jupiter Optimus Maximus on the Capitoline Hill in Rome,[39] temples of the Tuscan order were enlarged; with this adjustment in scale, the Etruscan round found its natural home.

The so-called Second Phase roofs that accompanied these larger temples present a completely new style adapted to suit the new monumental size. As figured friezes in relief characteristic of the so-called First Phase roofs would not be legible to the viewer from their new elevation, floral patterns in relief were substituted for figured friezes on the sizable revetment plaques that protected the beams and rafters; these plaques are generally subdivided into three zones, separated by a small half-round moulding (a roll), with the floral frieze at the bottom. A large new raking sima type carries tall, beaklike convex strigils across the top, separated by a small roll from a narrow painted flat fascia above a large Etruscan round base moulding that commonly carries a painted zigzag pattern rather than the painted upright scale pattern typical on the First Phase Etruscan round mouldings.[40] An openwork cresting placed above the raking sima adds even further height to this element. Eaves tiles have a painted underside with a zigzag pattern recalling that on the base moulding of the raking sima. Antefixes along the eaves of the roof have a tongue frame set off by a roll with painted diagonal bands from the central decoration, which is usually a female head or a silen head, alternating along the eaves. Antefixes placed in the open pediment are instead decorated with smaller heads in a tongue frame or full-figure antefixes with mythical creatures. The ends of the columen and mutulus beams in the open pediment are protected by terracotta plaques carrying figural decoration in high relief.

The earliest preserved roof of the Second Phase style on a monumental temple of the Vitruvian Tuscan order comes from Veii in the Portonaccio sanctuary, which hosted the cults of Aplu, the Etruscan Apollo, and Menerva, the Etruscan Athena. The temple is dated 510–500 BCE (table 4.8).[41] Typical are the podium and the plan with three cellae preceded by a row of columns. The temple is best known for the many statues placed along the ridge of the roof, thought to represent the Etruscan equivalents of Apollo, Herakles, Leto with the baby Apollo, and Hermes, among others in too fragmentary condition for closer identification.

The Veii Portonaccio roof includes all of the elements typical of Second Phase roofs: an openwork cresting attached to the top of a raking sima with a roll with painted diagonal bands separating the central flat fascia from the tall convex strigils above and an Etruscan round base moulding with a painted horizontal scale pattern; two-part revetment plaques with floral patterns in relief as the lowest of four different zones of decoration, each zone separated from the others by rolls with painted diagonal bands; antefixes with heads of females, silens, Gorgons, and Acheloos, separated from the encircling frame of long concave tongues by a roll with painted diagonal bands, ending in volutes; and decorated columen and mutulus plaques with relief decoration, the left mutulus plaque with a sloping top edge preserving a large Etruscan round crowning moulding with a painted wave pattern bordered by a rippled lower edge and a decoration of dolphins in relief on the plaque.

Table 4.8. Veii, Portonaccio temple, 510–500 BCE

L/W foundations	18.5 m/side
H raking sima cresting	26 cm
H raking sima	54.5 cm
H raking sima roll	3 cm
H raking sima round base moulding	9 cm
RH revetment plaque on slope	49.8
RH revetment plaque on horizontal architrave	44.6 cm
H revetment plaque roll	2.9 cm
H antefixes	41–46 cm
H left mutulus plaque at left edge/right edge	40.5/44 cm
H left mutulus plaque round crowning moulding	9.4 cm

Discussion

FOR DECORATED ROOFS OF THE FIRST PHASE STYLE using revetment plaques with figural scenes in relief, the Etruscan round was employed in three different places: as a base moulding on at least one early raking sima, as a crowning moulding on revetment plaques, and as an intermediary moulding on revetment plaques. The evidence suggests that the earliest occurrences of the Etruscan round, dating between 580 and 550–540 BCE, employed a double Etruscan round that marked the transition between raking sima and revetment plaque on the pedimental slopes. This was initially formed of two separate elements (one as the base moulding of the raking sima sitting directly above the crowning moulding of the revetment plaque below), but later, at least in one documented example from Caere, it was made as a separate element with two joined mouldings. Thereafter only a single rounded element marking the transition from raking sima to revetment plaques of the slopes becomes the norm, initially as a quarter-round moulding forming the crowning moulding at the top of the revetment plaque (540–530 BCE; H 8–8.3 cm) and later as a full half round (530–520 BCE; H 10.7–12.9 cm). This placement may have influenced the subsequent development in the form of later Second Phase raking simas that have an Etruscan round base moulding, but the presence of a half-round base moulding on the raking sima of the first temple of S. Omobono—the largest of any preserved on a First Phase roof—should not be forgotten. In any case, apart from the Etruscan rounds on both S. Omobono temples and one example from Caere, the other examples are all modest in size (H 8–9.5 cm during the period 550–530 BCE) and actually become smaller closer to the time of the introduction of the Second Phase roofs (H 7.5–7.7 cm from 520–500 BCE). The use of the flat half round with painted upright scale pattern as an intermediary moulding (H 7.2–7.9 cm) was limited and had less impact than the half-round crowning moulding on revetment plaques of the same roofs.

It is notable that the Etruscan round on First Phase roofs appears to be used only on temples, wherever the building type can be determined. The association of many of these examples, on temple podia as well as on architectural terracottas, with temples dedicated to Mater Matuta (at S. Omobono in Rome, Satricum, and probably Pyrgi) may also be significant. Another important feature is that, whether positioned as a base moulding, crowning moulding, or intermediary element on architectural terracottas, the Etruscan round carries a painted upright scale pattern, almost without variation.[42]

Second Phase terracotta roofs with Etruscan round mouldings are regularly associated with sizable temples. With the introduction of these terracotta roofs after 510 BCE, the raking sima with its Etruscan round base moulding is enlarged to monumental proportions suitable to the larger architecture: a typical Second Phase raking sima has a height of 34–52 cm (compared to First Phase raking simas, whose heights normally vary between 14.5 and 19 cm until ca. 530 BCE, when they rise to 21–32 cm) with the Etruscan round base moulding now reaching a height of 11–12 cm.[43] The Etruscan round on these roofs functions primarily as the base moulding for the raking simas of the pedimental slopes, commonly painted with a zigzag motif,[44] while a smaller half round (a roll) with painted diagonal bands separates the different intermediary zones on the raking simas, revetment plaques, and antefixes.

The inspiration for the Second Phase roofs has often been thought to have been drawn from Campania, although the ultimate source may go back to floral reliefs on the architecture of Asia Minor, as noted by John Hopkins in his contribution here; this phenomenon may be part of a general Ionicizing trend attributable to the westward movement of artisans from Asia Minor through Sicily to Magna Graecia, and through Campania to central Italy, beginning just after the mid-sixth century BCE. In Asia Minor revetment plaques with floral decoration in relief, dating 550–540 BCE, that could possibly have formed a model for Second Phase revetment plaques are known from Larisa am Hermos,[45] for example, with two or three zones separated by a bead-and-reel moulding rather than the roll with painted diagonal bands common to Second Phase revetment plaques; while some Asia Minor simas have zones separated by a roll, none carries painted diagonal bands, as far as can be determined.[46] The form, placement, and decoration of rolls on Campanian revetment plaques and on Second Phase roofs may instead owe something to the rolls separating different painted zones of decoration on Sicilian simas, which are often decorated with painted diagonal bands;[47] less convincing is a derivation from the flat Etruscan round intermediary moulding on the Veii-Rome-Velletri revetment plaques, because of the much smaller scale of the roll in relation to the overall size of the roof element and its regular decoration of diagonal bands rather than a painted upright scale pattern. The zigzag pattern painted on the undersides of eaves tiles is well documented on Campanian roofs, as are the tongue frames for antefixes and columen and mutulus plaques with figured scenes in relief.[48] Only the Etruscan round at the bottom of Second Phase raking simas may claim its origin from First Phase roofs of basically Etruscan style, such as that on the first temple of Mater Matuta at S. Omobono in Rome. Thus, the formative background for terracotta roofs of Della Seta's Second Phase appears to be Asia Minor, Sicily, Campania, and central Italy under Etruscan influence.

Conclusions

THROUGHOUT ITS LIFE ON THE ARCHITECTURE AND architectural terracottas of the sixth century BCE in central Italy, the Etruscan round moulding functioned as an important visual marker for transition points. On stone podia of temples, it stands as the uppermost projecting element below the footing for the mudbrick wall face or, later, as a base moulding. On terracotta roofs, it occurs as a base moulding or crowning moulding marking the transition from raking sima to revetment plaques on the pedimental slopes, as an intermediary moulding on revetment plaques to visually separate different zones of the plaque, and/or to single out special elements such as acroterion bases or, at least at Veii on the Portonaccio temple, columen and mutulus plaques.

In Rome, the Etruscan round on decorated terracotta roofs of the First Phase style is monumental in scale from its first appearance ca. 580 BCE as the base mould-ing (H 13.5 cm) on the raking sima of the first temple of Mater Matuta at S. Omobo-no, a temple of the Tuscan order. Almost as grand in size, in any case outstripping that of other examples of Etruscan round mouldings on roofs at most other sites outside of Rome,[49] is the half-round crowning moulding (H 10.7 cm) of the pedi-mental revetment plaques of the second temple of Mater Matuta at S. Omobono, another temple of the Tuscan order. Both of these half-round mouldings are closest in scale to that of the base mouldings (H 11–12 cm) on the tall raking simas that become a canonical part of Second Phase roofs from 510 BCE onward, following the monumentalization of the Tuscan temple with the construction of the Temple of Jupiter Optimus Maximus in Rome.

Ultimately, the origin of the Etruscan round moulding on terracotta roofs might go back to the late-seventh-century-BCE employment of a convex cover joint with horn acroteria for large semicylindrical ridge tiles, documented at Rome, but in the sixth century BCE the Etruscan round moulding is more common on the pedimental slopes of the roof than on the ridge and is characterized by the painted upright scale pattern that regularly decorates its surface. With the exception of the examples on the S. Omobono roofs, which are larger, most of the Etruscan rounds on First Phase roofs occur as crowning mouldings on revetment plaques and range in height from 7.5 to 9.5 cm. These are documented at Caere, Pyrgi, Tarquinia, and Vetulonia in Etruria, and at Satricum in Latium (but on a roof made in Etruria).

The large round base moulding on the raking sima of the first S. Omobono roof seems, on present evidence,[50] to have had no following until the Second Phase decorative system was introduced; at this point, ca. 510 BCE, the round base moulding replaces the crowning moulding on the revetment plaques to become the visual weight-bearing element for the tall raking simas of the Second Phase roofs, whose size exceeds that of any First Phase raking simas. In fact, the Etruscan round base moulding on raking simas is one of the characteristic features of the monumentalization of the Tuscan temple at the end of the sixth century BCE.

The role of the rounded moulding, originally highlighted by Lucy Shoe Meritt and Ingrid Edlund-Berry for Etruscan stone architecture of the fifth century BCE and later, can be shown by material from more recent excavations and studies to have been equally prominent for temple podia and architectural terracottas in the sixth century BCE, particularly in Rome during the period of the Etruscan kings, but also in Etruria itself, fully justifying its nomenclature as the "Etruscan round."

Notes

This essay is offered in recognition of Ingrid Edlund-Berry's contributions to the study of both Etruscan mouldings and architectural terracottas, and in gratitude for her many years of friendship and scholarly support.

Abbreviations used: D = depth; H = height; L = length; R = restored; W = width; Diam = diameter.

1. Shoe Meritt 1965, 81–140, pls. XXIII–XLIV; Shoe Meritt and Edlund-Berry 2000, XXII–XXIV, 81–140, pls. XXIII–XLIV.
2. Shoe Meritt (1965, 138): "There is one striking exception [to the use of beak-like strigils accompanied by small half rounds on terracotta revetments] which, although unique among preserved examples, may suggest a wider use of this form than we know. For the crown of a figured frieze at Satricum in the 6th century there was used a deep, crowning type quarter round with a beak below (LXIV, 1)." The revetment plaque she is referring to comes from the Etrusco-Ionian roof at Satricum (see infra).
3. Rome, Antiquarium forense, inv. R64.339 (RW ca. 17 cm): Winter 2009, 41, figs. 1.4 and 1.5, ill. 1.6.3 and ill. Roof 1-2, with earlier bibliography.
4. Rome, Capitoline Hill: Winter 2009, 45. This ridge tile type occurs at Piazza d'Armi at Veii 580–575 BCE, at Caere 560–550 BCE, at Acquarossa 550–530 BCE (H tile 13.5 cm; W tile 56–59.5 cm; D tile 30–36; H half round 22; W half round 12–14.5 cm), and at Castellina del Marangone 530–520 BCE: see Winter 2009, 45–47, fig. 1.6, ill. 1.8 (Acquarossa), 307 (Veii), 308 (Caere), 308–309, fig. 4.36 (Acquarossa), and 492, ill. 6.26 (Castellina del Marangone), with earlier bibliography.

5. The so-called First Phase of Etruscan terracotta roofs, characterized by figured friezes in relief, and the so-called Second Phase, characterized by floral patterns in relief, were first defined by Della Seta (1918, 128–132 [First Phase] and 132–144 [Second Phase]).

6. Colonna 1991; 2006, 154–155 (noting that there was a turning point in temple architecture ca. 580 BCE, but attributing this first example to Servius Tullius and dating it 575–560 BCE); Coarelli 2007, 308 (dating the temple to the mid-sixth century BCE and attributing it to Servius Tullius). Mertens-Horn 1995, 274 (attributed to Tarquinius Priscus); Mura Sommella 2000, 19–20 (attributed to Tarquinius Priscus); Winter 2009, 149–150 (dated 580 BCE and attributed to Tarquinius Priscus).

7. See Gjerstad 1960, 384–385, fig. 246; Shoe Meritt 1965, 22 n. 5; Shoe Meritt and Edlund-Berry 2000, xxiii, 22 n. 5.

8. Rome, Antiquarium Comunale, inv. 15823: Sommella Mura 1977, 94, fig. 20; Arata in Cristofani 1990, 127–128, no. 5.1.34 (identified as a revetment plaque). For the deep cavetto with widely separated, flat strigils in low relief, cf. the upper parts of raking simas from Veii and Caere (a flat fascia substitutes for the Etruscan round base moulding on the Rome sima): Winter 2009, 239–240, ill. 4.1 (Veii), dated 580–560/550 BCE.

9. Rome, Antiquarium Comunale, inv. 15813 (feline moving to right): Sommella Mura 1977, 68, figs. 4, 5 upper left; Arata in Cristofani 1990, 128, no. 5.1.36; Mura Sommella 2000, 19–20, figs. 12, 14 upper right; Winter 2009, 189–190, fig. 3.20. Inv. 15816 (feline moving to left): Sommella Mura 1977, 68, figs. 3, 5 upper right; Arata in Cristofani 1990, 128, no. 5.1.35; Mura Sommella 2000, 19–20, figs. 13–14; Winter 2009, 190, fig. 3.21.

10. Rome, Antiquarium Comunale, inv. 16083: Winter 2009, 190–191, fig. 3.22.

11. London, British Museum, inv. GR 1876.3–29.5: Andrén 1940, 30, no. II:9a, pl. H:1; Winter 2009, 294–295, ill. 4.13.2, citing additional fragments.

12. For the roof as a whole, see Winter 2009, 236–239, ill. Roof 4-11.1–2, with earlier bibliography.

13. Shoe Meritt 1965, 86–88, pl. XXIII, 3, 4; Shoe Meritt and Edlund-Berry 2000, 86–88, pl. XXIII, 3, 4 (thought to represent the base of the podium); Colonna 2005, 112, fig. 1 left (restored as the crowning moulding of the podium).

14. Shoe Meritt 1965, 117, pl. XXXIV, 1, 2; Shoe Meritt and Edlund-Berry 2000, 117, pl. XXXIV, 1, 2.

15. Riders: Rome, Museo Nazionale Etrusco di Villa Giulia, inv. 10033: Andrén 1940, 457, no. I:1a–c, fig. 40, pls. 137:484–485, 138:486–487; Shoe Meritt 1965, 138, pl. XLIV, 1; Knoop 1987, 51–63, 237–239, nos. 173–176a, figs. 6–10, 30–31, pls. 72–76; Shoe Meritt and Edlund-Berry 2000, 138, pl. XLIV, 1; Winter 2009, 448–449, ill. 6.12.2; Lulof (forthcoming). For the temple roof as a whole, see also Winter 2009, 398–400, ill. Roof 6-1, with additional bibliography.

16. Knoop 1987, 62–63, 66, 227–231, pls. A, D.

17. For the roof as a whole, see Winter 2009, 400, ill. Roof 6-2.1–2, with earlier bibliography.

18. Chariot race to right: Copenhagen, Ny Carlsberg Glyptotek, inv. H.I.N. 713–716, H.I.N. 713–719, H.I.N. 858, H.I.N. 863, H.I.N. 865: Winter 2009, 447, ill. 6.13.1, fig. 6.21, with earlier bibliography. Armed riders moving to left: Copenhagen, Ny Carlsberg Glyptotek, inv. H.I.N. 713–719: Winter 2009, 450–451, ill. 6.13.2, fig. 6.22, with earlier bibliography.

19. Santa Severa, Antiquarium di Pyrgi, inv. 41711: Winter 2009, 448, with earlier bibliography.

20. Berlin, Antikensammlung, inv. TC 2027X: Andrén 1940, 31, no. II:9d (described upside down); Winter 2009, 414, fig. 6.4.

21. Pisani Sartorio et al. in Cristofani 1990, 111–129, with earlier bibliography; Colonna 1991; Winter 2009, 316–318, ill. Roof 5-4.1–2, with additional bibliography.

22. See Gjerstad 1960, 380–384, fig. 245; Shoe Meritt 1965, 22 n. 5; Shoe Meritt and Edlund-Berry 2000, xxiii, 22 n. 5.

23. Rome, Antiquarium Comunale, inv. 15817 (chariot procession moving to right): Sommella Mura 1977, 76, figs. 5 bottom left, 8 top left; Arata in Cristofani 1990, 126, no. 5.1.30; Winter 2009, 366–368. Chariot procession moving to left: inv. 15883: Sommella Mura 1977, 71–78, figs. 5–7; Arata in Cristofani 1990, 126, no. 5.1.28; Winter 2009, 369–370, fig. 5.23 right. Inv. 15800 (with obliquely cut left edge indicating its placement at the apex of the right slope): Sommella Mura 1977, 71–78, figs. 5, 6, 9; Arata in Cristofani 1990, 126, no. 5.1.29; Winter 2009, 369–370, fig. 5.23 left.

24. Rome, Antiquarium Comunale, inv. 15955 + 15963: Gjerstad 1960, 402, fig. 265.3 (shown upside down); Arata in Cristofani 1990, 126–127, no. 5.1.31 (attributed to the architrave); Winter 2009, 363–364.

25. Rome, Antiquarium Comunale, inv. 15853: Gjerstad 1960, 448, fig. 281.1; Shoe Meritt 1965, 225, pl. LXXVI, 2; Sommella Mura 1977, 107–112, figs. 35, 36, 44; Arata in Cristofani 1990, 119–120, no. 5.1.1c, with additional bibliography; Mura Sommella 1993, 227, fig. 10; Shoe Meritt and Edlund-Berry 2000, 225, pl. LXXVI, 2; Winter 2009, 386, fig. 5.41; Winter 2011, 64, fig. 5.

26. Rome, Antiquarium Comunale, inv. 15854: Arata in Cristofani 1990, 129, no. 5.1.38 (identified as a possible column base); Mura Sommella 1993, 227–232, figs. 12–13 (identified as an acroterion base); Winter 2009, 386–387, fig. 5.42. Inv. IX5 3979, IX5 3981, 15873, 15874, 15875, 15876, 15880, 15881, 15882: Winter 2009, 386 n. 180; Winter 2011, 64, fig. 6.

27. See esp. Colonna 1984, 402–405; Fortunati 1989; Winter 2009, ch. 5.

28. Winter, Iliopoulos, and Ammerman 2009, 20–22.

29. For the Velletri roof, see Fortunati 1989 (dated 530 BCE); Fortunati in Cristofani 1990, 199–205; Winter 2009, 320–323, ill. Roof 5-7.1–2, with additional bibliography.

30. Chariot procession to right: Rome, S. Omobono: Rome, Antiquarium Comunale, inv. 15817: n. 23 supra. Esquiline Hill: Rome, Antiquarium Comunale, inv. 3371: Andrén 1940, 343–344, no. I:1, pl. 104:371; Martini in Cristofani 1990, 253–254, no. 10.1.2; Winter 2009, 366–368, fig. 5.21, with additional bibliography. Velletri: Naples, Museo Nazionale, inv. 21606: Andrén 1940, 409–410, no. I:1, pl. 126:442; Fortunati in Cristofani 1990, 203, no. 8.6.11; Winter 2009, 366–368, fig. 5.20, ill. 5.14.2, with additional bibliography. Chariot procession to left: Rome, S. Omobono: Rome, Antiquarium Comunale, inv. 15883 and 15800: n. 23 supra. Velletri: Naples, Museo Nazionale, inv. 21605: Winter 2009, 369–370, with additional bibliography.

31. Chariot procession to right: Velletri, Museo Civico, inv. 514–515: Andrén 1940, 409–410, no. I:1; Fortunati 1989, 70, no. II.1, pl. XII, fig. 5a; Fortunati in Cristofani 1990, 203, no. 8.6.13. Inv. 516: Fortunati 1989, 70, no. II.2, pl. XII; Fortunati in Cristofani 1990, 203, no. 8.6.14. Winter 2009, 362–363, ill. 5.13.1, with additional bibliography. Chariot procession to left: Rome, S. Omobono: Rome, Antiquarium Comunale, inv. 15955 + 15963: n. 24 supra. Rome, Capitoline Hill: Rome, Antiquarium Comunale, inv. G.R. 810: Winter 2009, 363–364, with previous bibliography. Velletri, Museo Civico, inv. 518–519: Andrén 1940, 410, no. I:2, fig. 13:3, pl. 126:443; Fortunati 1989, 71–72, no. II.4, pl. XIII; Fortunati in Cristofani 1990, 204, no. 8.6.15; Winter 2009, 363–364, fig. 5.18, ill. 5.13.2, with additional bibliography.

32. Velletri: Naples, Museo Nazionale, inv. 21600: Andrén 1940, 411–412, no. I:5, pl. 128:447; Fortunati in Cristofani 1990, 204, no. 8.6.17; Winter 2009, 365–366, fig. 5.19, ill. 5.14.1, with additional bibliography. Many fragments of the figured scene are preserved at Rome and Veii, but none document the type of crowning moulding: see Winter 2009, 365–366.

33. Tarquinia, excavation storerooms, inv. 259/49: Ciaghi 1999, 18, pl. 11.1; Winter 2009, 371.

34. Tarquinia, excavation storerooms, inv. 178/11: Ciaghi 1999, 14–20, pl. 8.1–2; Winter 2009, 360–361.

35. Rome, Antiquarium Comunale, inv. 15827, 15831, 15978, 16037: Sommella Mura 1977, 78, fig. 10; Arata in Cristofani 1990, 127, no. 5.1.32; Winter 2009, 365, with additional bibliography.

36. See Lulof 2010, 98, nn. 36, 38.

37. Etruscan round moulding: Vetulonia, Museo Civico Archeologico "Isidoro Falchi," inv. 107310, 107311/A–B, 107317: Cygielman and Shepherd 1987, 86, no. IV.1, pl. XIVc–d. Figured friezes: inv. 107306/A+B, 107307, 107309, 107324/A+B, 107324/D, 107324/E, 107324/G, 107324/F, 107320/A (moving to right); 107308, 107315 (moving to left): Cygielman and Shepherd 1987, 87–89, nos. V.1–V.11, pls. XV.a–b, XVI.a–c, XVII.a, c; Winter 2009, 370–371, with additional bibliography.

38. Vetulonia, Museo Civico Archeologico "Isidoro Falchi," inv. 107318/A–B, 107320/C–D: Cygielman and Shepherd 1987, 85–86, no. III, pl. XIV.a–b; Winter 2009, 387, with additional bibliography.

39. Mura Sommella 2000, 20–26 (with results of new excavations of the foundations); Colonna 2006, 154–155, fig. VIII.33. See also the contribution by John Hopkins in this volume.

40. A few transitional roofs may be represented by raking simas that have the morphology of the Second Phase simas but with the figured friezes typical of First Phase roofs. At Palestrina, a raking sima (see table below) has the larger form with tall, beak-like convex strigils across the top, separated by a roll from the field below, and the Etruscan round base moulding, but with a central figured frieze with a chariot procession/departing warrior scene in relief; the Etruscan round carries a painted zigzag pattern, common on Second Phase roof elements. Other more fragmentary examples with animals in relief on the central figured frieze above an Etruscan round base moulding come from the Palatine Hill in Rome, Vulci, and Tarquinia. See Winter 2009, 336–337, with earlier bibliography. All of these raking simas are probably datable 510–500 BCE.

Palestrina roof, 510–500 BCE

H raking sima	55.6 cm
H strigils	25 cm
H roll	2.8 cm
H half-round base moulding	6.6 cm

41. Colonna in Moretti Sgubini 2001, 40–43; Boitani 2004; Colonna 2006, 156, figs. VIII.37–40; Colonna in Torelli and Moretti Sgubini 2008, 59–63; Carlucci in Torelli and Moretti Sgubini 2008, 200–205. Cresting and raking simas: Rome, Museo Nazionale Etrusco di Villa Giulia, inv. VP 564, VP 565, VP 567: Shoe Meritt 1965, 212–213, pl. LXVI, 3, 4; Wikander 1994, 58, nos. 56–57, fig. 5.3; Shoe Meritt and Edlund-Berry 2000, 212–213, pl. LXVI, 3, 4. Inv. NP 09: Carlucci in Torelli and Moretti Sgubini 2008, 205, no. 14. The measurements given in table 4.8 refer to NP 09. Revetment plaques: Rome, Museo Nazionale Etrusco di Villa Giulia, inv. VEX 19 + VEX 20 (slope): Carlucci in Torelli and Moretti Sgubini 2008, 205, nos. 15, 16, with earlier bibliography. Inv. VEX 29 (horizontal architrave), possibly also combined with VEX 19: Carlucci in Torelli and Moretti Sgubini 2008, 205, no. 17, with earlier bibliography. Antefixes: Rome, Museo Nazionale Etrusco di Villa Giulia, inv. VEX 04, VEX 07, VEX 06, VEX 08, VP 329: Carlucci in Torelli and Moretti Sgubini 2008, 204, nos. 12.1–12.5, with earlier bibliography. Mutulus plaque: Rome, Museo Nazionale Etrusco di Villa Giulia, inv. VEX 03: Carlucci in Torelli and Moretti Sgubini 2008, 203, no. 8, with earlier bibliography.

42. The single known exception is on the second acroterion base from the second temple at S. Omobono in Rome, with a painted crescent pattern: see n. 26 supra.

43. See, e.g., Wikander 1994, nos. 15, 18, 30, 31, 41, 56, 57.
44. Occasionally the painted decoration is a horizontal scale pattern rather than the vertical one on Etruscan round mouldings of First Phase roofs, in some cases documentable as representing snake bodies ending in a snake head, as, e.g., at Pompeii: B. d'Agostino, "Le terrecotte architettoniche arcaiche," in de Waele 2001, 141–142, 170–174, and fig. on 145. I would like to thank Patricia Lulof for bringing this example to my attention.
45. Åkerström 1966, pl. 32.3–4; Winter 1993, p. 246 (dated 550–540 BCE).
46. E.g., Åkerström 1966, pls. 46–48.
47. See Wikander 1986, with earlier bibliography.
48. See Rescigno 1998, passim.
49. The single example of a half-round moulding with painted scale pattern that falls within the range of the two S. Omobono mouldings comes from Caere, on the Etruscan round attached to the bottom of a raking sima datable 530 or 530–520 BCE; see n. 20, supra. It should be noted that other roof elements similar to those of the second S. Omobono temple have also been found at Caere: Winter 2009, 467 (acroterion of Herakles and Athena), 468–469 (Leukothea and Palaimon?), and 473 (volute acroterion).
50. No raking sima is preserved from the second temple at S. Omobono but other fragmentary raking simas of the Veii-Rome-Velletri decorative system, and more completely preserved examples from the Caprifico temple, have a flat fascia across the base of the vertical plaque rather than a half-round moulding.

Bibliography

Åkerström, Å. 1966. *Die architektonischen Terrakotten Kleinasiens.* Lund: C. W. K. Gleerup.

Andrén, A. 1940. *Architectural Terracottas from Etrusco-Italic Temples.* Lund/Leipzig: C. W. K. Gleerup/O. Harrassowitz.

Boitani, F. 2004. "Il capolavoro e il suo contesto," "Il santuario in località Portonaccio," and "Il tempio." In "Il restauro dell'Apollo di Veio." *Kermes* 17:41–44.

Ciaghi, S. 1999. "Le terrecotte." In *Tarquinia: Scavi sistematici nell'abitato, campagne 1982–1988. I materiali.* Vol. I, ed. C. Chiaramonte Treré, 1–41. *Tarchna: Scavi e ricerche a Tarquinia, 2.* Rome: L'Erma di Bretschneider.

Coarelli, F. 2007. *Rome and Environs: An Archeological Guide.* Trans. J. J. Clauss and D. P. Harmon. Berkeley: University of California Press.

Colonna, G. 1984. "I templi del Lazio fino al V secolo compreso." *ArchLaz* 6:396–411.

———. 1991. "Le due fasi del tempio arcaico di S. Omobono." In *Stips Votiva. Papers Presented to C. M. Stibbe*, ed. M. Gnade, 51–59. Amsterdam: Allard Pierson Museum.

———. 2005. "Tra architettura e urbanistica: A proposito del tempio di Mater Matuta a Satricum." In *Omni pede stare: Saggi architettonici e circumvesuviani in memoriam Jos de Waele*, ed. S. T. A. M. Mols and E. M. Moormann, 111–117. Naples: Electa Napoli.

———. 2006. "Sacred Architecture and the Religion of the Etruscans." In *The Religion of the Etruscans*, ed. N. T. de Grummond and E. Simon, 132–168. Austin: University of Texas Press.

Cristofani, M., ed. 1990. *La grande Roma dei Tarquini.* Rome: L'Erma di Bretschneider.

Cygielman, M., and E. J. Shepherd. 1987. "Su alcune terrecotte architettoniche provenienti da Vetulonia." *StEtr* 53:77–93.

Della Seta, A. 1918. *Museo di Villa Giulia.* Rome: Danesi Editore.

de Waele, J. A. K. E. 2001. *Il tempio dorico del Foro Triangolare di Pompei.* Rome: L'Erma di Bretschneider.

Fortunati, F. R. 1989. "Il tempio delle Stimmate." In *Museo Civico di Velletri*, 57–87. Rome: Quasar.

Gjerstad, E. 1960. *Early Rome* III: *Fortifications, Domestic Architecture, Sanctuaries, Stratigraphic Excavations*. Lund: C. W. K. Gleerup.

Knoop, R. R. 1987. *Antefixa Satricana: Sixth-Century Architectural Terracottas from the Sanctuary of Mater Matuta at Satricum*. Assen/Maastricht: Van Gorcum.

Lulof, P. S. 2010. "The Architectural Terracottas from Caprifico." In *Il tempio arcaico di Caprifico di Torrecchia (Cisterna di Latina): I materiali e il contesto*, ed. D. Palombi, 25–111. Rome: Edizioni Quasar.

———. Forthcoming. *Three Central Italic Roof Systems: Architectural Terracottas from Satricum*.

Mertens-Horn, M. 1995. "Corinto e l'Occidente nelle immagini: La nascita di Pegaso e la nascita di Afrodite." In *AttiTaranto* 34:257–289.

Moretti Sgubini, A. M., ed. 2001. *Veio, Cerveteri, Vulci: Città d'Etruria a confronto*. Rome: L'Erma di Bretschneider.

Mura Sommella, A. 1993. "Ancora sulla decorazione plastica del tempio arcaico del Foro Boario: Statue e acroteri." In *Deliciae Fictiles* I, ed. E. Rystedt, C. Wikander, and Ö. Wikander, 225–232. *SkrRom* 4°, 50. Stockholm: Paul Åströms Förlag.

———. 2000. "'La grande Roma dei Tarquini': Alterne vicende di una felice intuizione." *BullCom* 101:7–26.

Rescigno, C. 1998. *Tetti Campani: Età arcaica. Cuma, Pitecusa e gli altri contesti*. Rome: Giorgio Bretschneider.

Shoe Meritt, L. T. 1965. *Etruscan and Republican Roman Mouldings*. MAAR 28. Rome: American Academy in Rome.

Shoe Meritt, L. T., and I. E. M. Edlund-Berry. 2000. *Etruscan and Republican Roman Mouldings. A Reissue of the Memoirs of the American Academy in Rome XXVIII, 1965*. Philadelphia: University Museum, University of Pennsylvania.

Sommella Mura, A. 1977. "L'area sacra di S. Omobono: La decorazione architettonica del tempio arcaico." *PP* 32:62–128.

Torelli, M., and A. M. Moretti Sgubini, eds. 2008. *Etruschi: Le antiche metropoli del Lazio*. Milan: Electa.

Wikander, C. 1986. *Sicilian Architectural Terracottas: A Reappraisal. SkrRom* 8°, 15. Stockholm: Paul Åströms Förlag.

Wikander, Ö. 1994. "The Archaic Etruscan Sima." In *Murlo and the Etruscans*, ed. R. D. De Puma and J. P. Small, 47–63. Madison: University of Wisconsin Press.

Winter, N. A. 1993. *Greek Architectural Terracottas from the Prehistoric to the End of the Archaic Period*. Oxford Monographs on Classical Archaeology. Oxford: Clarendon Press.

———. 2009. *Symbols of Wealth and Power: Architectural Terracotta Decoration in Etruria and Central Italy, 640–510 B.C. MAAR* Suppl. 9. Ann Arbor: University of Michigan Press.

———. 2011. "The Evolution of Bases for Acroteria in Etruria and Latium." In *Deliciae Fictiles* IV, ed. P. S. Lulof and C. Rescigno, 62–68. Oxford: Oxbow Books.

Winter, N. A., I. Iliopoulos, and A. J. Ammerman. 2009. "New Light on the Production of Decorated Roofs of the 6th c. B.C. at Sites in and around Rome." *JRA* 22:6–28.

V MONUMENTAL EMBODIMENT
SOMATIC SYMBOLISM AND THE TUSCAN TEMPLE

P. GREGORY WARDEN

> The whole of environment, from the moment we name
> it and think of it as such, is symbol. To understand
> how the situation can be managed we are forced to
> look at the past.
>
> —Joseph Rykwert, 1969

RECENT WORK AT THE SITE OF POGGIO COLLA IN
northern Etruria,[1] about 22 miles northeast of Florence, has produced valuable evidence for the nature of ritual for both the consecration and the deconsecration of Etruscan sacred space.[2]

The site includes an extensive area of settlement dominated by an acropolis sanctuary. The sanctuary prospered from at least the seventh century BCE until its destruction at the hands of the Romans around 178–177 BCE. There are at least four phases of occupation (fig. 5.1), the earliest of which can now be identified by traces of hut foundations on the plateau.[3] Somewhat later, possibly in the late sixth or fifth century BCE,[4] a monumental temple was built on the acropolis (Phase I). This temple was the visually defining element of a hilltop sanctuary placed dramatically at the junction of two discrete geographical areas, the Mugello and the Val di Sieve; it is clearly the type of sanctuary that Zifferero has defined as a "santuario di confine."[5] Judging from its remains, which include molded podium blocks and Tuscan sandstone bases, the temple was of the Tuscan type, and a set of massive foundations indicates that it had a southerly orientation, thus according with Etruscan practice. The five preserved Tuscan column bases have setting rings indicating that the wooden column shaft would have been ca. 70 cm in diameter. Following the Vitruvian recipe for a 7:1 ratio of column height to diameter, the columns would have been about 4.9 m high, and the width of the façade, again according to

Vitruvius, about three times that, or almost 15 m. The podium blocks themselves are monumental, just under 1 m in length with a powerful half-round as crowning molding. The entire temple could thus easily have been 13–15 m high at its apex. Placed conspicuously on the dominant promontory of Poggio Colla, decorated with brightly painted terracottas, it would have been visible from anywhere in the Mugello basin and from much of the Val di Sieve, as well as from the other nearby mountaintop sanctuaries, Monte Falterona and Monte Giovi.

The temple was destroyed and replaced by two subsequent courtyard complexes. The first of these complexes (Phase II) measures approximately 11 by 20 m and had a large central altar, as well as a dramatic change in axis: the courtyard complex is oriented to the natural edges of the rectangular plateau rather than to the cardinal points. The change in axis is difficult to explain, given that there is continuity of occupation at the site. One possibility is that a change from temple to courtyard complex, now with an altar rather than a temple, may have allowed the occupants to conceive of the sacred space in a different manner and freed them from the strictures of the temple orientation, which is of great importance in Etruscan religious planning. A third phase continued the courtyard plan of Phase II, but now the courtyard is slightly larger and there is clear evidence for a series of rooms around the large court.[6]

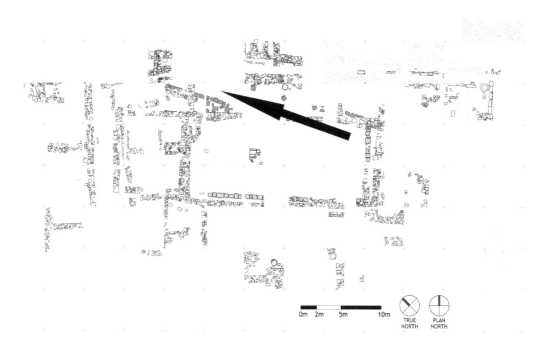

Fig. 5.1. Plan of the acropolis sanctuary at Poggio Colla, I–IV. The arrow indicates the orientation of the Phase I building (drawing by Jess Galloway).

Fig. 5.2. Reused blocks at Poggio Colla. The podium blocks have been turned upside down and used as the bottom course of a foundation (photo courtesy MVAP).

Phase I, which saw the construction of a large temple, and Phase II, with the reuse and adaptation of the remains of the destroyed temple, are especially pertinent here, as they document the monumentalization and the subsequent de-monumentalization of the sanctuary. What is especially interesting is the postdestruction treatment of the temple elements. It is uncertain why and how the temple was destroyed or dismantled, but it is clear that the temple parts were not abandoned or discarded. They were in fact either carefully placed in new contexts or intentionally interred, often upside down and aligned with the new (Phase II–III) axial arrangement of the sanctuary. The treatment of the temple is mirrored in the many votive or ritual deposits at the site that document specific ritual practices: deliberate fragmentation of objects, placement of objects in alignment with the axial layout of the sanctuary, and reversal, the purposeful turning upside down of dedicated objects, so as to turn them toward the earth. These practices are connected to the natural topography of the bedrock at the site, for instance the placement of gold objects and a deliberately broken block of the temple podium next to an underground fissure, or the layering of hundreds of bronze objects into channels in the bedrock. These ritual practices have been discussed elsewhere, as has the singular treatment of the monumental Tuscan column bases (six at the last count) and the molded blocks of the temple podium, which were sometimes reused, sometimes deliberately buried along the axes of the sanctuary (fig. 5.2), or in the unique case of the "Fissure Deposit," broken and ritually buried (fig. 5.3).[7]

Fig. 5.3. Fissure deposit, Poggio Colla. The upside-down podium block bears chisel marks that show that it was deliberately broken (photo courtesy MVAP).

The early temple at Poggio Colla thus underwent a ritual process associated with its destruction, a process that, it has been argued, mimics the processes of death and burial of the human body.[8] The most intriguing question is why. Why would a temple be treated like a body? Is the body a metaphor, or is there a more concrete symbolism at work? The answer may be connected to both the form and the setting of this type of temple: a Tuscan temple was not a static entity but a place of process, a setting for ritual that took place on the platform, and inside and in front of the temple. The temple not only embodied divinity as a house for the god(s) but also embodied divine will through its spatial rhetoric and ritual processes. It functioned as both a place of meaning and a setting for agency.

It is this congruence of form and ritual that I would like to investigate, for ritual is by definition human action—manifestation of the belief system. And the Tuscan temple, which by the time of the sixth century can be documented with all its trappings (pitched roof with terracotta tiles and decoration, the columnar porch, and the imposing stone podium), is the place for the enactment of ritual. We find evidence for the combination of form and ritual in sacred space in literary sources and also, increasingly, in archaeological contexts and material culture.[9] Ingrid Edlund-Berry has explored the way that Etruscans defined or consecrated ritual space,[10] and in cases where a temple, building, or sacred space was destroyed or abandoned, how that space might have been "deconsecrated." Both actions are done through ritual that is not restricted to sacred buildings; it also occurs at monumental structures of seemingly secular nature, such as the Archaic complex at Murlo.[11] Human figural decoration in both sacred and secular cases seems to have been treated ritually, as at Murlo or at the Portonaccio temple at Veii. The interment of terracotta "bodies" at these two sites—in the case of Veii even carefully and ritually placed upright in the earth[12]—mirrors the burial rituals accorded to humans. Fictile bodies and human bodies may be analogous in the way that they were treated, and the analogy, as we will see, may even apply to the temple itself.

Building and Body

THE IDEA OF THE BUILDING AS BODY IS A FUNDAMENtal trope of Western architectural tradition. In terms of preserved literary sources it begins with Vitruvius, who explicitly uses the body as metaphor for the temple, likening the proportions of an ideal body to the proportions of an ideal temple and situating this concept in earlier traditions of the classical world:

> Therefore since nature has designed the human body so that its members are duly proportioned to the frame as a whole, it appears the ancients had good reason for their rule, that in perfect building the different members must be in exact symmetrical relations to the whole general scheme. (*De arch. 3.1.4*)

The theme was taken up again by Renaissance architects and theorists like Alberti and Filarete, and it persisted not only in theory but in practice into the twentieth century, for instance in Le Corbusier's Modulor, a modernist take on the Vitruvian theory of the human as measure. The body/building relationship is also fundamental to phenomenological approaches to architecture, figuring prominently in the philosophy of both Husserl and Heidegger.

The idea of body as symbol or metaphor was explicated by Rykwert, who overtly argued for connections between body and building, for instance in neo-Vitruvian concepts like gender and the column, or with more original and controversial linkages like the hero as a column.[13] This approach has much to offer anyone interested in the intersection of visualization and belief system, or in a broader archaeological approach that seeks to investigate what might be termed the archaeology of the mind. This interest in the somatic aspects of architecture has been pursued in a more specific sense by theorists like Onians, who analyzed architecture and space in the light of contemporary developments in neuroscience and argued for "archaeology of the brain."[14] Onians's work has been particularly productive in reevaluating aspects of Greek planning, just as Wilson Jones has recently contributed to our understanding of the meaning of the Doric order.[15] More general considerations of architectural practice and the creative process have recently been summarized by Mallgrave.[16] For the Etrusco-Italic world, where so little remains of the written record, where the badly preserved monuments are often the only texts that we have, this approach may be productive. Can we apply some of these theoretical approaches to the Tuscan temple in the light of new evidence of the temple/body symbolism found in Poggio Colla? One promising approach is the concept of "biophilia," which has recently become popular with architects and architectural theorists.[17] The term "biophilia" connects to issues of both "lifelike forms" and "lifelike processes"[18] that one prominent contemporary architect has termed the "reassertion of the human body as the locus of experience."[19] Spatial experience is thus defined in both somatic and phenomenological terms.[20]

A phenomenological approach to the Tuscan temple must consider Etruscan ritual in its spatial context. Ritual is performative, by its very nature an act of embodiment, and the enactment of ritual would have allowed the viewer to conceive space somatically. Unfortunately, evidence for the actual performance of ritual in Etruria is slight. We have what results from ritual, what Fay Glinister has called "sacred rubbish,"[21] as well as evidence for sacrifice and sacrificial processions, and knowledge of Etruscan doctrine as it connected to prophecy and divination.[22] We can be certain that sacrifices took place in front of the temple, that the podium platform would have been used as a vantage point for divination, and that the space in front of the temple would have been structured to reflect a spatial order that was divine.[23]

An interesting example of "biophilia" is the correspondence of this sacred space to the organs of sacrificial animals, most famously the Piacenza liver.[24] The body of the priest/magistrate took center stage, but the ritual that would have been practiced on the platform of the Tuscan temple might also have been corporate, a manifestation of the corpora of Etruscan society, enacted by a number of bodies that represented the ranking of the social landscape: god, priest, and worshiper in the body of the temple, bringing the temple to life. For as Pierre Bourdieu has argued, the body "does not represent what it performs, it does not memorize the past, it *enacts* the past, bringing it back to life. What is 'learned by body' is not something that one has, like knowledge that can be brandished, but something that one is."[25] We know little about Etruscan philosophy and concepts of embodiment, but extrapolating from other areas of the Mediterranean, it might be worth noting that at least as early as the Hellenistic period, the relationship of body to mechanics and medicine figured prominently in Greek philosophy.[26] Furthermore, there are wellknown aspects of Etruscan ritual that are connected to the body through sacrifice; the interpretation of divine will, or even possibly extispicy, results from the study of parts of the sacrificial victim that, in Etruscan belief, would have reflected divine space. In the case of hepatoscopy, there is even the intriguing suggestion that the priest might have been able to bring to bear special biological knowledge.[27]

The Tuscan Temple

have been summarized by Izzet, who analyzed the topic from the perspective of the viewer, as visual experience, focusing on the visual meanings of the building, its decoration, and its setting.[28] This approach raises other questions. How did the building, in its environment, work as a space through which a visitor/viewer/participant moved? If we can examine the temple as a "building which was meaningfully constructed, seen, and visited,"[29] then we might also apply a phenomenological point of view, examining the temple as space that was meant to be experienced through ritual and performance. If evidence from contexts such as Poggio Colla suggests that the temple was treated as a kind of sacred body, as a living thing, then how did this type of structure work as a setting for ritual, as a platform for performing sacred action, as a space in which ritual might have been viewed by a broader audience?

Etruscan religious structures were extremely varied in type and could range from a simple pile of stone and ash to monumental structures of grand design. Temples themselves could also vary, but by the sixth century BCE, when temple plans were seemingly standardized, two types were predominant: the Greek peripteral temple set on a shallow set of steps, and the frontal Tuscan type described by Vitruvius (4.7), presumably of local derivation. In a major sanctuary such as Pyrgi, both types of temple could be built side by side. Although the Tuscan temple has been much discussed, the nature of the evidence makes reconstruction difficult. Remains are often ephemeral: a podium and the shattered roof, fragmentary fictile decoration, or perhaps the occasional temple model.[30] And Vitruvius notwithstanding, the form of the temple was adaptable and changeable; the constant is not form but ritual practice, for a *templum* was originally a consecrated and sacred space rather than a structure.[31] It is only in the sixth century BCE that we begin to find evidence for the kind of structure, the *aedes* or house of the god(s), that qualifies as monumental and "codified."[32] While the suddenness and date of the process remain debatable, the phenomenon is unquestionable. As Izzet notes, by the sixth century there is a spatial aesthetic that is distinct and closely connected to ritual practice:[33] a temple that conforms to an Etrusco-Italic aesthetic[34] described by Vitruvius, even though his recipe for building such a structure, based on a normative and possibly reductive approach, admittedly does not always fit the actual evidence. But what recipe ever does?

Vitruvius, in keeping with Roman tradition, defines the Tuscan temple as a Capitolium with three cellae. However, some preserved temples that we would identify as Tuscan in form, for instance Fiesole, have a single cella, and the three-cella reconstruction along Vitruvian lines of other temples, such as the Belvedere temple at Orvieto, is based on such slim evidence as to be untenable.[35] The Etrusco-

Italic or Tuscan temple was both a specific form and a certain kind of spatial setting, and Vitruvius is primarily interested in the former. In general, a Tuscan temple was easily recognizable. It was raised on a tall stone podium that could be articulated with characteristic Etruscan half-round moldings at both top and bottom. The columns of Tuscan type would have been in front, one or two rows deep. A tetrastyle façade, as described by Vitruvius, would have been common, but other possibilities also existed. In the early examples, the pediment was often open and roofed, and the roof would have been protected and decorated with elaborate terracotta cladding; the crest or ridge of the roof might also have been encrusted with fictile decoration.

The decoration of the temple and its possible meaning to the viewer have been discussed by Izzet,[36] but the temple as a vehicle for ritual, a virtual machine for performance, bears further investigation. The relevant formal elements are an unabashed frontality, a strict insistence on axiality, the raising of the temple on an elevated platform on which ritual action would often have taken place (and could have been easily viewed), and the opening up of the façade with wide intercolumniations that would have let the viewer's gaze penetrate into the temple, thus creating ambiguities of internal or external space.

The interplay between interior and exterior in the Tuscan temple is very different from that in the Greek peripteral temple. The open front porch of the Italic temple was more of a scrim than a curtain. The widely spaced columns and frontality afforded a view of a façade open at the columnar level with a broad central intercolumniation,[37] and in earlier periods often open at the pedimental level with the so-called pedimental roof. The god's house, the *aedes*, was visible from the outside, behind a porch that served as a stage for priestly performance. The *aedes* thus becomes a backdrop for human action, action that connects the participant/viewer, through the bodily action of the priest, to the divine power that resides offstage, behind the scenes. The scenographic aspects of a spatial tripartite division of sacred space (most remote), priestly space (intermediate), and human space (nearest and most easily attainable) is paralleled in other tripartite divisions: three parts vertically (podium, porch, and pediment/roof) and three parts horizontally (wider center intercolumniation flanked by open areas). In every spatial reading of this sort, the priest was central, literally front and center. The division of interior and exterior is in this case bridged by the body, connecting to "the seemingly reasonable assumption that conditions as distinct as being in and outside an architectural enclosure require equally distinct ways of thinking about the body and the settings it inhabits."[38]

The action of looking into the temple, the sequence from spectator into or through the podium/porch and into the house of the divinity, or vice versa, is enhanced by the building's frontality (fig. 5.4) as well as by its axiality, which as Paolo Portoghesi has pointed out, unequivocally inserts and aligns the body of the viewer

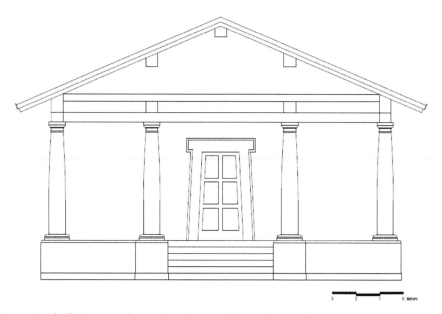

Fig. 5.4. Façade of a Tuscan temple, according to Vitruvius (drawing by Jess Galloway).

with the priest (on the podium) and the statue of the divinity (the *simulacrum*) in the *aedes* behind him/her: "La nozione di frontalità nasce dalla tendenza dell'uomo a immedesimarsi in ciò che costruisce, come se il suo corpo entrasse virtualmente nello spazio dell'oggetto costruito."[39] The importance of seeing and being seen as a way of connecting to the divinity is emphasized by Vitruvius in his discussion of temple orientation (4.5), a passage that has received less attention than his famous discussions of proportionality, harmonics, or even the layout of the Tuscan temple. When there is a choice in siting a temple, Vitruvius suggests (peculiarly) that a temple should face west[40] so that "those who approach with offerings and sacrifices will look toward the image within the temple beneath the eastern part of the heavens."[41] The theatrical aspect of the temple tableau is important for both the worshiper and the *simulacrum*, for the participant "will view both the temple and the rising heaven, while the images (*simulacra*) themselves will seem to be rising as well, to view the supplicants and sacrificers."[42] And finally, Vitruvius concludes that when temples are placed on public roads, they should be sited so that passersby can see the image in the temple and salute (pay their respects to) the divinity.[43] What is visible becomes real; the connection of human and divine is engaged through the act of seeing.

Such transparency in the temple front is illustrated by the newly excavated urban temple (fig. 5.5) at Marzabotto.[44] Its plan is Greek, peripteral, and without a podium, but its setting is Etrusco/Italic, set axially and aligned to the orthogonal street plan of Marzabotto. The other telling Italic aspect of its design is the façade, which is treated as a Tuscan temple porch, albeit in this case without the podium. The tetrastyle façade has a very wide central intercolumniation and two smaller flanking intercolumniations, opening up the front of the temple in the Tuscan manner.[45] Whether the opening up of the façade is for the cult statue of Tina/Tinia (allowing it to see the edges of the city, as suggested by Vitruvius?) or for the population (allowing it to see the statue), it is clear that the feature is purposely designed not to block but to enhance the visual interaction in front of the temple. In fact the rear flank of the temple's colonnade is closed, an awkward pentastyle.

Axiality is another fundamental aspect of Tuscan temple planning. This insistence on an axial approach was surely connected to the *etrusca disciplina* and the quartering of space as a reflection of divine order.[46] This aspect of Etruscan religion has been much discussed,[47] and even if the nuances of the ordering of space may not be clear, what is certain is the idea of a temple platform that served as an elevated place from which the priest could look over a divinely ordered space. Axiality reflected divine will that was interpreted through the priest's body. Frontality thus results, as Portoghesi noted, from a human need to insert the notion of the body into the spatial context. In the case of the Tuscan temple, the axiality and frontality of the temple created awareness of the divine body in the cella, the priestly body on the stage, and the participatory bodies of the audience. In this sense the temple became a corporate entity at times of ritual, tying together all the bodies in the sacred and ritualized space. Izzet has also pointed out that the steps of a Tuscan temple, placed only at the front, serve to control the visitor.[48] This sense of being controlled, of dominated space in a Lefebvrian sense, is fundamental to the experience: the control is the result not of the will of an architect but of the will of the gods, communicated here by the human planners in the same way as the will of the gods is interpreted through ritual.

The relationship between the body of the officiating priest and the audience would of course have helped shape and define space, for as performance theorists have noted, "the spectators experience the actors as well as themselves as embodied minds, as people engaged in the permanent process of becoming, and as living organisms gifted with consciousness. This can happen because of the bodily co-presence of actors and spectators."[49] In a similar manner, the space could have defined the performance: "It is the performative space that enables particular pos-

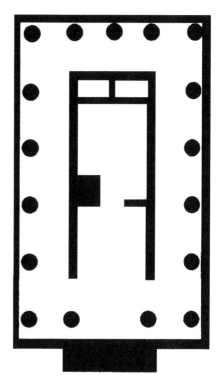

Fig. 5.5. Plan of Tina/Tinia temple at Marzabotto (after Sassatelli and Govi 2005).

sibilities for the relationship between actors and spectators, for movement and perception, which it also organizes and structures."[50]

There is a profound difference, however, between theatrical performance and ritual performance, in that the former can be described as ephemeral[51] and even unique,[52] while the latter may gain much of its power through repetition, especially when doctrinally grounded. Religious ritual is by its nature conservative, but the rituals that took place on the Etruscan temple stage would still have engaged scenographic values that are fundamentally somatic and are at the heart of any sort of performance; they are thus perceivable

> on various levels: the mimetic platform of the stage, on which the actor's body works as both a signifier and a sign . . . ; the receptive arena of the audience, where the spectator's body reacts on multiple planes to the experience before her . . . ; and the uncontainable receptacle of memory—somatic, intellectual, emotional—on which and in which the performance event replays its effect.[53]

In the case of ritual performance, doctrinal memory might have been the most important element, a key part of the control of the audience exerted by the officiating performer to bring order and meaning to a world of omen and mystery.

The alignment of the temple as a platform for viewing may have been connected to specific spatial talents and interests of the controlling elite.[54] Studies suggest that "scene processing"[55] and the ability to connect to spatial orientation are a specific functionality of certain individuals, and it has also been argued, for instance by Mircea Eliade, that orientation is fundamental to defining the sacred: "For nothing can begin, nothing can be done, without previous orientation—and any orientation implies a fixed point. It is for this reason that religious man has sought to fix his abode at 'the center of the world.' "[56] Orientation is thus both physical and existential, even if, as Barrie has pointed out in his critique of Eliade,[57] the physical realities of sacred architecture are usually more complex, nuanced, and dynamic, given that space is not experienced statically. And the physicality of spatial experience is mirrored by the physicality of religious experience; recent research suggests that even such intangibles as an individual's religiosity are connected to discernible physical determinants.[58]

The hierarchies and orientation of the temple reflected the social landscape of the Etruscans, and monumental temples from the sixth century onward seem to have been a distinctly urban manifestation.[59] This makes sense, given the amount of wealth and manpower that must have been manifest to create such a structure—to quarry the large amount of stone for the podium and column bases, to harvest the timber for the columns and the roofing system, or to manufacture the extensive surfaces of tile, revetments, and other decorative elements. Whatever the mechanisms, even when a temple is not situated in a strictly urban setting, as at Poggio Colla, the Etruscan temple seems to have been an inherently urban phenomenon. In the case of Marzabotto, our only well-preserved Etruscan city, the alignment of temples on the acropolis is directly connected to the urban plan (although the exact orientation might result from astronomical reckoning),[60] and the newly discovered temple of Tina/Tinia is an integral part of the city's fabric and the orthogonal layout.[61] Even more interesting is the evolution—or more possibly conflation—of house, shrine, and sacred area that takes place in some urban contexts, for instance at Tarquinia in the case of the celebrated Building Beta,[62] dated as early as the middle of the seventh century BCE. This shrine takes the form of a rectangular structure set axially in a rectangular precinct. The axiality and frontality, whether or not this was an actual *aedes* or temple of the *oikos* type, as suggested by Colonna,[63] are likely precursors of temple planning of the following century.

The Ritual and Social Contexts

THE SHEER MONUMENTALITY AND THE CONCOMITANT patronage necessary to build a large temple argue for an urban context.[64] The Tuscan temple may also have been urban in the way that it processed performance through the filter of Etruscan society. We know little of the way that ritual performance was viewed, or of the makeup of the audience. Would the viewing of ritual have been restricted to the elite? Etruscan visual culture does associate sacrifice with elaborate processions and games connected to funerary ritual, but the Etruscan interest in spectacle may not have existed just in the funerary sphere. Etruscan material culture suggests that banqueting was also an important part of sanctuary life.

It is not hard to imagine that Etruscan ritual as it was performed in the sanctuary was a kind of spectacle that could have involved, as viewer if not as participant, a range of Etruscan society. Ritual and spectacle reinforced social boundaries, including the role of divinity in both the social and the spatial context. In this sense the form and setting of a Tuscan temple would have defined an Etruscan conceptualization of human–divine interaction. The Greek temple, set on its pedestal and meant to be viewed from a distance, creates a world that we cannot inhabit. The house of the god is shrouded from our view, surrounded by a protective phalanx of columns.[65] Interaction takes place in front, on an altar seen by the divinity but also at a remove. In Etruscan religion knowledge of the gods and their will, the *cognitio deorum*,[66] was expressed through bodily presence and action, through the agency of the officiating priest.

But if Etruscan religion was participatory, it would probably also have been strictly and hierarchically arranged, with clear delineation of both social and religious boundaries. Using the analogy of later Roman performance, where the physical placement of individuals mirrored their social ranking,[67] we might wonder whether the social landscape was perhaps reflected in the ritual setting of the Tuscan temple, with the performing priest, representing the pinnacle of the elite, placed front and center, physically closer to the gods, indeed backed or flanked by gods. The analogy of priest and god, or of priest as bodily vessel of the god, would have been evident: analogous thinking is inherently a visual activity.[68] Indeed, performance can enhance metaphor comprehension,[69] even on a biological or neural level, as has been argued by Lakoff and Johnson,[70] who situated metaphorical thinking in "perceptual and motor systems."[71]

Thus the interpretation of ritual would have been an inherent result of the semiotic systems of a culturally constructed and interpreted environment. The spatial relationships would also have provided an underlying structure for the sense of community; current performance theory would refer to "containment," "verticality," "near–far," and even "center–periphery,"[72] the latter perhaps more in social and doctrinal terms than spatially. Display would not have been restricted to ritual performance: Etruscan sanctuaries displayed gifts and votives, and these too would have been agents for social ranking.[73]

The articulation of boundaries was especially important to the aesthetic of the Tuscan temple (fig. 5.4). The decoration of the roof in fact enhanced its edges, just as the characteristic Etruscan moldings of the podium articulated and defined the transitional elements, the place where the podium began and ended. The powerful Etruscan round defined the boundaries of the podium, creating a visual stop for the eye of the viewer rather than the smoothing and flowing of transitions that are characteristic of Greek architecture. This very different aesthetic of the Etruscan use of moldings was noted by Lucy Shoe Meritt: "It was instantly obvious that here was a world of a totally different architectural concept; the idea that Etruscan and Roman architecture was simply a version of Greek architecture was not true."[74]

The Etruscan roof also functions in a singular and characteristic way, with figural decoration that literally walks the sky, silhouetted on the ridge, connecting human and divine, although admittedly this kind of decoration is found on both religious and secular structures.[75] The roof thus not only shelters and protects,[76] but in the case of a temple may also serve to connect the earthbound human ritual action with a broader divine order.[77] The pediment of the temple is in early structures conceived as an open and roofed space that may mirror the caves or underground fissures that were early places of worship. In later cases, as at Talamone, the closed pediment can mirror ritual through narrative.[78]

The scenographic aspects of both the layout and the façade of the Tuscan temple created two different spaces, two spheres of activity that involved two groups: the elite priest, who performed ritual on the temple platform; and a larger group of participants, who would have faced the temple and provided the audience for ritual. Recent theoretical work on the psychological and cognitive aspects of ritual and religion has proposed that there are two types of religion: doctrinal and imagistic.[79] The Etruscan religion that we know from later Roman sources is profoundly doctrinal, set down in books that were passed from generation to generation until the very end of classical antiquity. The layout of the Tuscan temple, however, suggests that the reality of religious experience might have been more complex, at least as it was performed, with a more imagistic understanding of ritual by the people watching the performance. In fact, a sociological model of ritual would posit that ritual is "an occasion on which normal behavioral rules and hierarchical positions are temporarily suspended, creating a sense of equal membership in the group," perhaps even resulting in a "community-based *locus of control* in which non-elites can participate."[80]

Even if we cannot know exactly how the officiating priest would have connected to a larger audience in front of the temple, there is evidence that large-scale performances would have taken place in sanctuaries, that performance and ritual could be inextricably linked. The evidence is etic, Livy's description (5.1.1–3) of the events of 403 BCE: during the protracted struggle between Rome and Veii, the Romans elected more magistrates to help with the effort while the Etruscans elected a king. Livy contrasts the due process of Roman government with the autocratic systems of the Veientines, but he also provides a fascinating glimpse of Etruscan patronage and religious organization when he describes the new king's unsuitability. In an act of personal arrogance (*superbia*—and how could this not bring to mind the Tarquins?) and impiety in response to not being made the officiating priest, this individual had interrupted an important religious festival (*sollemni ludi*) by withdrawing his retinue, his dependents (*servi*), from the spectacle. As Camporeale points out in a recent analysis of this passage, we thus have evidence of the close connection between Etruscan spectacle and ritual, of the organization of Etruscan religion (an officiating elite Etruscan appointed as *sacerdos*), and of a non-elite population that would have participated in the ritual.[81]

Further evidence for the use of Etruscan temples and altars can be extrapolated from funerary contexts, where altars follow the general aesthetic of temples— probably because of similar ritual demands. With the characteristic high podium, frontal steps, and clear axiality, they thus provide "new information about the performative aspects of Etruscan sacred structures and of the symbolic meaning of the human body in the context of ritual."[82] These structures are found from the seventh century onward and, as Camporeale points out, they were intended for spectacles or performances probably attended by persons related to or connected with the deceased, and these "performances would have been analogous to those that took place in the sanctuaries in honor of the gods."[83] A good example is the monumental stone altar that forms part of the Melone del Sodo II complex at Cortona.[84] The high altar (fig. 5.6) rises to the level of the top of the stone drum of the tumulus with an imposing and very steep set of steps. The steps are flanked by antae illus-

Fig. 5.6. Cortona, Melone del Sodo II, altar (photo G. Warden).

trating remarkable human–animal combats that must have symbolized the spilling of sacrificial blood, possibly even its transformative power.[85] The altar platform was a place for the priest/magistrate to perform rituals that would have been dramatically situated in the context of the tumulus that towers in the background, with the body of the priest/performer becoming the element that, through ritual action, would have connected living to dead, human to divine.[86]

Monumentality: Podium, Body, and Roof

THE MONUMENTALIZATION OF ARCHITECTURAL FORMS that took place in central Italy in the seventh and sixth centuries BCE was connected to state formation, urbanization, and to changes in the power structure of the Etruscan elite. The change from unstructured sacred space to codified temple sanctuary may not have been sudden,[87] and certainly some of the spatial concepts later manifest in the monumental temple and its sanctuary must have existed before the sixth century BCE. The creation of temples with stone elements and tile roofs is also part of a much larger and more complex development in both the sacred and the urban spheres.[88] Indeed, the present state of the evidence, which admittedly could change very quickly, suggests that the earliest buildings with tile roofs—for instance the complexes at Murlo and Acquarossa,[89] or the recently excavated series of buildings at Casale Marittimo—were not temples. The seventh-century complex at Murlo combines monumentality and new terracotta roofing systems with the expression of very sophisticated ideological messages in its decorative scheme.[90]

These messages are connected to the ideology of the Etruscan elite, for the architectural innovations of the seventh century BCE were both in practice and in symbolism an elite phenomenon. At Murlo there is in fact evidence of coeval elite and non-elite architecture, where the traditional thatched huts continued to serve utilitarian, servile functions.[91]

The settlement of Casale Marittimo, which awaits full publication, documents the characteristics of the change toward monumentality in the Orientalizing period in Etruria: an early, eighth-century settlement with huts, a seventh-century building (Building Beta) with tile roof, which the excavator has interpreted as a kind of Regia, and then a later seventh-century building (Gamma), again with tile roof but now also with gorgon antefixes.[92] Inscribed bucchero *kyathoi* associated with these buildings allow for this development to be firmly dated in the mid-seventh century BCE. The change from rounded huts with thatched roofs to rectilinear structures with tile roofs would have been dramatic visually but also must have reflected important changes in social organization. The economics of this change warrant further investigation, but the new monumental buildings with stone foundations, pisé walls, and terracotta roofing systems would certainly have required more manpower and greater use of natural resources than earlier structures. In this sense the new Tuscan temple reflected the growing power of the Etruscan elites: the power not only to order divine space and to interpret the will of the gods, but also to control large populations and to muster the physical and human resources necessary to build structures that glorified the human as well as the divine.

Monumentality is thus much more than sheer size. A work can be monumental in its style as well as in its materiality, and I would argue that a work might be monumental in its subject. Monumentality can result from what is depicted: the mythic narratives that are imaged from the seventh century onward can be inherently monumental in theme as well as in scope. The impression of monumentality can also result from the deep historicity of architectural forms, constituting a monumentality of tradition, where physical form can embody the power of social and political structure and the reality of "historical or mythic heft."[93]

The new structures of the seventh century, with their rectilinear plans and terracotta roofs, were a startling departure from the past not only in form but also in color and texture. The natural materials of the traditional huts—mud and wood, which would have faded and organically blended in with their surroundings over time—were now replaced by human-made terracotta, sometimes brightly painted. The innovation of the tile roof had other implications as well; apart from requiring a rectangular plan, it also necessitated a regular system of raftering and thus a plan that followed rational order—much as, somewhat later, temple planning would impose its rational order over natural space. It is not farfetched to wonder whether the Etruscan interest in rational space might have begun with the architectural revolution of the seventh century. Or could it be the other way around? Are the innovations of this period the result of the Etruscan belief system?

The earliest buildings of this type—for instance the complexes at Poggio Civitate (Murlo)—are planned with a basic module that is used as a measure for the entire complex. There is probably no other way to lay out complex architecture of this type, but it is worth remembering that such modules are often based on parts of the human body, for instance "foot" in English, or "piede" or "braccio" in Italian. The tile roof was thus revolutionary conceptually as well as visually. As a form in itself it would have symbolized power and, as a corollary, monumentality. This symbolism explains why in Etruscan usage, tiles had important functions other than serving as part of the cover of a building; they were, for example, inscribed surfaces that signified sacred or funerary importance.[94] Tiles could also symbolize unity, perhaps because a single tile could serve as signifier for a roof—with the roof as a potent symbol of human agency[95]—and thus of a space that connects the human and the divine. A good example of this kind of symbolism, expressed simply and elegantly by a single tile, is the conjugal urn from the Tomb of the Calisna Sepu at Monteriggioni,[96] just north of Siena (fig. 5.7). The tile is placed purposely and impossibly upside down on the heads of a reclining couple, uniting them in the afterlife through the symbolism of the roof.[97] A single tile in this case embodies a monumental function.

In Etruria the construction of monumental temples goes hand in hand with a concomitant interest in depicting the human body on a more monumental scale. A similar interest in monumentality is found in Greece in the second half of the seventh century BCE, but what sets Etruria apart is that the earliest monumental sculpture is found in funerary contexts, seemingly quite separate from the normative schemes of display in the sanctuary. The earliest Etruscan life-size sculpture in stone consists of single figures whose identification remains enigmatic but whose function was certainly to display simulacra of the human body.[98] The figures are at first awkwardly realized, as in the famous Pietrera woman, and the lack of transition between discrete elements suggests that the sculptor used a small-scale figure as a model and blew it up to a much larger size.[99] Brendel has a different explanation: "One receives the impression that these figures indeed represent the first attempt at statuary, as if upright stone stelae had only gradually, hesitatingly been transformed into a kind of statue, in order to impart greater reality to the images."[100] The newly discovered stone figures from Casale Marittimo[101] have some of the same awkwardness, a similar lack of transition from one part of the body to another, as if once again the sculptor had found it difficult to depict the modulation and surface of the human body in such an unforgiving medium and on an uncomfortably large scale. As was the case with ar-

Fig. 5.7. Urn from the Tomb of the Calisna Sepu, Monteriggioni. Florence Archaeological Museum (photo G. Warden).

chitecture, there are different aspects of monumentality at work: the larger scale of the figure, the necessary virtuosity of engaging a new medium, and the sheer visual drama of the human figure displayed in an entirely new way. A culminating moment, then, is the aforementioned monumental stone altar at Cortona with its large, sanguinary human–animal combats placed prominently at the antae, literally flanking the ceremonial approach to the sacred space (fig. 5.6). Architecture and funerary ritual are now combined in the context of a monumentality that symbolizes the transcendent nature of the Etruscan elites. The environment is monumental not only in scale but also thematically, because of the heroic subject matter, the impenetrable material, and the sophisticated spatial context.[102]

If monumentality can be expressed in ways that are mutable, the phenomenon of monumentality in the seventh century BCE was also widespread. It occurs not just in temple planning, but also in other types of architecture, in sculpture, in funerary architecture and custom (as documented by Tuck in this volume), and eventually even in larger urban settings.[103] The massive stone walls that girdle the great Etruscan cities, for example, rise naturally out of the bedrock and thus symbolize the natural as well as the sacred power of the city. I would argue that all this results from the expression of the power of the Etruscan elites, power that is firmly rooted in the control of what today we would call the sacred and the secular. Temple, tomb, and wall: Etruscan space is sacred space. It is therefore not surprising that Roman law, perhaps based on these traditions, recognized three types of sacred property: *res sacrae*, temples and altars; *res religiosae*, tombs and funerary monuments; and *res sanctae*, the walls of the city.[104]

Fig. 5.8. Tumulus in the Via S. Iacopo, Pisa (photo G. Warden).

Fig. 5.9. Tuscan column as funerary marker at Marzabotto, north necropolis (drawing by Jess Galloway).

Fig. 5.10. Funerary stela, Marzabotto (photo G. Warden).

Conclusions

RITUAL, "BY MEANS OF CRITICAL OBSERVATION and an assumption of a relationship of a body and its environment,"[105] connected the body of the elite Etruscan to observable signs within the spatial context of the *templum*, a space that according to the *etrusca disciplina* mirrors divine order. For the Etruscans, as was noted by Seneca, things do not signify meaning because of their existence, but rather, they exist as signifiers, as bearers of meaning that, of course, can be interpreted only by the theocratic elite.[106]

The elite body is the connecting element, and there is evidence for the display of the elite body in funerary contexts at least as early as the Orientalizing period: the recently excavated tumulus (fig. 5.8) in Via S. Iacopo at Pisa[107] is earlier than the first monumental codified temples at the end of the Archaic period. The funerary rituals would probably have been connected to the cult of the ancestors. At Pisa the tumulus is surrounded by a row of upright stones, presumably the stelae and cippi of the descendants of the elite Etruscan commemorated (in this case not buried, for the structure is a cenotaph) by the tumulus. The descendants are thus a silent and eternal audience for the performances that take place on the tumulus stage, the altar at the apex of the mound. The statues are individual descendants of the ancestor memorialized by the tumulus, circling the funerary monument as quiet witnesses to ancestral memory as it was celebrated in a funerary setting. In this sense, ritual binds the performer to the audience in a spatial rhetoric that mirrors the social landscape of the Etruscans in much the same way as it is mirrored by the spatial rhetoric of the Tuscan temple.

Thus, if the temple can be conceived and treated as a body, then the opposite can also be true: the human body through performance and ritual action[108] is visualized as an architectonic entity. Rykwert's human column—or Onian's suggestion of the peristyle as phalanx—are thus more than metaphor. The Etruscans clearly thought of the human body in such terms, at least in funerary contexts, and the interment of the "dead" Poggio Colla temple can be thought of as a kind of mortuary context. In an overt example, funerary markers at Etruscan sites like Marzabotto can take the form of a Tuscan column[109] (fig. 5.9) that clearly symbolizes the body of the deceased and serves as a permanent memorial, where monumentality results not just from size or scale but from symbolism and function. The metaphor is even more explicit in the case of an exceptional and singular stela from Marzabotto (fig. 5.10) that shows a figure standing on an altar.[110] The altar (or podium?) is of the characteristic hourglass shape with broad Etruscan rounds at top and bottom. An elite female figure is situated on the altar, standing firmly as a column while performing a libation, while above her head sprouts an elegant palmette.[111] The human body, displayed now through ritual performance and as important for its agency as for its meaning, connects earth and sky. Temple and body, body and temple: disparate elements are connected, and the will of the gods is revealed.

Notes

I met Ingrid Edlund-Berry at Murlo, where I had the good fortune to work from 1970 to 1978, and I have valued her friendship to this day. She continues to work with us at Poggio Colla, where her insight into the architectural remains has contributed to the success of the project. I have appreciated her common sense and the cautionary approach that she has taken to difficult problems, which is always based on a sound appreciation of the limits of the evidence. This contribution, which admittedly tries to push the evidence farther than she might consider judicious and which attempts to incorporate theory in order to make up for the lack of evidence, is dedicated to her.

I must also express my gratitude to my colleagues at Poggio Colla, especially Michael Thomas, co-director of the Mugello Valley Archaeological Project; Ann Steiner, director of research; Gretchen Meyers, director of materials; and Jess Galloway, architect. The Mugello Valley Archaeological Project and excavations at Poggio Colla would not be possible without the support of Dr. Fulvia Lo Schiavo, Superintendent, and Dr. Luca Fedeli of the Soprintendenza per i Beni Archeologici della Toscana. I am most grateful for their encouragement.

1. Summarized in Warden, Thomas, and Galloway 1999; Warden et al. 2005. Most recently: Warden 2009b; Warden 2010.
2. Edlund-Berry 1994.
3. The artisan areas and settlement surrounding the sanctuary are summarized by Thomas (2000).

4. A terminus post quem is provided by Orientalizing and Archaic bucchero in underlying strata.

5. Zifferero 1995.

6. There is now evidence of yet another phase, but it is as yet too early to know whether it is a full phase or a subphase.

7. For preliminary results: Warden, Thomas, and Galloway 1999 and Warden et al. 2005. For discussion of the ritual deposits: Warden 2009a. For the temple as body: Warden 2010.

8. For which see Scheid 1984; and Warden 2010.

9. Edlund 1987.

10. For recent work on consecrated space, see Briquel 2008 with previous bibliography.

11. Edlund-Berry 1994.

12. Bonghi Jovino 2005, 43.

13. Most notably in Rykwert 1996, for instance ch. 7, "The Hero as Column," or in ch. 3, "The Body and the World," such topics as "Fabric of Man, Fabric of the World."

14. Onians 1988 and 2002.

15. Wilson Jones 2002.

16. Mallgrave 2010.

17. Mallgrave 2010, 205.

18. Wilson 1984, 1; Mallgrave 2010, 205.

19. Holl 2006, 116; Mallgrave 2010, 205.

20. For phenomenology and experiencing space as movement in Etruscan architecture: Meyers 2003, esp. 27. In the context of prehistory and archaeology: Tilley 1994.

21. Glinister 2000. See also Warden 2009a.

22. For Etruscan ritual and priests: de Grummond 2006; van der Meer 1979.

23. See Stevens 2009, with previous bibliography. Also: Aveni and Romano 1994a and 1994b; Weinstock 1946.

24. van der Meer 1987.

25. Bourdieu 1984, cited by Frasier and Greco 2005, 90.

26. Von Staden 1996, 98: "a teleological and mechanistic version of the body therefore offers a further example of the interactive nature of the early Hellenistic scientific community."

27. Turfa and Gettys 2009.

28. Izzet 2000; 2001.

29. Izzet 2000, 35.

30. For a recent and excellent summary of Etruscan temples of various types: Colonna 2006, esp. 152–164. For sanctuaries in general: Colonna 1985. For a fundamental discussion of the Tuscan temple: Lake 1935.

31. For a full analysis of *"templum"* in Roman context but relevant to Etruscan antecedents, see Cipriano 1983.

32. As Izzet (2007, 128) has aptly put it, "After the ambiguity of earlier buildings, where ritual was one of many activities that took place in a given location, the sudden appearance of a recognizable architectural form in which ritual was housed must be a deliberate attempt to fix ritual spatially. It is important to stress that the mere development of a distinct and archaeologically recognizable architectural language for religious buildings is one of the most significant expressions of the importance of demarcating the ritual sphere."

33. Colonna (1985, 60–65) discusses the temple as *"categoria architettonica."* The bibliography on the Tuscan temple is vast, but is summarized in Colonna 1985, 62, and Izzet 2000.

34. Given the nature of the evidence and its geographical scope, it is probably safer to refer to this kind of structure as an Etrusco-Italic temple, but for the sake of convenience I will use the Vitruvian terminology, "Tuscan temple."

35. See Colonna 2006, 162, fig. VIII.41 for the plan of the Belvedere temple. The identification of three cellae rests on the location of a mere two stones, now not readily visible. For other dubious tripartite reconstructions: Damgaard Andersen 1993a, 74.

36. Izzet 2000.

37. The ratio of 3:4:3 is given by Vitruvius (4.7) for a tetrastyle temple of the Tuscan type. The arrangement is illustrated in Rowland and Howe 1999, 234, fig. 73.

38. Leatherbarrow 2002, 269, who points out that the notions of being inside and outside can also theoretically be seen as one.

39. "The concept of frontality results from man's need to situate himself into what he builds, as if his body were entering virtually the space that he constructed." Portoghesi 1999, 360.

40. A western orientation is far from the norm, judging from the evidence of actual temples.

41. Rowland and Howe 1999, 59.

42. Rowland and Howe 1999, 59.

43. "uti praeterentes possint respicere et in conspectus salutations facere."

44. Sassatelli and Govi 2005; Rameri 2005.

45. See Sassatelli and Govi 2005, pls. 2 and 3 for a reconstruction and plan.

46. For the etrusca disciplina and the temple, Rowland and Howe 1999, 152.

47. The Vitruvian connection of sacred space and the etrusca disciplina is summarized in Meyers 2003, 44–45; and Meyers 2005, 76–77.

48. Izzet 2000, 52: "In an Etruscan temple it was physically impossible to get up onto the podium in any other way than that which was intended by the builders: the front." It might be argued that the intention is not that of the builders but of the gods.

49. Fischer-Lichte 2010, 33.

50. Fischer-Lichte 2010, 33.

51. Hall 2010, 18–19.

52. Fischer-Lichte 2010, 32–33.

53. Griffiths 2010, 223.

54. As well as the Etruscan talent for land surveying, which also involved quartering space, according to Howe in Rowland and Howe 1999, 152. See also Howe 2005, 62 and fig. 21.

55. Epstein, Higgins, and Thompson-Schill 2005, 73–83.

56. Eliade 1959, 22.

57. Barrie 2010, 167–168.

58. Colzato, Hommel, and Shapiro 2010, 1: "People's attentional processing style reflects biases rewarded by their religious beliefs."

59. A good summary of temple development in its urban framework is provided by Colonna (1986).

60. The evidence is still inconclusive: Gottarelli 2005. For more convincing arguments: Stevens 2008.

61. Sassatelli and Govan 2005.

62. Colonna 2006, 147, fig. VIII.24, with previous bibliography.

63. Colonna 2006, 146–147. The exact function of the building, despite the certain indications of votive activity and the inclusion of what seems to be an altar within the building, is unclear.

64. Much work needs to be done on the economic agency of temples and sanctuaries. Evidence from Rome connects Roman temples to specific vows and thus to Roman elite society. The evidence from Etruria is, as always, far less clear. See Edlund-Berry 2009, 101–105.

65. For the idea of the peripteral colonnade as phalanx, see Onians 2002, 51.

66. Ceccarelli 2007, 322.

67. For social ordering: Hillier and Hanson 1984. For spatial rhetoric and its relationship to the concept of the cosmos: Catalano 1978.

68. Stafford (1999, 8) points out that knowledge is a heuristic activity "always in pursuit of equivalencies for one thing or another."

69. Wilson and Gibbs 2007.

70. Lakoff and Johnson 1999, 555, for experiences that "become neurally linked."

71. Lakoff and Johnson 1999, 555.

72. As for instance elaborated by McConachie (2002), in an analysis of actual performances based on Lakoff and Johnson's theories of spatial relationships.

73. See Becker 2009 for the economic agency of the temple and its connections to social ranking. On a broader level: Renfrew and Sherman 1992.

74. Shoe Meritt 1965, XV. See also Shoe Meritt and Edlund-Berry 2000. It was my good fortune to know the late Prof. Meritt and to witness firsthand her vast knowledge of the aesthetics of Etrusco-Italic moldings. For moldings and the history of the Tuscan temple: Edlund-Berry 2008.

75. Poggesi et al. 2005, 278, fig. 8.

76. Etruscan roofs had prominent overhangs that protected the mud and timber walls; according to Vitruvius the overhang would have been one-quarter the height of the columns.

77. Human figures are found on roofs as early as the Villanovan period, and the human mask is a common form of decoration as well. Damgaard Andersen 1993b, 54–57.

78. For the possible connection of the blind Oedipus on the Talamone pediment to ritual, Warden 2008, 13.

79. McCauley and Lawson 2002; Sørensen 2005.

80. Hermanowicz and Morgan 1999, 210.

81. Camporeale 2010, 158.

82. Warden 2010.

83. Camporeale 2009, 229, with bibliography and documentation for games and spectacles in Etruscan sanctuaries, for which see also Thuillier 1993. The combination of tomb and spectator area (often stepped) could also be the precursor of the Italic/Roman tradition of combining temple and theater, often in an axial arrangement.

84. Zamarchi Grassi 1992, pls. 25–29; Bruschetti and Zamarchi Grassi 1994, 46.

85. Warden 2009c.

86. For a more detailed discussion in the context of Etruscan belief in sacrifice as a transformative ritual: Warden 2009c and Camporeale 2009. The Etruscan ancestor cult is discussed in detail by Damgaard Andersen (1993b).

87. As for instance suggested by Izzet 2000, 35.

88. Brandt and Karlsson 2001.

89. Winter 2009, 567: "From their earliest appearances, tiled roofs in Etruria are associated with domestic architecture and only later with buildings of clearly sacred or civic nature." I am not certain that the distinction between domestic, civic, and sacred would have

been perceived thusly by the Etruscans, for elite architecture could embody all three aspects; however, given the present state of the evidence, it does seem clear that the codified temple is a later phenomenon.

90. Tuck 2006, 130–135.

91. Carroll, Rodriguez, and Tuck 2009.

92. Esposito 2007, 90–91.

93. Miller 2010, 25: "The reality of this historical or mythic heft, which we conventionally call 'monumentality . . .'"

94. Tiles were sometimes used to ritually seal tombs, or inscribed tiles could be placed in tombs as markers (memorials?) of the deceased. A good example is the tile from the Tomb of the Tassinae at Chiusi: it bears the name of a woman buried in the tomb. Rastrelli 1985, 120–121.

95. As for the instance on the Chiusine cippus in Berlin that shows a *prothesis* under an open but elaborately roofed building. Damgaard Andersen 1993a, 82, fig. 10.

96. Cristofani et al. 1975–1977, 168, fig. 246. The context of the tomb is discussed in detail, 161–189; this remarkable urn held the ashes, in separate sections of the box, of the "founders" of the dynasty. The upside-down tile, for whose placement the heads of the man and woman have been carefully cut, has never been satisfactorily explained other than as a way of protecting the couple from underground water, an explanation that is both banal and difficult to accept. The singular placement of the tile, upside-down in a way that mirrors Etruscan ritual, with the careful cutting of the heads (are we to believe that this took place in the tomb, after the fact?) is better explained by conjugal symbolism.

97. For the concept of the roof as uniting force, one might consider the Etruscan practice of covering the couple with a canopy at weddings, as documented on Chiusine funerary iconography.

98. Brendel (1995, 92) referring to the earliest Etruscan statues from the Pietrera tomb: "We must assume that they represented the dead in their last dwelling place in order to endow the departed with an abiding form such as only art can provide. They were the substitute bodies for the owners of the tomb." They may alternately have represented the ancestors of the deceased.

99. For this figure and others from the Pietrera tumulus: Camporeale 1967. A. M. Esposito in Celuzza and Cianferoni 2010, 157–158.

100. Brendel 1995, 93.

101. Esposito 2007, 104–105. Idem in Celuzza and Cianferoni 2010, 123–124.

102. Warden 2009c, 206.

103. For urbanization: Damgaard Andersen 1997.

104. Laurence 1996, 117.

105. Howe in Rowland and Howe 1999, 152.

106. Seneca, *Quaestiones Naturales* 2.32.2.

107. Bruni 1998, 105–107; Floriani and Bruni 2006, 20–22.

108. Mitchell 2007, 338: A focus on body agency demands a move toward a phenomenologically informed analysis.

109. Sassatelli 1992, 37, fig. 8.

110. Sassatelli 1992, 47, fig. 18. Also illustrated in Camporeale 2009, 233, fig. 14.9, although this illustration cuts off the bottom half of the altar.

111. Considered a divinized figure by Camporeale (2009, 232–233).

Bibliography

Aveni, A., and G. Romano. 1994a. "Orientation and Etruscan Ritual." *Antiquity* 68:545–563.

———. 1994b. "Orientazioni di templi e rituali etruschi." *RdA* 18:57–67.

Barrie, T. 2010. *The Sacred In-Between: The Mediating Roles of Architecture*. London: Routledge.

Becker, H. 2009. "The Economic Agency of the Etruscan Temple: Elites, Dedications, and Display." In *Votives, Places, Rituals in Etruscan Religion: Studies in Honour of Jean MacIntosh Turfa*, ed. M. Gleba and H. Becker, 87–99. Leiden: Brill.

Bonghi Jovino, M. 2005. "Depositi votivi e sacralità: Dall'analisi del rituale alla lettura interpretativa delle forme di religiosità." In *Depositi votivi e culti dell'Italia antica dall'età arcaica a quella tarda-repubblicana. Atti del Convegno di Studi, Perugia, 1–4 giugno 2000*, ed. A. Comella and S. Mele, 31–46. Bari: Edipuglia.

Bourdieu, P. 1984. *The Logic of Practice*. London: Blackwell.

Brandt, J. R., and L. Karlsson, eds. 2001. *From Huts to Houses: Transformations of Ancient Societies*. Stockholm: Paul Åströms Förlag.

Brendel, Otto J. 1995. *Etruscan Art*. 2nd ed. Baltimore: Johns Hopkins University Press.

Briquel, D. 2008. "L'espace consacré chez les Étruques: Réflexions sur le rituel étrusco-romain de fondation des cités." In *Saturnia Tellus: Definizioni dello spazio consacrato in ambiente etrusco, italico, fenicio-punico, iberico e celtico. Atti del Convegno Internazionale svoltosi a Roma dal 10 al 12 novembre 2004*, ed. X. D. Raventós, S. Ribichini, and S. Verger, 27–47. Rome: Consiglio Nazionale delle Ricerche.

Bruni, S. 1998. *Pisa etrusca: Anatomia di una città scomparsa*. Milan: Longanesi.

Bruschetti, P., and P. Zamarchi Grassi. 1994. *Cortona etrusca: Esempi di architettura funeraria*. Cortona: Calosci.

Camporeale, G. 2009. "The Deified Deceased in Etruscan Culture." In *New Perspectives on Etruria and Rome: Papers in Honor of Richard D. De Puma*, ed. S. Bell and I. Nagy, 220–250. Madison: University of Wisconsin Press.

———. 2010. "Il teatro etrusco secondo le fonti scritte: Spettacolo, ritualità, religione." In *Material Aspects of Etruscan Religion*, ed. L. B. van der Meer, 155–164. Leuven: Peeters.

Camporeale, Giovannangelo. 1967. "Appunti su alcuni frammenti plastici della Pietrera." *StudEtr* 35:595–601.

Carroll, A., A. Rodriguez, and A. Tuck. 2009. "Light Framed Architecture at Poggio Civitate: A Comparison of Elite and Non-Elite Domiciles." *Rasenna* 2.1. http://scholarworks.umass.edu/rasenna/vol2/iss1/4/

Catalano, P. 1978. "Aspetti spaziali del sistema giuridico-religioso romano." *ANRW* II.16.1, 440–553.

Ceccarelli, L. 2007. "The Role of Votive Objects in Roman Religious Practices between the Fourth and Second Centuries B.C." In *Cult in Context: Reconsidering Ritual in Archaeology*, ed. D. A. Barrowclough and C. Malone, 321–327. Oxford: Oxbow Books.

Celuzza, M., and G. C. Cianferoni, eds. 2010. *Signori di Maremma: Élites etrusche fra Populonia e Vulci*. Florence: Edizioni Polistampa.

Cipriano, P. 1983. *Templum*. Biblioteca di ricerche linguistiche e filologiche 13. Rome: Università "La Sapienza."

Colonna, G., ed. 1985. *Santuari d'Etruria*. Milano: Electa.

———. 1986. "Urbanistica e architettura." In *Rasenna: Storia e civiltà degli Etruschi*, ed. G. Pugliese Carratelli, 371–530. Milan: Scheiwiller.

———. 2006. "Sacred Architecture and the Religion of the Etruscans." In *The Religion of the*

Etruscans, ed. N. T. de Grummond and E. Simon, 132–168. Austin: University of Texas Press.

Colzato L. S., B. Hommel, and K. L. Shapiro. 2010. "Religion and the Attentional Blink: Depth of Faith Predicts Depth of the Blink." *Frontiers of Psychology* 1:1–7.

Cristofani, M., M. Cristofani Martelli, E. Fiumi, A. Maggiani, and A. Talocchini, eds. 1975–1977. *Corpus delle urne etrusche di età ellenistica*, 1, *Urne volterrane* 1. 2 vols. Florence: Centro Di.

Damgaard Andersen, H. 1993a. "Archaic Architectural Terracottas and Their Relation to Building Identification." In *Deliciae Fictiles*, ed. E. Rystedt, C. Wikander, and O. Wikander, 71–86. Stockholm: Paul Åströms Förlag.

———. 1993b. "The Etruscan Ancestral Cult—Its Origin and Development and the Importance of Anthropomorphization." *AnalRom* 21:8–66.

———. 1997. "The Archaeological Evidence for the Origin and Development of the Etruscan City in the 7th and 6th Centuries B.C." *Acta Hyperborea* 7:343–382.

de Grummond, N. T. 2006. "Prophets and Priests." In *The Religion of the Etruscans*, ed. N. T. de Grummond and E. Simon, 27–44. Austin: University of Texas Press.

Edlund, I. E. M. 1987. *The Gods and the Place: Location and Function of Sanctuaries in the Countryside of Etruria and Magna Graecia (700–400 B.C.)*. Lund: Swedish Institute.

———. 1992. *The Seated and Standing Statue Akroteria from Poggio Civitate (Murlo)*. Rome: Giorgio Bretschneider.

Edlund-Berry, I. E. M. 1994. "Ritual Destruction of Cities and Sanctuaries: The 'Un-Founding' of the Archaic Monumental Building at Poggio Civitate." In *Murlo and the Etruscans*, ed. R. D. De Puma and J. P. Small, 16–28. Madison: University of Wisconsin Press.

———. 2008. "The Language of Etrusco-Italic Architecture: New Perspectives on Tuscan Temples." *AJA* 112:441–447.

———. 2009. "The Historical and Religious Context of Vows Fulfilled in Etruscan Temple Foundations." In *Votives, Places, Rituals in Etruscan Religion: Studies in Honour of Jean MacIntosh Turfa*, ed. M. Gleba and H. Becker, 101–106. Leiden: Brill.

Eliade, M. 1959. *The Sacred and the Profane: The Nature of Religion*. San Diego: Harcourt, Brace, Jovanovich.

Epstein, R. A., J. S. Higgins, and S. I. Thompson-Schill. 2005. "Learning Places from Views: Variation in Scene Processing as a Function of Experience and Navigational Ability." *Journal of Cognitive Neuroscience* 17:73–83.

Esposito, Anna Maria. 2007. "Casale Marittimo: L'insediamento e le necropoli." In *Etruschi di Volterra*, 90–111. Volterra: Federico Motta.

Fischer-Lichte, E. 2010. "Performance as Event—Reception at Transformation." In *Theorizing Performance: Greek Drama, Cultural History, and Critical Practice*, ed. E. Hall and S. Harrop, 29–42. London: Duckworth.

Floriani, P., and S. Bruni. 2006. *La Tomba del Principe: Il tumulo etrusco di via San Iacopo*. Pisa: Edizione ETS.

Fraser, M., and M. Greco, eds. 2005. *The Body*. London: Routledge.

Glinister, F. 2000. "Sacred Rubbish." In *Religion in Archaic Republican Rome and Italy*, ed. E. Bispham and C. Smith, 54–70. Edinburgh: Edinburgh University Press.

Gottarelli, A. 2005. "Templum solare e città fondata: La connessione astronomica della forma urbana della città etrusca." In *Culti, forma urbana, e artigianato a Marzabotto: Nuove prospettive di ricerca*, ed. G. Sassatelli and E. Govi, 101–138. Bologna: Ante Quem.

Griffiths, J. M. 2010. "Acting Perspectives: The Phenomenology of Performance as a Route to

Reception." In *Theorizing Performance: Greek Drama, Cultural History, and Critical Practice*, ed. E. Hall and S. Harrop, 219–231. London: Duckworth.

Hall, E. 2010. "Towards a Theory of Performance Reception." In *Theorizing Performance: Greek Drama, Cultural History, and Critical Practice*, ed. E. Hall and S. Harrop, 10–28. London: Duckworth.

Hermanowicz, J. C., and H. P. Morgan. 1999. "Ritualizing the Routine: Collective Identity and Affirmation." *Sociological Forum* 14:197–214.

Hillier, B., and J. Hanson. 1984. *The Social Logic of Space*. Cambridge: Cambridge University Press.

Holl, S. 2006. "Questions of Perception—Phenomenology of Architecture." In *Questions of Perception: Phenomenology in Architecture*, ed. S. Holl, J. Pallasmaa, and A. Pérez-Gómez. San Francisco: William Stout.

Howe, T. N. 2005. "Vitruvian Critical Eclecticism and Roman Innovation." *MAAR* 50:41–65.

Izzet, V. 2000. "Tuscan Order: The Development of Etruscan Sanctuary Architecture." In *Religion in Archaic Republican Rome and Italy*, ed. E. Bispham and C. Smith, 34–53. Edinburgh: Edinburgh University Press.

———. 2001. "Form and Meaning in Etruscan Ritual Space." *Cambridge Archaeological Journal* 11:185–200.

———. 2007. *The Archaeology of Etruscan Society*. Cambridge: Cambridge University Press.

Lake, A. K. 1935. "Archaeological Evidence for the 'Tuscan Temple.'" *MAAR* 12:89–149.

Lakoff, G., and M. Johnson. 1999. *Philosophy in the Flesh: The Embodied Mind and Its Challenge to Western Thought*. Jackson: Basic Books.

Laurence, Ray. 1996. "Ritual, Landscape, and the Destruction of Place in the Roman Imagination." In *Approaches to the Study of Ritual: Italy and the Ancient Mediterranean*, ed. J. C. Wilkins, 111–121. Accordia Specialist Studies on the Mediterranean 2. London: Accordia Centre.

Leatherbarrow, D. 2002. "Sitting in the City, or the Body in the World." In *Body and Building: Essays in the Changing Relation of Body and Architecture*, ed. G. Dodds and R. Tavernor, 268–288. Cambridge, Mass.: MIT Press.

Mallgrave, H. F. 2010. *The Architect's Brain: Neuroscience, Creativity, and Architecture*. Malden: Wiley-Blackwell.

McCauley, R., and E. Thomas Lawson. 2002. *Bringing Ritual to Mind: Psychological Foundations of Cultural Forms*. Cambridge: Cambridge University Press.

McConachie, B. 2002. "Using Cognitive Science to Understand Spatiality and Community in Theater." *Contemporary Theatre Review* 12:97–114.

McEwen, I. K. 2003. *Vitruvius: Writing the Body of Architecture*. Cambridge, Mass.: MIT Press.

Meyers, G. E. 2003. "Etrusco-Italic Monumental Architectural Space from the Iron Age to the Archaic Period: An Examination of Approach and Access." PhD diss., University of Texas at Austin.

———. 2005. "Vitruvius and the Origins of Roman Spatial Rhetoric." *MAAR* 50:67–86.

Miller, K. 2010. Review of E. Hollis, *The Secret Life of Buildings* (2010) and R. Harbison, *Travels in the History of Architecture* (2010). *Times Literary Supplement* 5592, June 4, 25–26.

Mitchell, J. P. 2007. "Towards an Archaeology of Performance." In *Cult in Context: Reconsidering Ritual in Archaeology*, ed. D. A. Barrowclough and C. Malone, 336–339. Oxford: Oxbow Books.

Morgan, W. H. 1960 (1914). *Vitruvius: The Ten Books of Architecture*. New York: Dover.

Onians, J. 1988. *Bearers of Meaning: The Classical Orders in Antiquity, the Middle Ages, and the Renaissance*. Princeton: Princeton University Press.

———. 2002. "Greek Temple and Greek Brain." In *Body and Building: Essays in the Changing Relation of Body and Architecture*, ed. G. Dodds and R. Tavernor, 44–63. Cambridge, Mass.: MIT Press.

Poggesi, G., L. Donati, E. Bocci, G. Milenucci, L. Pagnini, and P. Pallecchi. 2005. "Prato-Gonfienti: Un nuovo centro etrusco sulla via per Marzabotto." In *Culti, forma urbana, e artigianato a Marzabotto: Nuove prospettive di ricerca*, ed. G. Sassatelli and E. Govi, 267–300. Bologna: Ante Quem.

Portoghesi, P. 1999. *Natura e architettura*. Milan: Skira.

Prayon, F. 1991. "*Deorum sedes*: Sull'orientamento dei templi etrusco-italici." In *Miscellanea Pallottino*, ed. R. Staccioli, F. R. Fortunati, P. Pensabene, and F. Taglietti, 1285–1295. *ArchCl* 43.

Rameri, M. 2005. "La geometria della pianta del tempio urbano di Marzabotto (Regio I, insula 5)." In *Culti, forma urbana, e artigianato a Marzabotto: Nuove prospettive di ricerca*, ed. G. Sassatelli and E. Govi, 73–88. Bologna: Ante Quem.

Rastrelli, A. 1985. "La tomba a camera delle Tassinae (Chiusi)." In *Artigianato artistico: L'Etruria settentrionale interna in età ellenistica*, ed. A. Maggiani, 120–121. Milan: Electa.

Renfrew, C., and S. Sherman, eds. 1982. *Ranking, Resource, and Exchange*. Cambridge: Cambridge University Press.

Rowland, I., and T. N. Howe. 1999. *Vitruvius: Ten Books on Architecture*. Cambridge: Cambridge University Press.

Rykwert, J. 1969. "The Sitting Position—A Question of Method." In *Meaning in Architecture*, ed. C. Jencks and G. Baird, 232–243. London: Barrie and Jenkins.

———. 1996. *The Dancing Column: On Order in Architecture*. Cambridge, Mass.: MIT Press.

Sassatelli, G. 1992. *La città etrusca di Marzabotto*. Bologna: Grafis Edizioni.

Sassatelli, G., and E. Govi. 2005. "Il tempio di Tina in area urbana." In *Culti, forma urbana, e artigianato a Marzabotto: Nuove prospettive di ricerca*, ed. G. Sassatelli and E. Govi, 9–62. Bologna: Ante Quem.

Scheid, J. 1984. "*Contra facere*: Renversements et déplacements dans les rites funéraires." *AION* 6:117–139.

Shoe Meritt, L. S. 1965. *Etruscan and Republican Roman Moldings*. *MAAR* 28. Rome: American Academy in Rome.

Shoe Meritt, L. S., and I. E. M. Edlund-Berry. 2000. *Etruscan and Republican Roman Mouldings*. Philadelphia: University of Pennsylvania Museum.

Sørensen, J. 2005. "Charisma, Tradition, and Ritual: A Cognitive Approach to Magical Agency." In *Mind and Religion: Psychological and Cognitive Foundations of Religiosity*, ed. H. Whitehouse and R. N. McCavley, 167–186. Walnut Creek, Calif.: Alta Mira Press.

Stafford, B. 1999. *Visual Analogy: Consciousness as the Art of Connecting*. Cambridge, Mass.: MIT Press.

Stevens, N. L. C. 2009. "A New Reconstruction of the Etruscan Heaven." *AJA* 113:153–164.

Thomas, M. L. 2000. "The Technology of Daily Life in a Hellenistic Etruscan Settlement." *EtrStud* 7:107–108.

Thuillier, J.-P., ed. 1993. *Spectacles sportifs et scéniques dans le monde étrusco-italique*. *CÉFR*. Rome: École française de Rome.

Tilley, C. 1994. *A Phenomenology of Landscape: Places, Paths, and Monuments*. Oxford: Berg.

Tuck, A. 2006. "The Social and Political Context of the 7th Century Architectural Terracottas at

Poggio Civitate (Murlo)." In *Deliciae Fictiles, III: Architectural Terracottas in Ancient Italy: New Discoveries and Interpretations. Proceedings of the International Conference Held at the American Academy in Rome, November 7–8, 2002*, ed. I. E. M. Edlund-Berry, G. Greco, and J. Kenfield, 130–135. Oxford and Rome: Oxbow Books and the American Academy in Rome.

Turfa, J. M., and S. Gettys. 2009. "The Skill of the Etruscan Haruspex." *BABesch* 84:41–52.

van der Meer, L. B. 1979. "Iecur Placentinum and the Orientation of the Etruscan Haruspex." *BABesch* 54:49–64.

———. 1987. *The Bronze Liver of Piacenza: Analysis of a Polytheistic Structure*. Amsterdam: J. C. Gieben.

Von Staden, H. 1996. "Body and Machine: Interactions between Medicine, Mechanics, and Philosophy in Early Alexandria." In *Alexandria and Alexandrianism. Papers Delivered as a Symposium Organized by the J. Paul Getty Museum and The Getty Center for the History of Art and the Humanities and held at the Museum April 22–25, 1993*, 85–98. Los Angeles: J. Paul Getty Museum.

Warden, P. G., ed. 2008. *From the Temple and the Tomb*. Dallas: Meadows Museum.

———. 2009a. "Remains of the Ritual at the Sanctuary of Poggio Colla." In *Votives, Places, Rituals in Etruscan Religion: Studies in Honour of Jean MacIntosh Turfa*, ed. M. Gleba and H. Becker, 107–121. Leiden: Brill.

———. 2009b. "Vicchio (Fı). Poggio Colla: Campagna de Scavo 2008." *Notiziario della Soprintendenza per i Beni Archeologici della Toscana*, 4: 402–405. All'Insegna del Giglio.

———. 2009c. "The Blood of Animals: Predation and Transformation in Etruscan Funerary Representation." In *New Perspectives on Etruria and Rome: Papers in Honor of Richard D. De Puma*, ed. S. Bell and I. Nagy, 198–219. Madison: University of Wisconsin Press.

———. 2010. "The Temple Is a Living Thing: Fragmentation, Enchainment, and the Reversal of Ritual at the Acropolis Sanctuary of Poggio Colla." In *The Archaeology of Sanctuaries and Ritual in Etruria*, ed. N. T. de Grummond, 55–67. *JRA* Suppl. 81.

Warden, P. G., M. L. Thomas, and J. Galloway. 1999. "The Etruscan Settlement of Poggio Colla (the 1995–98 Excavations)." *JRA* 12:231–246.

Warden, P. G., M. L. Thomas, A. Steiner, and G. Meyers. 2005. "The Etruscan Settlement of Poggio Colla (1998–2004 Excavations)." *JRA* 18:252–266.

Weinstock, S. 1946. "Martianus Capella and the Cosmic System of the Etruscans." *JRS* 36:100–129.

Wilson, E. A. 1984. *Biophilia*. Cambridge, Mass.: Harvard University Press.

Wilson, N. L., and R. W. Gibbs. 2007. "Real and Imagined Body Movement Primes Metaphor Comprehension." *Cognitive Science* 31:721–731.

Wilson Jones, M. 2002. "Doric Figuration." In *Body and Building: Essays in the Changing Relation of Body and Architecture*, ed. G. Dodds and R. Tavernor, 64–77. Cambridge, Mass.: MIT Press.

Winter, N. A. 2009. *Symbols of Wealth and Power: Architectural Terracotta Decoration in Etruria and Central Italy. MAAR* Suppl. 9. Ann Arbor: University of Michigan Press.

Zamarchi Grassi, P., ed. 1992. *La Cortona dei principes*. Cortona: Calosci.

Zifferero, A. 1995. "Economia, divinità, e frontiera: Sul ruolo di alcuni santuari di confine in Etruria meridionale." *Ostraka* 4:333–350.

**THE CAPITOLINE TEMPLE AND THE
EFFECTS OF MONUMENTALITY ON
ROMAN TEMPLE DESIGN**

JOHN N. HOPKINS

THROUGHOUT ANTIQUITY, AUTHORS PRAISING THE
Roman cityscape turned time and again to the Temple of Jupiter Optimus Maximus
on the Capitoline Hill as a work of architectural "genius." Among others, Dionysius
of Halicarnassus portrays it as one of the most resplendent and colossal temples
to have survived from the Archaic Mediterranean, and Pliny the Elder describes
its Archaic central acroterial statue of Jupiter on a quadriga as a masterpiece of
architectural sculpture, "more admired than gold."[1] Cassiodorus and others place it
at the pinnacle of Roman architectural achievement.[2] Overall, ancient sources paint
a grand image of the temple from its initial construction near the end of the sixth
century BCE through its thousand-year dominance of the Roman cityscape.[3]

In modern histories of Rome and its architecture, the storied sanctuary has a
far less prominent role. The religious significance of the triad housed there and its
role as the chief sanctuary of Jupiter receives attention, and occasionally scholars
remark on reconstructions of the building under Sulla, Vespasian, and Domitian;
but most brush quickly past the initial design of the temple and the effects of the
Archaic structure on Roman architecture.[4] This has been due in part to a lack of
evidence for the Archaic temple and a reluctance to lend credence to literary descriptions in the absence of archaeological corroboration; yet recent excavations
have uncovered substantial remains that verify ancient accounts of the temple's design and magnificence. In this essay I assess this new evidence and compare it with
remains of temples from around Italy and the Mediterranean, in order to suggest a

sense of the status that the Capitoline had in early Rome; I then consider the profound effect of the monumental building on ancient viewers and suggest a new way to conceive of its role in defining Roman temple architecture.

Fitting the Capitoline into the History of Roman Architecture

THREE PRIMARY ISSUES HAVE KEPT THE CAPITOLINE Temple out of discourse on Roman architecture: arguments over its size, its plan, and its patrons.[5]

The size of the Archaic Capitoline Temple has been a source of controversy for over a century. In the late eighteen hundreds, Luigi Canina proposed a plan based on Vitruvian theory and Dionysius of Halicarnassus's description of the temple. His reconstruction gained popularity, and Rodolfo Lanciani's identification of colossal remains of the temple around the Palazzo Caffarelli reinforced modern belief in the ancient stories of its early grandeur.[6] Einar Gjerstad further investigated remains on the Capitoline Hill and also concluded that the temple was colossal, but instead of resolving concerns about its size, his study inspired Ferdinando Castagnoli and architectural historian Cairo Fulvio Giuliani to reevaluate the remains systematically and to argue that the temple could not have been as big as had been previously thought.[7] Thus a debate began that raged on through the twentieth century. In 2000, a new series of excavations (led by Anna Mura Sommella) reopened arguments, and once again, archaeologists have championed a colossal plan (fig. 6.1:A), while architectural historians, especially John Stamper, have disparaged the reconstruction and suggested a smaller building (fig. 6.1:B).[8]

Proponents of the diminutive plan suggest that architects in early central Italy, especially in Rome, would not have been able to engineer a temple of great size, much less the complex roof it would require. In recent work I have addressed these concerns in detail, arguing that central Italic architects did in fact possess all the necessary skills to build a colossal temple, and that they did just that; it is worth briefly reiterating a few aspects of this debate here.[9] First, while Stamper and others suggest that early Romans could not build on a large scale, recent excavations reveal that they were perfectly capable of doing so. Comprising approximately 32,000 m³ of stone, the *foundations* of the Capitoline Temple (which remain in situ) are themselves among the most colossal stone structures produced in the entire Archaic Mediterranean world (fig. 6.2).[10] Along with plentiful evidence of other large-scale construction—at the Temple of Castor and the twin temples at S. Omobono in Rome—their existence establishes that in this period Romans could quarry, transport, and lay stone in enormous quantities with great precision.[11]

The Romans were capable of building a vast temple; whether or not they could roof it, however, remains a question. The primary concern about the roof of the

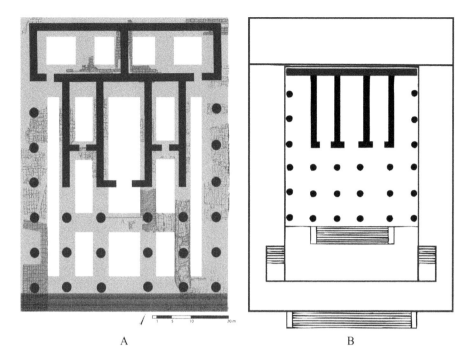

A   B

Fig. 6.1. Proposed plans of the Capitoline Temple.
A: after Mura Sommella 2000b, fig. 5; B: after Stamper 2005, fig. 16 (drawing by J. Hopkins).

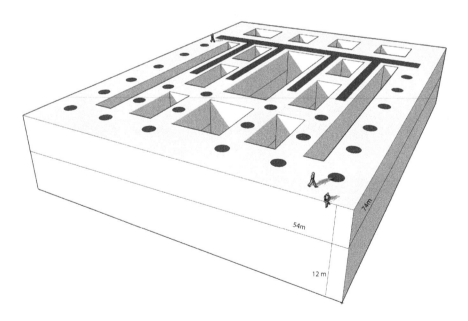

Fig. 6.2. Axonometric reconstruction of Capitoline Temple foundations (drawing by J. Hopkins).

Capitoline pertains to its wide spans. Recently, Stamper has reinforced the suggestion of Giuliani and others that Romans could not cap Gjerstad's and Mura Sommella's proposed wide central intercolumniation (fig. 6.1:A) with post-and-lintel construction.[12] He is right. Under such a system, the weight of a heavy tile roof over an unsupported 10.5-meter span would crack the central lintel.[13] It is worth noting, however, that post-and-lintel was not the only construction and roofing system available to early Romans; for wide spans like that in the Capitoline, they had another option: a truss. Examples of trussed roofs at Agrigento, Gaggera, Corfu, Murlo, and Tarquinia predate the Capitoline by more than fifty years, and by the late sixth century architects in the western Mediterranean were spanning distances approaching 12 m.[14] Overall, simple wooden trusses can structurally support spans as wide as 15 m, and complex king and queen post wooden trusses spanned as much as 24 m in the old Basilica of S. Peter.[15] With even the simplest truss, Romans could easily have roofed the Capitoline's central span. In short, they possessed all the necessary skills to build the proposed colossal temple.

The question remains as to whether or not they did build it. The primary evidence for considering this possibility lies in the plan and dimensions of existing substructures and the size of the terracottas associated with the building. The foundations of the Capitoline Temple consist of intersecting walls surrounded by

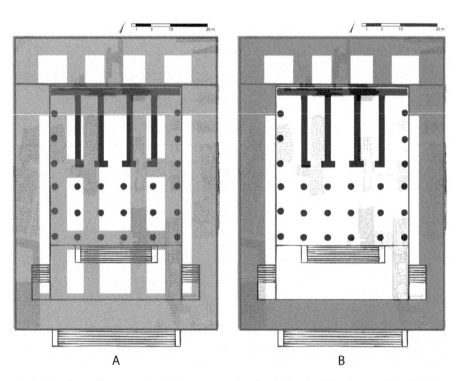

A   B

Fig. 6.3. Plan after small reconstruction by Stamper over extant foundations. A: all foundation walls highlighted; B: foundations unused in small reconstruction highlighted (drawings by J. Hopkins).

a thick perimeter foundation that measures 74 × 54 m (fig. 6.2). Because the foundations form intersecting walls and not a solid platform, any reconstruction must align walls and columns in the superstructure with the foundation walls below.[16] It would be impractical to build foundations if they were not expected to support something in the superstructure, and furthermore, if walls and columns rested in part on earth and in part on stone, the two materials would receive the weight of the heavy stone and terracotta superstructure differently: some walls would sink, others would not, and the building would be structurally unsound.

Colossal reconstructions fit well on the remaining substructures. A diminutive structure would by necessity have more closely spaced columns and walls, which would not align with the foundations; instead they would rest partly on solid stone and partly on earthen fill (fig. 6.3:A). Arguments for a small temple also run into trouble when trying to account for the resulting unused mass of foundations surrounding the proposed diminutive building, since a survey of Archaic Mediterranean sanctuaries reveals no example of a temple that does not occupy all of its foundations. This presents a conundrum: a small temple covering a fraction of the substructure at Rome would be an anomaly.[17] Still more striking, the Capitoline foundations were fully embedded in the hill; a reconstruction that does not occupy their entire surface implies that architects sank nearly 20,000 m³ of stone 8 m into a hilltop around the small temple for no purpose but to reinforce pavement (fig. 6.3:B).[18]

Lastly, excavations in 1999–2000 recovered fragments of the Capitoline's revetments. Remains include a lotus calyx and leaves from palmettes—all of extraordinary size—that indicate a frieze some 60 cm tall (fig. 6.4).[19] By comparison, the next tallest anthemion frieze from Archaic central Italy is at Pyrgi and measures just 32 cm tall, or 53 percent of the size of the Capitoline's; at Satricum, they are just 28 cm, or 47 percent as tall.[20] At other sites—Ardea, Lanuvium, Orvieto, and elsewhere in central Italy—similar plaques are even smaller. The Capitoline revetments, nearly twice the size of their closest rival, suggest a temple building that is also much larger than those at Pyrgi and elsewhere, and its foundations reveal just such a correspondence. Thus, for tectonic reasons and by comparison with its contemporaries, one should imagine that the temple's superstructure covered the surface of its foundations.

The second reason scholars have been reluctant to highlight the Capitoline's role in the history of Roman architecture is that its superstructure no longer exists, and reconstructions must therefore be based on

Fig. 6.4. Reconstruction of Capitoline revetments (drawing by J. Hopkins, after Mura Sommella 2000b, fig. 12, and Mura Sommella 2000a, fig. 27).

a reading of textual descriptions against the remaining substructures. Those substructures do provide a rare and substantial indication of where walls and columns could have been, but the details of any plan must accord with Dionysius of Halicarnassus's record of the temple:

> It stood on a high base and was eight hundred feet in circuit, each side measuring close to two hundred feet; indeed one would find the excess of the length over the width to be but slight, in fact not a full fifteen feet. For the temple that was built in the time of our fathers after the burning of this one [the Archaic temple] was erected upon the same foundations, and having three rows of columns on the side facing south and single colonnades on the sides, it differed from the ancient structure in nothing but the costliness of the materials. The temple consists of three parallel shrines, separated by party walls; the middle shrine is dedicated to Jupiter while on one side stands that of Juno and on the other that of Minerva, all three being under one pediment and one roof.[21]

Many scholars are reluctant to give credence to Dionysius's account because he was writing with conspicuous political and social bias nearly a half-millennium after the early years of Rome's history.[22] I myself am a steadfast critic of the use of Livy, Dionysius, and other late Republican sources to reimagine early Rome and do not suggest that they be used without great prudence. But using Dionysius to help reconstruct the Capitoline Temple is markedly different from using his work as evidence of a battle fought at the start of the Republic or a law code introduced by a king.[23] If relying on his word in those cases, one is expecting Dionysius to have detailed information about an event that occurred five hundred years before he was writing, that is, a passing event that transpired centuries in the past and was remembered only in poorly preserved written or oral record.[24] For the Capitoline Temple, however, Dionysius is not reaching back through time to a lost building of the sixth century, depending on ancient hearsay for details of its design, but rather he is recalling a temple that stood just a generation before him, "in the time of our fathers." Pliny, Cicero, and others state clearly that the original temple survived down to 83 BCE, just twenty years before Dionysius's birth, and recent excavations have upheld their testimony.[25] No doubt the structure underwent refurbishment—perhaps its roof was even partially replaced—but the temple built in the late sixth century survived down to the latest days of the Republic. The Archaic temple that Dionysius describes would have been seen by half the Romans who were alive while he wrote, and records of it would have been abundant.

Even so, one need not blindly trust Dionysius, as recent excavations have gone a long way to corroborate his description and lend validity to the image his text presents. Remains indicate not only that the first temple was Archaic in date, but even that it was completed between 520 and 500, precisely when Dionysius suggests.[26] Excavations also reveal that the original temple was enormous, just as he characterizes it, and, moreover, that its width and length are extraordinarily close to the dimensions he provides.[27] He further remarks that the late Republican reconstruction used the original foundations and changed nothing of the superstructure's plan; excavations uncovered *imperial* concrete buttresses reinforcing segments of the Archaic foundations, but found no changes to the plan of the original substructures and no interference whatsoever before the Empire, again supporting Dionysius's account.[28] The repeated corroboration of Dionysius in the archaeological record and the temple's endurance through the Republic until just before Dionysius's time suggest that his account should stand.[29] As he describes it, the temple had three rows of six columns, creating a deep porch. Behind the porch, three cellae occupy the center of the temple with colonnades flanking either side (fig. 6.5).

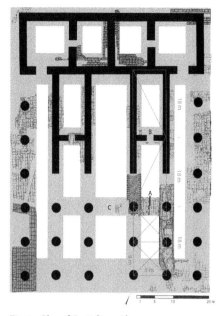

Fig. 6.5. Plan of Capitoline with measurements (drawing by J. Hopkins).

As to the precise location of columns and cella thresholds, any proposal based on known remains can only be hypothetical, but as an exercise, a brief look at proportions in the foundations may offer some clues. The interaxial distance between the second and third (and the fourth and fifth) longitudinal foundation walls is 9 m (fig. 6.5). A measurement between the midpoints of the short transverse foundation walls (A–B on the plan) yields a length of exactly double that. Applied to the superstructure, these proportions may indicate the position of columns, spaced 9 m apart longitudinally, as well as cella doors that align precisely with the foundations. Though conjectural, the scheme may be corroborated by the location of the single long transverse wall that connects internal longitudinal foundations (fig. 6.5:C). A similar wall (only partially connecting longitudinal foundations) is found in just one other contemporaneous Mediterranean temple, and there it supports the third colonnade of the porch (fig. 6.6).[30] Remarkably, the proportions outlined above situate the third colonnade of the Capitoline directly over the partial transverse foundation. For now the scheme is only conjecture. In any case, Dionysius's description of a deep tripteral porch fronting cellae flanked by colonnades fits noticeably well with the extant foundations, especially when viewed alongside evidence for temples and foundations in the contemporaneous Mediterranean.[31]

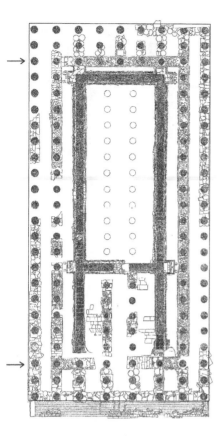

Fig. 6.6. Plan of Temple of Hera at Samos with third colonnade indicated (after Reuther 1957, Z1).

The third reason scholars segregate the temple from Roman architectural history is Rome's political environment during its construction. Some believe the temple is the product of Etruscan influence on Rome and therefore not a work of Roman architecture. While the role of Etruscan culture in early Rome and the roots of central Italic temple architecture are hotly debated issues, the Capitoline Temple's place in Roman architectural history should not depend on the outcome of these disputes. This is not to say that the Capitoline Temple is not a significant part of Etruscan architectural history. At present it is difficult to discern who built it, and it may very well have been the product of Etruscan influence on Rome. Yet to restrict the building to the architectural history of one people limits the appreciation of its influence. Whatever cultural constructs led to its creation, the building did not cease to exist or to play a role in architectural history after its last stone was laid; it stood for centuries—in reconstruction, for over a millennium—and would have continued to impress and instruct viewers and worshipers long after its completion at the end of the sixth century. What is more, in the coming centuries, as the cityscape morphed around it and cultural shifts affected those who viewed it, its new environment and the differing experiences of those who saw and reacted to it would have prompted ever-changing, new interpretations of the building and its significance.[32]

By way of comparison, one might say that removing the temple and its influence from Roman architectural history would be tantamount to removing Independence Hall from American architectural history. Though it was built during British rule in 1755, scholars regard it not simply as a British building in America, and not as a precursor to American style, but as an emblem of change that fundamentally shaped American public architecture: its influence can be seen in myriad designs of dramatically different purpose, style, and form from centuries later.[33] The Capitoline has a contested early history that may place its origins under the sway of Etruscan people, but like Independence Hall, its influence goes beyond its cultural "origins."[34] The temple is squarely in the city of Rome, high on the most prominent hill. It remained one of the city's preeminent temples throughout the Republic and Empire, and authors refer to it consistently as a Roman building. If it had no other influence, it at least served as a springboard for the design of Roman capitolia, temples that were erected as emblems of Rome's subjugation of other (sometimes Etruscan) cities. This temple should therefore hold a prominent place in the history of Roman architecture.

The Design of the House of Jupiter and Its Effects on Roman Temples

SO-CALLED *OIKOS* TEMPLES WERE COMMON THROUGHout the Mediterranean in the seventh century, marking religious architecture with several fundamental features, including frontality, side and rear walls, and an absence of lateral and rear colonnades. Beginning in the sixth century, however, these features fade from major temple construction outside of central Italy. In the Greek world a radical shift in temple design beginning at the turn of the century led to a change in scale, materials, and especially plan.[35] By then, architects at Corfu, Olympia, Thermon, Isthmia, and elsewhere were replacing *oikos*-type buildings with temples circumscribed by colonnades and large stone steps.[36] The new design allowed access to the peripteron from any point and fundamentally altered both the image of the temple and a worshiper's interaction with it. Such temples were found throughout the Greek world by the late sixth century, when the Capitoline was constructed.

By this time a change in architecture had also occurred in central Italy, but the shift was chiefly in size and building material.[37] While architects there began building a few bigger temples out of new materials like stone and terracotta, they maintained the frontality of earlier *oikos* temples, often with a single room fronted by columns. The earliest known temple to endure this kind of monumentalization was the first temple at S. Omobono in Rome (fig. 6.7:A). In it architects raised the *oikos*-type temple on a tall podium with an Italic round moulding and stairs to the front.[38] Also atop the podium, walled side chambers, or alae, flanked the *oikos* structure, and at the front the architects seem to have articulated the façade with columns *in antis*.[39] Another similar but much larger temple with alae and columns *in antis* appeared soon after at Tarquinia, Ara della Regina I (fig. 6.7:C).[40] Overall, though, most temples remained small through the early and mid-sixth century, and alongside these two temples, the Capitoline was among the first in the region to experience monumentalization. At the time it was designed, the primary features of *oikos* temples still prevailed in central Italy, sometimes highlighted by a high podium and stair. The austere design distinguished these temples, but it also limited variation among them.

With the Temple of Jupiter, architects in Rome pioneered a new form of architecture, incorporating innovative intersecting foundation walls, lateral colonnades, a deep multicolonnaded porch, and anthemion revetments into a traditional

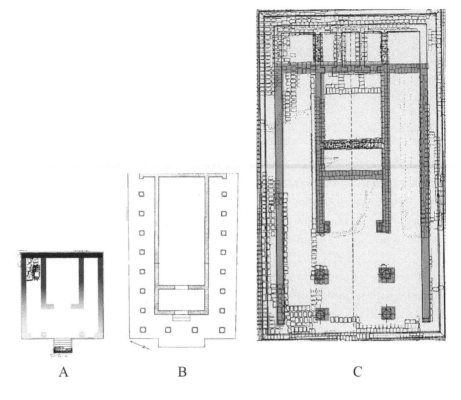

A   B   C

Fig. 6.7. Plans of three central Italic temples, to scale. A: S. Omobono, plan with hypothetical elements shaded gray (after *Il viver quotidiano in Roma archaica*, pl. V); B: Satricum, Temple I (from De Waele 1981, pl. 7); C: Tarquinia, Ara della Regina phase I (after Bonghi Jovino 1997, fig. 17 and Colonna 2006, VIII.34) (drawings by J. Hopkins).

central Italic temple with frontal disposition and a high podium supporting a rare triple cella. A full discussion of the roots of the Capitoline's own design is beyond the scope of this essay, but a brief look at each element is essential for determining which aspects were already common in the region and which—as outright innovations or the result of foreign influence—were new.

In the substructure, builders used a series of interconnecting longitudinal and transverse walls to support walls, colonnades, and thresholds in the superstructure. It is difficult to find comparanda for these foundations in central Italy; most Archaic central Italic temples have pillars (not walls) under columns.[41] Yet comparisons abound in the Greek world from Paestum to Metapontum, Agrigento, Corinth, Delos, Ephesus, and elsewhere. Throughout Archaic Greek sanctuaries, architects built foundation walls underneath all load-bearing elements: peripteroi, naos, and opisthodomos/adyton walls and colonnades inside naoi and pronaoi.[42] In the Greek world, just as with the Capitoline, longitudinal and transverse walls universally support walls, colonnades, and thresholds in the superstructure. The broad analogy suggests that the Roman temple foundations are akin to Greek substructures, not to central Italic foundations. One particularly striking comparandum suggests more than a vague association. In both the Samian Heraion—another colossal tripteral temple—and the Capitoline Temple, architects employed only longitudinal foundation walls to support colonnades, with one exception: conspicuous in their plans is the architects' use of the same partial transverse foundation under only the third colonnade (figs. 6.5 and 6.6).[43] Foundations are visible only to those who witness a temple's construction, and for one architect to copy or mirror another's foundation design suggests either an intimate knowledge of the construction process, or that the same architect is at work. Further than this, speculation is imprudent; whatever the relationship between Rome and Samos, it is clear that the Capitoline Temple employed a type of foundation that was new to central Italy, perhaps inspired by distant architects, perhaps an outright innovation, but otherwise absent in the region.

The side columns and colonnaded porch are also anomalous for central Italy. The only regional precursor might be Temple I at Satricum (fig. 6.7:B).[44] It was finished ten to twenty years before the Capitoline, ca. 525, but because it is just one-eighth the overall size of the Roman temple, one can imagine that it took far less time to build and may have been begun after the Temple of Jupiter.[45] In any case, scholars have long held that the Satricum temple was the beneficiary of substantial Greek inspiration if not outright design and construction.[46] In contrast to their absence in central Italy, side and frontal ptera were an indispensable part of Greek temple architecture; one hardly needs to describe or enumerate examples: they flank the naos of nearly every temple in the Greek world built from the early sixth century onward.[47]

As for the Capitoline's frontal forest of columns, there is no earlier temple and no earlier foundation in central Italy that even vaguely suggests a triple colonnaded porch. Even in the Greek world it is hard to find a precedent. Architects at Syracuse, Metapontum, Selinunte, and further from Rome at Samos and Ephesus had already experimented with double colonnades.[48] In the years preceding the Capitoline's completion, only architects at Athens, Ephesus, and Samos were more daring and had begun temples with triple colonnaded porches.[49] Few scholars are willing to see early Rome as an open city, with contacts and architects from as far away as Athens or especially Ionia, but there is simply no precedent for anything like the Capitoline's tripteral hexastyle façade in central Italy or even the Italic peninsula and Sicily.[50] What is more, the colossal scale of the Capitoline is mirrored only in temples in Ionia and Athens. Similar temples in Sicily, at Agrigento and Selinunte, were not begun until the turn of the sixth century, contemporaneously with and subsequent to the Capitoline. While it is possible that the Romans imagined the colossal tripteral design on their own, its popularity in Ionia just before the construction of the Capitoline seems a striking coincidence. Furthermore, this kind of complex architecture cannot be copied from sight. Scholars have long known that the implementation of a forested facade, the construction of the stacked pillars, and the complex trabeation of a multicolonnaded porch would require the aid of architects who had built this kind of structure before.[51]

In the end, wherever they came from, none of these aspects of the Capitoline appear in other local structures, and they suggest either extraordinary innovation or outside influence that is absent in earlier known temples in the region.

Before the Capitoline, just two temples in all of Italy may have employed sculpted anthemion friezes as the primary sima decoration. Again, one is the temple at Satricum; the other is at Minturnae on the Latial–Campanian border.[52] It too has been tied to Greek prototypes, and given its small size, like the Satricum temple, it too may have been begun after the Capitoline. What is most striking about the anthemion, though, is that in the form it takes on the Capitoline, it is absent not only in central Italy, but in the entire western Mediterranean. It was popular as painted decoration and in perforated simas throughout the Mediterranean, but in the Capitoline it takes on a sculpted form with a superimposed cavetto that is found previously only in Asia Minor, at Magnesia, Mytilene, and a few other sites.[53] Once again, the temples at Satricum and Minturnae are far smaller than the Capitoline and may have been begun after it. In any case, the Roman temple is among the first in the region—or in fact in the western Mediterranean—to employ the decoration, and in the Capitoline revetments sculptors brought the design fully into a central Italic style of delicately outlined and painted palmettes interspersed with lotus calyces for the very first time.[54] The new sima decoration did more than simply replace established frieze iconography; it caused a complete shift in the role of roof decoration. Anthemion revetments are much larger than their figural predecessors, and so decorated terracotta simas and architraves became far more prominent; by the same token, the repetition of floral design did not require the viewer's analytical attention in the same way that scenes on figural friezes did, and so acroteria, antefixes, and columen plaques became the focus of large, complex decoration on temples.[55]

It is hard to speak of the Eastern style of the Capitoline revetments without remembering the similarity of the Capitoline Temple's size, foundations, and plan to late sixth- and early fifth-century temples in Sicily, at Agrigento and Selinunte, which were also looking to Asia Minor. Barbara Barletta argues that Ionicizing monumental decoration in the Greek West indicates a connection not just between the sculptural styles of Sicily and Ionia, but also between architecture and architects working across the Mediterranean.[56] Among many others, Irad Malkin and Nicolas Purcell speak of vast shipping networks in the Archaic period, exchanges connecting east and west, north and south to a degree that had never before been seen: architects, artists, merchants, rulers, all traveling from Persia to Phoenicia, Egypt, Ephesus, Corinth, Agrigento, and, it seems, to Rome.[57] The architects of the Capitoline Temple adopted new sculptural styles popular also in Asia Minor, alongside a similarly Eastern foundation plan, colossal proportion, and colonnades at precisely the same time and in some cases before Selinunte and Agrigento saw a similar architectural shift.[58] The simultaneity of changes at these sites suggests Romans were not drawing on south Italic and Sicilian statements of monumentality, as some have previously suggested, but that alongside these powers of the West, they were participating in the creation and promotion of a new western Mediterranean monumentality—of scale, opulence, and fine craftsmanship—that drew on Eastern influence.

Still, the Capitoline was by no means a Greek temple; its frontal disposition and triple cella are not common features of temples built in the Greek East or West. This should not be surprising. While the religious functions and architectural history of Greek temples allowed for peripteral design,[59] early central Italic sanctuary architecture is defined largely by a viewer's frontal approach.[60] As Dieter Mertens has pointed out, only two peripteral temples existed in central Italy through the end of the fifth century, both in communities heavily influenced and inhabited by Greeks, and still a frontal staircase dictated these buildings' primary façades.[61] Temples surrounded by colonnades were not popular in central Italy, probably for religious or architectural historical reasons: divination, augury, foundation ritual, or some other religious practices[62] seem to have required a frontal disposition, and by the sixth century, architectural tradition in central Italy dictated that the rear of a building be closed.[63] The resulting frontality of the Capitoline Temple expresses its fundamental Central Italic religious function,[64] and architects did not sacrifice the needs of the people who commissioned the building to architectural form.

The Capitoline's triple cella may similarly be Central Italic in origin. Contact with Punic architects, who used triple cellae in their temples, could have influenced the new arrangement, but it is not clear whether Punic temples already had triple cellae in the sixth century.[65] Closer to Rome, a three-room building at Murlo that dates to the late seventh century hosted some kind of sacred activity; excavators hesitate to brand this a triple cella or even a religious building, but it may be the closest remaining predecessor to a three-room temple.[66] Also, at Tarquinia, Building Beta underwent a mid-century renovation that left a three-room structure; scholars working there compare it to megaron houses, but if its predecessor was indeed a temple, one could imagine that the new structure there also had a religious purpose.[67] For now, the origins of the triple cella remain unclear, but by all rights, the Capitoline is the first to incorporate it into a monumental colonnaded structure on a podium.

In sum, the lateral colonnades, deep porch, tripteral façade, foundation grid, and triple cella—the entire plan of the building—and the decoration of its roof come from diverse sources and meet in the Capitoline with more traditional elements of Central Italic design, including a podium, frontal disposition, and frontal staircase. No known central Italic building had previously combined these features.[68] Thus, while this Roman temple was not necessarily the first to use each of them, it seems to have been the first to combine them, and moreover, it is the first known in central Italy to employ at least two and probably five of these traits. Furthermore, the abundance of temples that drew on this collection of elements immediately after the Capitoline suggests that although it may not have given birth to any one of these features, it did engender their popularity and fusion in central Italic (and later Roman) religious architecture.

Few scholars have remarked on the Capitoline's impact past the Archaic period, and those who do consider its influence have often been criticized for speaking in excessively broad terms. This is primarily because they tend to suggest that the Capitoline became the standard for a temple type or imply that a link from the design of an Imperial temple to the Capitoline was absolute, leaping over centuries of design and tectonic change. Colonna, Boëthius, and others uphold it as a model of the early central Italic temple; yet it is clear from the wildly inconsistent plans of temples in central Italy that they are not based on the Capitoline, or on any other single predecessor.[69] Stamper sees the Capitoline as a direct influence on temples like Mars Ultor and the Pantheon, but one could hardly mistake the Capitoline for either of these buildings, both of which incorporate major stylistic and tectonic innovations from the intervening centuries.[70]

A fundamental problem in these assessments of the Capitoline's legacy is their implication that any influence the temple had was unaffected by the temporal, cultural, or social circumstance of the designers of new, later temples; in fact, they seem not even to imagine designers. Yet if one is to conceive of a building that copies or is influenced by the Capitoline, one must conceive of an architect for that new building; in the eyes of different builders from different towns, periods, and backgrounds, the Capitoline and its elements would have been perceived, assessed, and used in varied ways.[71] It is not surprising, then, that one cannot find in the architectural record a line of temples from the Capitoline down to the Empire that exhibit a uniform impact; the temple was not a model or a *typical* Italic or Roman temple. Instead, I suggest that its influence on the history of Roman temple design was diffuse. It was a touchstone, a temple that people borrowed from and emulated but did not wholly reproduce.[72] It helped define religious architecture not because it prompted *copies*, but because its grandeur—its monumentality—popularized elements that individually and collectively came to exemplify magnificence in Italic and Roman temples. When seen in this light, the significance of the Capitoline reaches far beyond its role as a part of the Archaic city. When the temple was finished, its life as a monument had only just begun,[73] and as a sanctuary that was used, seen, and encountered, it would go on to affect viewers and architects who themselves commissioned and designed temples throughout central Italy and the Roman Empire.

Less than half a century after the completion of the Capitoline, temples at Ardea (Acropolis, Casalinaccio), Vulci (Fontanile di Legnisina), Veii (Portonaccio),

Satricum (Temple II), Lanuvium, Rome (Castor), Pyrgi (Temples A and B), Orvieto, and Marzabotto (Temple C, Tinia Temple) combined at least four elements first popularized in the Temple of Jupiter (fig. 6.8). Of known central Italic temples built between ca. 510 and 450, at least three have lateral colonnades, five employ a grid of foundation walls, eleven have podia, at least seven and probably all have anthemion friezes, nine have deep porches, six have triple cellae, and at least nine have frontal colonnades, six of which are dipteral and at least one tripteral. This is to say that of the thirteen known temples built in the wake of the Capitoline for which both architectural and terracotta evidence is preserved, a clear majority assemble the elements of the Roman temple in one form or another, and the list covers only elements for which there is direct archaeological evidence. For example, at the sanctuary at Vulci, no terracottas have as yet been found, and therefore it does not add to the number of sanctuaries with anthemion revetments. Yet no sima revetments using motifs other than the anthemion have been found at sanctuaries dating to the fifth century, suggesting that after the Capitoline, all temples adopted its revetment style. At Veii, it is clear that the temple had a deep porch, but whether it was dipteral or had four columns *in antis* is unclear, and so only the porch is highlighted in the list above, not the style of colonnade. Many of the Capitoline's elements were probably incorporated far more frequently than this list suggests.

Furthermore, this list considers only elements that remain in the *Capitoline's* archaeological record. Most of the temple's superstructure is missing, and so it is impossible to know whether the building also had mouldings on the podium, what kind of columns and capitals adorned it, whether or not it had ridgepole sculpture, columen plaques, full-bodied acroteria and antefixes, and various other details. It probably did incorporate several of these features, many of which became popular just after the Capitoline's completion.

Several elements that the temple featured for the first time in central Italy endured in temple architecture through the Roman Republic and Empire. The triple cella is found not only in later capitolia; architects also used it in temples throughout the Republic, even in some with only one or two dedicatees.[74] Architects would continue to use the anthemion frieze throughout central Italy and in Rome until the late Republic, in Hellenistic structures like the Temple at Talamone and Temple of Apollo at Civita Castellana, and after its popularization through the roof sculpture of the Capitoline, the motif remained a principal decoration in all varieties of architecture through the Empire, in monuments like the Tomb of the Sempronii and the Ara Pacis Augustae.[75] Multiple frontal colonnades also remained common. They are found immediately after the Capitoline at Pyrgi, Ardea, Orvieto, and elsewhere, and they remained popular in Roman temples like those to Castor, Victoria, and Venus Genetrix, and in the Pantheon. Though Vitruvius does not provide a name for the temple plan commonly called a *peripteros sine postico*, after the Capitoline the type remained popular in Roman architecture, as evidenced by buildings like Temple C in Largo Argentina and the Temple of Mars Ultor in the Forum of Augustus. The deep, open porch was also ubiquitous in later temples; central Italic architects immediately adopted it at Pyrgi, Lanuvium, Orvieto, and elsewhere, and it was used in Roman temples through the Empire, the most famous examples of the style being the Temple of Portunus and the Maison Carrée.

Had the Capitoline been just another small temple in central Italy, it is hard to say what impact it might have had. Perhaps as the symbolic head of Roman state religion (if such a concept existed in the Archaic period) it would have exerted great influence, but one can imagine that the monumental image of the building contributed at least marginally to the popularity of its elements in later Roman architecture. Scholars have long tried to envision the experience of a Roman or visitor standing in the low riverside valley, looking up at the colossal temple on the Capitoline.[76] The pervasive use of its pioneering features in temples around central Italy seems to indicate that those viewers were astounded and greatly influenced by the enormous sanctuary that towered above. Still, the Capitoline's monumentality and influence lie not only in its size, but also in its fine craftsmanship. The engineering required to build and roof such a structure and the delicate execution of its anthemion revetments—and any other lost sculpture—contributed to its grand image.[77] Temples incorporating these elements—colonnades, decorative sculpture, plan, and deep foundations—incorporated the monumentality of the Capitoline. Perhaps these later buildings (at Orvieto, Ardea, and elsewhere in central Italy and the later Roman Empire) were not as colossal as the famous Temple of Jupiter, but they possessed something of the monumental Capitoline, something of its opulence.

In this sense, the Temple of Capitoline Jupiter sparked a sea change in central Italic and Roman temple architecture. Before it, architects relied on a small number of elements for variation in new religious buildings; changing proportions, adding a few columns *in antis*, and employing a different revetment scene or perhaps a unique moulding defined the designer's options. After the Capitoline, temple architects had a vastly larger trove of embellishment to use in their design. Previously, a temple might introduce one or two new architectural elements; the Capitoline Temple popularized at least six. Yet the building was not an archetype for later religious architecture. Rather, it had a nuanced impact; through its monumental impression on viewers, it promoted more of what became traditional elements of Roman temple design than all temples before it, combined. Architects throughout central Italy quickly and ceaselessly pulled from its components, and there would be no such radical change or addition to the design of Roman temples until centuries later, when stone architraves and peripteral designs entered the architect's vocabulary. Even then, the deep porch, forest of columns, lateral colonnades, triple cellae, deep foundations, and floral revetments first made popular in the Capitoline Temple continued to pervade Roman architecture.

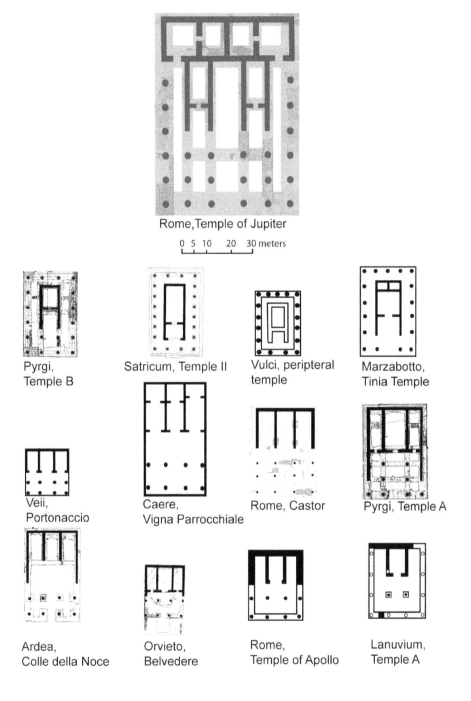

Rome, Temple of Jupiter

0 5 10 20 30 meters

Pyrgi, Temple B

Satricum, Temple II

Vulci, peripteral temple

Marzabotto, Tinia Temple

Veii, Portonaccio

Caere, Vigna Parrocchiale

Rome, Castor

Pyrgi, Temple A

Ardea, Colle della Noce

Orvieto, Belvedere

Rome, Temple of Apollo

Lanuvium, Temple A

Fig. 6.8. Scale renderings of thirteen preserved temples from central Italy, ca. 510–450 (drawing by J. Hopkins).

Notes

I offer my most sincere thanks to Ingrid Edlund-Berry both for her comments on this work and her steadfast support and advice throughout my doctoral work; I am grateful to know and work with such a generous scholar. I am also thankful to Penelope Davies, Gabriele Cifani, Anna Mura Sommella, and Nancy Winter for their comments as I have worked on this great building, and to Gretchen Meyers and Michael Thomas for including me in the conference and book. I am indebted to the peer-review readers for their suggestions.

1. Dion. Hal. 4.52.5–6; Plin *HN* 35.157. Pliny is probably making this comparison in part to suggest that Domitian's reconstruction (with its gilt roof) was excessive, evidence of an extravagant tendency.
2. E.g., Amm. Marc. 16.10.14; 22.16.12; Cassiod. *Var.* 7.6.1; Plut. *Vit. Popl.* 13.
3. E.g., Plut. *Vit. Popl.* 13; Fest. 274; Cic. *Cat.* 3.9; Cassiod. *Var.* 7.6.1.
4. When it does find its way into textbooks, this is to highlight its role as a precursor to Roman capitolia, rather than to recognize its wider effects on later temple design. The exception is John Stamper's recent work on Roman temple architecture (2005), though as will be clear, I disagree with his reconstruction and arguments about the Capitoline's influence. Many texts exclude the temple completely; examples that do include it, but only briefly among a list of precursors to "Roman style" are Boëthius, Ling, and Rasmussen 1994; Sear 1989; Gros 1996; Coarelli, Rossi, and Schezen 1980. Only recently with new excavations that firmly date its remains to the sixth century have a few scholars brought the temple into the sphere of Roman architecture, but the scope of their books allows only a mention of the building: Gros 2006; Davies and Janson 2007.
5. Until recently the date was an issue as well, but see Mura Sommella 2000a, 21–23; Danti 2001.
6. Lanciani 1875. For a historiography of the temple, see Ridley 2005.
7. Gjerstad 1953–1973, 3:178–186; contra: Castagnoli 1955; Castagnoli 1966–1967, 13–14; Castagnoli 1974, 435; Giuliani 1982, 31; Castagnoli 1984.
8. For a colossal temple, see Mura Sommella 2000a; 2000b; 2009. For a small temple, see Stamper 2005, 21–27; cf. Tucci 2006, 386–390.
9. Hopkins 2010b.
10. Two 45.5 × 6.9 × 12.75 m walls, four 45.5 × 4 × 12.75 m walls, two 53.5 × 8 × 12.75 m walls, and one 53.5 × 5 × 12.75 m wall, plus all transverse walls and three rear longitudinal walls. Measurements of the Capitoline Temple were taken on 28 January 2008 with both a Leica Disto A6 and a tape measure; see also Danti 2001.
11. On the Temple of Castor, see Nielsen and Poulsen 1992. On the twin temples at S. Omobono, see Hopkins 2010a, ch. 4.
12. Giuliani 1982, 31; Stamper 2005, 27.
13. On the Capitoline's unsupported span as 10.5 m and not 12, see Hopkins 2010b.
14. On the Gaggera roof and other western Greek sites, see Hodge 1960, 17–42; Klein 1998. On Murlo, see Turfa and Steinmayer 1996. On Tarquinia, measurements taken by author on site; cf. Bonghi Jovino 1997. A recent article has suggested a large post-and-lintel roof for the building, but it includes columns down the center, for which there are no foundations and no evidence; see Chiesa and Binda 2009. A truss is more likely.
15. Adam 1984, 212.
16. Stamper (2005, fig. 15) draws a mass of foundations, but archaeologists have dug between

the walls, finding their sides and no uninterrupted foundation platform; see Danti 2001. For a full discussion of this, see Hopkins 2010b.

17. On Orientalizing and Archaic temples, see Brizio 1889, 258–260; Pernier 1926, 164; Galieti 1928, 75–94; Stefani 1944, 231; Stefani 1953, 35–43; Stefani 1954, 7–12; Colonna and Pallottino 1970, 23–43, 275–287; De Waele 1981, 19–41; Colonna 1981; Beaufort et al. 1982; Pisani Sartorio 1982, 51–56; Colonna 1984; Chiarucci and Gizi 1985, 47; Colonna 1985; Massabò 1988–1989, 108–125; *Il viver quotidiano* 1989, 13–36; Nielsen and Poulsen 1992, 78–79; Boëthius et al. 1994; Bonghi Jovino 1997, 87–89; Damgaard Andersen 1998, esp. 87–95 and diagrams; De Waele and Cantilena 2001, 88–92; Colonna 2006. The Ara della Regina Phase I might seem an exception; its substructures, however, serve both to support the superstructure and to extend the hillside, allowing the temple to perch over a precipice (this would become popular in the Hellenistic period). The substructure therefore has two functions, but the second function distinguishes the Tarquinia foundations from the Capitoline. See Bonghi Jovino 1997, 87–89. For Greek temples in general: Dinsmoor 1975, 69–113, 123–146; Lawrence and Tomlinson 1983, 141–159, 160–173. On specific buildings and on building practices, see Bacon et al. 1902, 141; Orsi 1903, 374–376; Hogarth et al. 1908, pl. 12; Buschor 1930, 72; Courby 1931, pls. II, III; Fowler and Stillwell 1932, pls. I, V; Orsi 1933, 23–26, fig. 3; Rodenwaldt 1939, pls. 3, 22; Gruben 1963, 78–89; Feye 1970; Adamesteanu, Mertens, and D'Andria 1975, 109; De Franciscis 1979, fig. 6; Camp and Dinsmoor 1984, 11; Lambrinoudakis and Gruben 1987, abb. 13; Mertens, Schützenberger, and Sponer-Za 1993, 5–15, pls. 4–7, 20; De La Genière, Greco, and Donnarumna 1997, 337, 44; Cook and Nicholls 1998, 109–176; De La Geniere et al. 1999, 501–502, 505, 507; De Waele and Cantilena 2001, 88–92; Cooper 2008, 229–234.

18. Hopkins 2010b. For the elevation of the Capitoline foundations, see Danti 2001. For the elevation of the Capitoline Hill in the area of the temple, see Jordan 1885, Tafel II, 66ff.; Alvarez et al. 1996, 752–753. On the changing geomorphology of the Capitoline, see Alvarez et al. 1996, 751–752; Ammerman and Terrenato 1996; cf. Colini 1965.

19. Mura Sommella 2000a, 24–26.

20. Andrén 1940, 474–475.

21. Dion. Hal. 4.61.3–4 (after Cary 1937).

22. On Dionysius in particular, see Gabba 1991; Wiseman 1993. Criticism of textual histories of early Rome is extensive. Recently Wiseman 1995; 2008.

23. Purcell (2003, 28–30) has suggested (and especially in relation to the Capitoline) that Romans had a much more enduring historical consciousness of buildings and cults than of historical events, and moreover that the tradition of marking the year with a new nail in the doorpost of the Capitoline Temple reveals one way that modern scholars might see buildings as stronger and more enduring physical reminders of Rome's past than reports of legal, political, or sociological changes. Thus he goes so far as to suggest 509 as the start of a "Capitoline year," rather than the actual start of the Republic or expulsion of the kings. In fact, as I argue in the next few lines of this essay, there is good reason to believe that the history and design of the Capitoline are stronger than just Romans' heightened historical sensibility for architecture.

24. This is precisely the kind of detail that scholars like Wiseman and Gabba suggest Dionysius would not have had, regardless of his historical scruples.

25. E.g., Cic. *Cat.* 3.9; Dion. Hal. 4.52.5–6; Plin. *HN.* 33.16; on the excavation results see the paragraph below and Danti 2001.

26. On the foundations, see Danti 2001, 334–341. On the terracottas, see Mura Sommella 2000a, 21–33.

27. Cifani 2008, 101. In a recent talk, Mura Sommella accounts for the discrepancy between

Dionysius's exact measurement and the rear foundations, explaining that his measure would have been around the colonnade, not around the podium and certainly not around the subterranean foundations that remain today; see Mura Sommella 2009.

28. Mura Sommella 2009; cf. Mura Sommella 2000a; Mura Sommella 2000b; Danti 2001, 323–328; Mura Sommella 2001, 262–264; Mura Sommella 2002, 303–323.

29. Scholars are quick to point out that Dionysius does not mention the rear rooms of the building, but there are many ways to account for this. For example, if they had a religiously distinct function or were architecturally separated, perhaps by a different roof, Dionysius may have chosen not to include them in his description. The rooms would be part of the *templum* and *area capitolina*, but not of the temple proper. Or perhaps the rear rooms were not reconstructed after the area burned; Dionysius states that he is recording the similarities between the new and old buildings. Perhaps the temple's function or the purposes that the rear rooms served did not persist into the late Republic. One last explanation is proposed by Mura Sommella (2009): Dionysius says that apart from the front, there was a single colonnade on the sides; as Mura Sommella points out, he could very well be including the rear of the temple, in which case the rear foundation wall would be a rear colonnade. In this case the temple is peripteral, but still decidedly frontally disposed.

30. The temple in question is the so-called Polykrateion Temple (Dipteros II) at Samos, begun sometime between 550 and 530. Recent publication has made clear that the temple was underway and the transverse wall in question was laid by around 530: Hellner and Kienast 2009, 8. Cf. Buschor 1930, 72; Reuther 1957, Z1. For more on the similarities of their plans, see infra n. 43.

31. For a list of temples and publications on their plans as relates to foundations: supra n. 17.

32. Jacques Rancière (2004, 12–15; 2009, esp. 13, 17, 59, 109–112) argues that there is no one right conception of an object or an experience, and furthermore, that neither is a viewer passive, nor is her/his gaze the terminus of the effects of a work of art. Rather, the experience of that viewer will dictate her/his actions, and in the case of the Capitoline Temple, as I discuss below, its viewers' experiences will have dictated the differing adoption of many of its aspects in the construction of later temples.

33. Roth 1979, 2–52; Whiffen and Koeper 1981, 3–106; Handlin 1985, 9–38.

34. On the inherent problem with ascribing such an origin and on the continued effects of any work of art past its creation, see supra n. 32.

35. Exceptions to the popularity of peripteral temples in Greek territories are mostly found in southern Italy, where it is possible architects were working under similar influences as those in central Italy.

36. Even Barletta (2001), who takes a cautious view on the purported dominance of peripteral temples in early Greek architecture, concludes that in the sixth century the design took off, supplanting older frontal temples. For a brief recent synthesis, see Pedley 2005, 62–68; Lawrence 1967, 88–142.

37. E.g., Colonna 1984; 2006.

38. On remains of the podium, moulding, and stair: Gjerstad 1953–1973, 3: fig. 245; Ioppolo 1971–1972, 14; Pisani Sartorio and Virgili 1979, fig. 2; *Il viver quotidiano* 1989, fig. 12. For a full examination of the evidence and arguments, see Hopkins 2010a, ch. 3.

39. Recently: Colonna 1991.

40. It is unclear if one roof covered the *oikos* temple and surrounding enclosure at Gabii: Colonna 1981, 55; Colonna 1984, 400. On Tarquinia: Bonghi Jovino 1997; Colonna 2006.

41. E.g., Tarquinia: Bonghi Jovino 1997, 87–89, fig. 17; Colonna 2006, VIII.34; single stone blocks are used to support columns in other building types as well, for example at the Regia, where there is not a wall beneath the courtyard colonnade, but rather individual posts. For later temples that continue this trend: Vulci: Massabò 1988–1989; Orvieto: Pernier 1926; Ardea: Stefani 1954; Lanuvium: Galieti 1928, 75–118; Marzabotto (Tinia Temple): Sassatelli and Govi 2005, 13–30. Exceptions postdating the Capitoline are Marzabotto Temple C: Vitali, Brizzolara, and Lippolis 2001, 35–44; Brizio 1889, 258–260, pls. I–X; Pyrgi A and B: Colonna 1965; Colonna and Pallottino 1970, 36–43, 275–287; Rome Castor: Nielsen and Zahle 1985, 6. Scholars have argued that each of these sites experienced significant Greek influence. I suggest Greek influence on the Temple of Castor elsewhere; see Hopkins 2010a, ch. 1. On the other sites, see Colonna 1965, 192; Mertens 1980, 49.

42. Cf. Archaic temples at Samos, Ephesus, Didyma, Delos, Athens, Delphi, Corinth, Perachora, Corfu, Metapontum, Paestum, Agrigento, Selinunte, Syracuse, and elsewhere (Mertens 2006, 97–155, 216–309). On Archaic temples in general, see Dinsmoor 1975, 69–113, 123–146; Lawrence and Tomlinson 1983, 141–159, 160–173. On the correlation between foundations and superstructures in Greek architecture, see e.g., Cook and Nicholls 1998, 11–12; Cooper 2008, 230–234. On specific sites, e.g., Metapontum: Adamesteanu, Mertens, and D'Andria 1975, 109; Assos: Bacon et al. 1902, 141, pl. 1; Samos Heraia: Buschor 1930, 1–162, esp. 72; Hellner and Kienast 2009, 8, 143–148, 202; Temple of Apollo at Delos: Courby 1931, pls. II, III; Locri: De Franciscis 1979, 59–100, figs. 5–34; Paestum (Foce del Sele): De La Genière, Greco, and Donnarumna 1997, 337–344; De La Genière et al. 1999, 501–507; Corinth: Fowler and Stillwell 1932, pl. I, V; Didyma: Gruben 1963, esp. 78–85; Ephesus: Hogarth et al. 1908, pls. I, XII; Naxos: Lambrinoudakis and Gruben 1987, 569–621, ill. 13; Paestum (Hera I): Mertens, Schützenberger, and Spooner-Za 1993, 5–15, pls. 4–7, 20; Syracuse (Olympieion): Orsi 1903; Apollo Alaei: Orsi 1933, 22–27, figs. 3–4; Corfu: Rodenwaldt 1939, pls. 3, 22. In my survey I found only three Archaic Greek temples that do not follow this design: the Temple of Dionysus on Naxos, the Marasà sanctuary at Locri, and the Temple of Apollo Alaei. These have foundation walls under all superstructure walls and colonnades, but pillars supporting the three or four naos/opisthodomos columns (that is, interior columns).

43. Supra n. 30. While the temple at Samos was not complete for centuries, the foundation wall under the third colonnade was built by around 530, and the triple colonnade porch itself was underway before the close of the century: Hellner and Kienast 2009, 8, 143–148, 202. I suggest in forthcoming work that in the period between 530 and 500, when construction on the Samian temple stopped and architects and craftsmen were unoccupied, it is possible that they may have come west, bringing to Sicily and central Italy the designs, tectonics, and construction knowledge that pervaded the west thereafter.

44. De Waele 1981, 7–68; Chiarucci and Gizi 1985, 47–53.

45. The latest ceramic in the fill of the Capitoline foundation trenches dates to the early–mid sixth century, suggesting it may have been begun as early as ca. 550. On Satricum, see De Waele 1981.

46. Colonna 1965, 192; Mertens 1980, 49; Lulof 2006; Winter 2006.

47. Supra n. 42.

48. Syracuse-Apollo, Syracuse-Olympieion, Selinunte-C, Metaponto-A II and similar, Metaponto-B I, Locri-Marasà, see Mertens 2006, 108, 11, 21, 51, 37.

49. Cifani (2008, 292) makes this comparison. None of these temples was completed until long after the close of the century; a marked difference from the Capitoline, which was finished quickly.

50. Davies (2007), Rendeli (1989), and others have looked to Ionia in regard to the Capitoline's dimensions; only Cifani (2008, 292) has suggested a direct connection based on the frontal colonnades.

51. Mertens 1994, 196–197.

52. Andrén 1940, 149, pl. 39.488; Winter 2006.

53. Åkerström 1966, 97, pl. 52.3; cf. pl. 63.7 for other examples at Aklan and Gordion; Winter 1993, 259. For an overview of painted and perforated anthemion terracottas in the west, see Barletta 1983, esp. 21–22 with references; Wikander 1986, esp. 21–24, 32, 40, 42.

54. On the appearance at Agrigento, see Barletta 1983, 270–271.

55. Winter 2009, 1–2. I came to understand this profound change through extended conversations with Nancy Winter, whom I thank for her suggestions.

56. Barletta 1983; 1993; 2000.

57. E.g., Sherratt and Sherratt 1993; Horden and Purcell 2000, esp. 342–400; Malkin 2005; Morris 2005. More and more scholars do not see Etruria as the necessary point of entry for goods to Rome, but rather think of Rome as having a direct line to Mediterranean trade and cultural contact: e.g., Colonna 1976, 28–29; Cornell 1980; Bartoloni 1981, 91; Zevi, Bartoloni, and Cataldi Dini 1982, 258; Bietti Sestieri 1992; Holloway 1994, 103–164; Cornell 1986, no. 714; Bouma et al. 1995; Ginge and Becker 1996; Naso 2001, 226; Waarsenburg 1995, 2001.

58. The colossal temples in Sicily include Temple G and the Olympieion at Agrigento. Both have been tied to Ionic roots, and both were begun at the end of the sixth or beginning of the fifth century.

59. There are exceptions, especially the Oikos of the Naxians on Delos and the Naxian Temple of Dionysus, but these prove the rule.

60. On approach in early Italy, see Meyers 2003.

61. For Pyrgi B and Satricum Temple II, see Mertens 1980. On approach to buildings in central Italy and earlier frontal religious precedents, see Colonna 1981, 1984, 1985, 2006; Meyers 2003, 1–5.

62. See Warden in this volume for a discussion of the relationship between the design of the Tuscan temple and the performance of ritual.

63. Colonna 1981; 1984; 1985; 2006.

64. Alzinger (1982, 24–26) was the first to suggest that Romans adapted a Greek temple for their own religious needs, but he is less specific as to how.

65. Pensabene 1990.

66. Nielsen and Tuck 2001, 44–45; Kreindler and Tuck 2010.

67. Bonghi Jovino 1999.

68. For a list and plan of temples predating the Capitoline, e.g., Damgaard Andersen 1998, 22–29.

69. Colonna 1985, 60; Boëthius, Ling, and Rasmussen 1994, 41–42; Gros 2001, 136–137.

70. Stamper 2005, 132, 204–205.

71. Among many others, Derrida (1987) and Heidegger (1971) highlight the importance of time and circumstance on the study of art and objecthood.

72. Recently Jean-Claude Golvin (1987) and (more explicitly) Katherine Welch (2007, 138–141) have described the effects of the Colosseum in a similar manner. While no amphithe-

ater after it copies it outright, they argue that its design was so influential as to "canonize" the building type.

73. Supra nn. 32, 70.

74. E.g., the Temples of Castor and Pollux and of Saturn in Rome and the Temple of Jupiter in Pompeii (often referred to as a capitolium).

75. On the tomb, see Davies 2009.

76. Especially Colini (1965, 175), who recalls that however impressive its size might seem to us, "even more impressive must it have appeared to the first inhabitants of Rome who saw it rising from the plane of the Velabrum." Recently, Meyers 2003, 178–188.

77. See the contribution by Meyers to this volume.

Bibliography

Adam, J.-P. 1984. *La construction romaine: Matériaux et techniques*. Paris: A. and J. Picard.

Adamesteanu, D., D. Mertens, and F. D'Andria. 1975. *Metaponto I. NSc* Suppl. 29. Roma: Accademia Nazionale dei Lincei.

Åkerström, Å. 1966. *Die architektonischen Terrakotten Kleinasiens*. Lund: C. W. K. Gleerup.

Alvarez, W., A. J. Ammerman, P. R. Renne, D. B. Karner, N. Terrenato, and A. Montanari. 1996. "Quaternary Fluvial-Volcanic Stratigraphy and Geochronology of the Capitoline Hill in Rome." *Geology* 24:751–754.

Alzinger, W. 1982. "Tuscanicae dispositiones und griechische Tektonik." In *Pro arte antiqua: Festschrift für Hedwig Kenner*, ed. H. Kenner, W. Alzinger et al., 23–27. Vienna: A. F. Koska.

Ammerman, A. J., and N. Terrenato. 1996. "Nuove osservazioni sul Colle Capitolino." *BullCom* 97:35–46.

Andrén, A. 1940. *Architectural Terracottas from Etrusco-Italic Temples*. Lund: C. W. K. Gleerup.

Bacon, F. H., J. T. Clarke, R. Koldewey, and H. W. Bell. 1902. *Investigations at Assos: Drawings and Photographs of the Buildings and Objects Discovered during the Excavations of 1881–1882–1883*. Cambridge, Mass.: Archaeological Institute of America.

Barletta, B. A. 1983. *Ionic Influence in Archaic Sicily: The Monumental Art*. Göteborg: Paul Åströms Förlag.

———. 1993. "Some Ionic Architectural Elements from Selinus in the Getty Museum." *Studia Varia from the J. Paul Getty Museum* I:55–65.

———. 2000. "Ionic Influence in Western Greek Architecture: Towards a Definition and Explanation." In *Die Ägäis und das westliche Mittelmeer: Beziehung und Wechselwirkungen 8 bis 5. Jhdt. v. Chr.*, ed. F. Krinzinger, 203–216. Vienna: Verlag der Österreichischen Akademie der Wissenschaften.

———. 2001. *The Origins of the Greek Architectural Orders*. Cambridge: Cambridge University Press.

Bartoloni, G. 1981. "Precisazioni sulla produzione di ceramica geometrica in Italia." *PP* 36:90–101.

Beaufort, J., et al. 1982. *Satricum: Una città latina*. Florence: Alinari.

Bietti Sestieri, A. M. 1992. *La necropoli laziale di Osteria dell'Osa*. Rome: Quasar.

———. 1992. *The Iron Age Community of Osteria dell'Osa: A Study of Socio-Political Development in Central Tyrrhenian Italy*. New York: Cambridge University Press.

Boëthius, A., R. Ling, and T. Rasmussen. 1994. *Etruscan and Early Roman Architecture*. New Haven: Yale University Press.

Bonghi Jovino, M. 1997. "La phase archaïque de l'Ara della Regina à la lumière des recherches récentes." In *Les plus religieux des hommes: État de la recherche sur la religion étrusque*.

Actes du colloque international, 17–19 novembre 1992, ed. F. Gaultier and D. Briquel, 69–95. Paris: La documentation française.

———. 1999. "Tantum ratio sacrorum gerebatur: L'Edificio Beta di Tarquinia in epoca orientalizzante e alto-arcaica." In *Koina: Miscellanea di studi archeologici in onore di Piero Orlandini*, ed. M. Castoldi, 87–103. Milan: Edizioni ET.

Bouma, J. W., et al. 1995. "The Economy of an Early Latin Settlement, Borgo Le Ferriere-Satricum, 800–200 B.C." In *Settlement and Economy in Italy, 1500 B.C.–A.D. 1500: Papers of the Fifth Conference of Italian Archaeology*, ed. N. Christie, 183–195. Oxford: Oxbow Books.

Brizio, E. 1889. "Relazione sugli scavi eseguiti a Marzabotto presso Bologna dal Novembre 1888 a tutto maggio 1889." *MonAnt* 1:250–262, pls. I–X.

Buschor, E. 1930. "Heraion von Samos: Frühe Bauten." *AM* 55:1–162.

Camp, J. M., and W. B. Dinsmoor. 1984. *Ancient Athenian Building Methods*. Princeton: American School of Classical Studies at Athens.

Cary, E., trans. 1937. *The Roman Antiquities of Dionysius of Halicarnassus*. Cambridge, Mass.: Harvard University Press.

Castagnoli, F. 1955. "Peripteros sine postico." *RM* 62:139–145.

———. 1966–1967. "Sul tempio 'Italico.'" *RM* 73–74:10–14.

———. 1974. "Topografia e urbanistica di Roma nel IV secolo a.C." *StRom* 22:425–443.

———. 1984. "Il tempio romano: Questioni di terminologia e di tipologia." *PBSR* 52:3–20.

Chiarucci, P., and T. Gizi. 1985. *Area sacra di Satricum: Tra scavo e restituzione. Catalogo della mostra, Museo Civico Albano, 20 aprile–2 giugno 1985*. Rome: Paleani.

Chiesa, F., and B. Binda. 2009. "Una possibile reconstruzione dei tetti arcaici." In *L'Ara della Regina di Tarquinia: Aree sacre, santuari mediterranei*, ed. M. Bonghi Jovino and F. Chiesa, 65–91. Milan: Cisalpino.

Cifani, G. 2008. *Architettura romana arcaica: Edilizia e società tra Monarchia e Repubblica*. Roma: L'Erma di Bretschneider.

Coarelli, F., A. Rossi, and R. Schezen. 1980. *Templi dell'Italia antica*. Milan: Touring Club Italiano.

Colini, A. M. 1965. "Il Colle Capitolino nell'antichità." *Capitolium* 40:175–185.

Colonna, G. 1965. "Il santuario di Pyrgi alla luce delle recenti scoperte." *StEtr* 33:191–219.

———. 1976. "Le fasi protourbane dell'età del ferro dal IX al VII secolo a.C. (periodi IIB, III, IV)." In *Civiltà del Lazio primitivo. Palazzo delle Esposizioni, Roma, 1976*, ed. M. O. Acanfora, 25–36. Rome: Multigrafica.

———. 1981. "Varrone e i più antichi templi romani, Varrone e Vulca." *PP* 36:51–59.

———. 1984. "I templi del Lazio fino al V secolo compreso." *ArchLaz* 6:396–411.

———, ed. 1985. *Santuari d'Etruria*. Milan: Electa.

———. 1991. "Le due fasi del tempio arcaico di S. Omobono." In *Stips votiva: Papers Presented to C. M. Stibbe*, ed. M. Gnade, 51–59. Amsterdam: Allard Pierson Museum, University of Amsterdam.

———. 2006. "Sacred Architecture and the Religion of the Etruscans." In *The Religion of the Etruscans*, ed. N. T. de Grummond and E. Simon, 132–168. Austin: University of Texas Press.

Colonna, G., and M. Pallottino. 1970. *Pyrgi: Scavi del Santuario Etrusco (1959–1967). NSc* Suppl. 24. Rome: Accademia Nazionale dei Lincei.

Cook, J. M., and R. V. Nicholls. 1998. *Old Smyrna Excavations: The Temples of Athena*. London: British School at Athens.

Cooper, F. A. 2008. "Greek Engineering and Construction." In *Oxford Handbook of Engineering and Technology in the Classical World*, ed. J. P. Oleson, 225–255. New York: Oxford University Press.

Cornell, T. J. 1980. "Rome and Latium Vetus, 1974–79." *AR* 26:71–89.

Courby, F. 1931. *Les temples d'Apollon*. Paris: De Boccard.

Damgaard Andersen, H. 1998. "Etruscan Architecture from the Late Orientalizing to the Archaic Period (c. 640–480 B.C.)." 5 vols. PhD diss., University of Copenhagen.

Danti, A. 2001. "L'indagine archeologica nell'area del Tempio di Giove Capitolino." *BullCom* 102:323–338.

Davies, P. J. E. 2009. "The Tomb of the Sempronii: Identity and Ideology." Paper read at 9th International Conference on the Social Context of Death, Dying, and Disposal, 9–12 September 2009, Durham University, UK.

Davies, P. J. E., and H. W. Janson. 2007. *Janson's History of Art: The Western Tradition*. Upper Saddle River, N.J.: Pearson, Prentice Hall.

De Franciscis, A. 1979. *Il santuario di Marasà a Locri Epizefiri*. Naples: G. Macchiaroli.

De La Genière, J., G. Greco, and R. Donnarumna. 1997. "L'Héraion de Foce del Sele: Découvertes récentes." *CRAI* 141:333–353.

De La Genière, J., G. Greco, R. Donnarumna, and D. Theodorescu. 1999. "L'Héraion du Sele: Nouvelles découvertes." *CRAI* 143:501–508.

Derrida, J. 1987. "Restitutions of the Truth in Pointing [Pointure]." In *The Truth in Painting*, trans. G. Bennington and I. McLeod, 293–329. Chicago: University of Chicago Press.

De Waele, J. A. K. E. 1981. "I templi della Mater Matuta a Satricum." *MededRom* 43:7–68.

De Waele, J. A. K. E., and R. Cantilena. 2001. *Il tempio dorico del foro triangolare di Pompei*. Rome: L'Erma di Bretschneider.

Dinsmoor, W. B. 1975. *The Architecture of Ancient Greece: An Account of Its Historic Development*. New York: Norton.

Feye, J. 1970. "Il Tempio G di Selinunte e l'architettura dei templi siciliani." *BABesch* 71:88–99.

Fowler, H. N., and R. Stillwell. 1932. *Corinth*, I: *Introduction: Topography, Architecture*. Cambridge, Mass.: Harvard University Press.

Gabba, E. 1991. *Dionysius and the History of Archaic Rome*. Berkeley: University of California Press.

Galieti, A. 1928. "Il tempio italico rinvenuto nell'acropolis di Lanuvium." *BullCom* 56:75–118, 199–249.

Ginge, B., and M. J. Becker. 1996. *Excavations at Satricum (Borgo Le Ferriere) 1907–1910. Northwest Necropolis, Southwest Sanctuary, and Acropolis*. Amsterdam: Thesis.

Giuliani, C. F. 1982. "Architettura e tecnica edilizia." In *Roma repubblicana fra il 509 e il 270 a.C*, ed. P. Pensabene, I. Dondero, and L. Campus, 29–36. Rome: Quasar.

Gjerstad, E. 1953–1973. *Early Rome, I–VI*. Lund: C. W. K. Gleerup.

Golvin, J.-C. 1987. "L'amphithéâtre romain." *Dossiers d'Archéologie* 116:6–15.

Gros, P. 1996. *L'architecture romaine: Du début du IIIe siècle av. J.-C. à la fin du Haut-Empire*. Paris: Picard.

———. 2001. *L'architecture romaine: Du début du IIIe siècle av. J.-C. à la fin du Haut-Empire*. 2nd ed. Paris: Picard.

———. 2006. *L'architecture romaine: Du début du IIIe siècle av. J.-C. à la fin du Haut-Empire*. 2nd ed., rev. Paris: Picard.

Gruben, G. 1963. "Das archaische Didymaion." *JdI* 78:78–182.

Handlin, D. P. 1985. *American Architecture*. London: Thames and Hudson.

Heidegger, M. 1971. "The Origin of the Work of Art." In *Poetry, Language, Thought*, trans. A. Hofstadter, 17–87. New York: Harper Collins.

Hellner, N., and H. J. Kienast. 2009. *Die Säulenbasen des zweiten Dipteros von Samos: Grundlage für die Rekonstruktion des Tempels in seinen Bauphasen*. Bonn: Deutsches Archäologisches Institut.

Hodge, T. 1960. *The Woodwork of Greek Roofs*. Cambridge: Cambridge University Press.

Hogarth, D. G., C. Harcourt-Smith, A. H. Smith, B. V. Head, and A. E. Henderson. 1908. *The Archaic Artemisia*. London: British Museum.

Holloway, R. R. 1994. *The Archaeology of Early Rome and Latium*. London: Routledge.

Hopkins, J. N. 2010a. "The Topographical Transformation of Archaic Rome: A New Interpretation of Architecture and Geography in the Early City." PhD diss., University of Texas at Austin.

———. 2010b. "The Colossal Temple of Jupiter Optimus Maximus in Archaic Rome." In *Arqueología de la construcción, 2: Los procesos constructivos en el mundo romano: Italia y provincias orientales (Siena, Certosa di Pontignano, 13–15 de Noviembre de 2008)*, ed. S. Camporeale, H. Dessales, and A. Pizzo, 15–33. Archivo Español de Arqueología Suppl. 57. Merida: Archivo Español de Arqueología.

Horden, P., and N. Purcell. 2000. *The Corrupting Sea: A Study of Mediterranean History*. Malden, Mass.: Blackwell.

Ioppolo, G. 1971–1972. "I reperti ossei animali nell'area archeologica di S. Omobono (1962–1964)." *RendPontAc* 44:3–46.

Jordan, H. 1885. *Topographie der Stadt Rom im Alterthum*. Berlin: Weidmannsche Buchhandlung.

Klein, N. L. 1998. "Evidence for West Greek Influence on Mainland Greek Roof Construction and the Creation of the Truss in the Archaic Period." *Hesperia* 67:335–374.

Kreindler, K., and A. Tuck. 2010. "Political Uses of Religion in Early Central Italy: The Case of Poggio Civitate." Paper read at the 2010 Annual Meeting of the Archaeological Institute of America, 6–9 January, Anaheim, Calif.

Lambrinoudakis, V., and G. Gruben. 1987. "Das neuentdeckte Heiligtum von Iria auf Naxos." *AA* 98:569–621.

Lanciani, R. 1875. "Il tempio di Giove Ottimo Massimo." *BullCom* 3:165–189.

Lawrence, A. W. 1967. *Greek Architecture*. Baltimore: Penguin.

Lawrence, A. W., and R. A. Tomlinson. 1983. *Greek Architecture*. New York: Penguin.

Lulof, P. S. 2006. "'Roofs from the South': Campanian Architectural Terracottas in Satricum." In *Deliciae Fictiles, III: Architectural Terracottas in Ancient Italy: New Discoveries and Interpretations*, ed. I. E. M. Edlund-Berry, G. Greco, and J. Kenfield, 235–242. Oxford: Oxbow Books.

Malkin, I. 2005. *Mediterranean Paradigms and Classical Antiquity*. London: Routledge.

Massabò, B. 1988–1989. "Il santuario etrusco di Fontanile di Legnisina a Vulci—Relazione delle campagne di scavo 1985 e 1986: Il tempio." *NSc*: 103–135.

Mertens, D. 1980. "Parallelismi struturali nell'architettura della Magna Grecia e dell'Italia centrale in età arcaica." In *Attività archeologica in Basilicata, 1964–1977. Scritti in onore di Dinu Adamesteanu*, ed. M. Padula, 37–82. Matera: Meta.

———. 1994. "Elementi di origine etrusco-campana nell'architettura della Magna Grecia." In *Magna Grecia, Etruschi, Fenici: Atti del trentatreesimo Convegno di studi sulla Magna Grecia: Taranto, 8–13 ottobre 1993*, 195–209. Taranto: Istituto per la storia e l'archeologia della Magna grecia.

———. 2006. *Città e monumenti dei greci d'occidente: Dalla colonizzazione alla crisi di fine V secolo a.C.* Rome: L'Erma di Bretschneider.

Mertens, D., M. Schützenberger, and R. Sponer-Za. 1993. *Der alte Heratempel in Paestum und die archaische Baukunst in Unteritalien*. Mainz: von Zabern.

Meyers, G. E. 2003. "Etrusco-Italic Monumental Architectural Space from the Iron Age to the Archaic Period: An Examination of Approach and Access." PhD diss., University of Texas at Austin.

Morris, I. 2005. "Mediterraneanization." In *Mediterranean Paradigms and Classical Antiquity*, ed. I. Malkin, 30–55. London: Routledge.

Mura Sommella, A. 2000a. "'La grande Roma dei Tarquini': Alterne vicende di una felice intuizione." *BullCom* 101:7–26.

———. 2000b. "Le recenti scoperte sul Campidoglio e la fondazione del tempio di Giove Capitolino." *RendPontAc* 70:57–79.

———. 2001. "Notizie preliminare sulle scoperte e sulle indagini archeologiche nel versante orientale del Capitolium." *BullCom* 102:262–264.

———. 2002. "'La grande Roma dei Tarquini': Alterne vicende di una felice intuizioine." In *Il classico nella Roma contemporanea: Mito, modelli, memoria. Atti del convegno Roma 18–20 ottobre 2000*, ed. F. Roscetti, L. Lanzetta, and L. Canatore, 303–323. Rome: Istituto Nazionale di Studi Romani.

———. 2009. "Il Tempio di Giove Capitolino: Una nuova proposta di lettura." In *Gli etruschi e Roma: Fasi monarchica e alto-repubblicana*, ed. G. M. Della Fina, 333–372. Annali della Fondazione per il Museo "Claudio Faina" 16. Orvieto: Quasar.

Naso, A. 2001. "The Etruscans in Lazio." In *The Etruscans outside Etruria*, ed. G. Camporeale, 220–235. Los Angeles: Getty Publications.

Nielsen, E. O., and A. S. Tuck. 2001. "An Orientalizing Period Complex at Poggio Civitate (Murlo): A Preliminary View." *EtrStud* 8:35–63.

Nielsen, I., and B. Poulsen. 1992. *The Temple of Castor and Pollux*. Rome: De Luca.

Nielsen, I., and J. Zahle. 1985. "The Temple of Castor and Pollux on the Forum Romanum: Preliminary Report of the Scandinavian Excavations, 1983–1985." *ActaArch* 56:1–30.

Orsi, P. 1903. "L'Olympieion di Siracusa: Scavi del 1893 e 1902." *MonAnt* 13:369–391.

———. 1933. *Templum Apollonis Alaei ad Crimisa promontorium*. Rome: Società Magna Grecia.

Pedley, J. G. 2005. *Sanctuaries and the Sacred in the Ancient Greek World*. New York: Cambridge University Press.

Pensabene, P. 1990. "Il tempio di Saturno a Dougga e tradizioni architettoniche di origine punica." In *L'Africa Romana: Atti del VII convegno di studio*, ed. A. Mastino, 251–293. Sassari: Gallizzi.

Pernier, L. 1926. "Il tempio etrusco-italico di Orvieto." *Dedalo* 6:137–164.

Pisani Sartorio, G. 1982. "L'area sacra dei templi della Fortuna e della Mater Matuta nel Foro Boario." In *Roma repubblicana fra il 509 e il 270 a.C*, ed. P. Pensabene, I. Dondero, and L. Campus, 51–56. Roma: Quasar.

Pisani Sartorio, G., and P. Virgili. 1979. "Area sacra di S. Omobono." *ArchLaz* 2:41–47.

Purcell, N. 2003. "Becoming Historical: The Roman Case." In *Myth, History, and Culture in Republican Rome*, ed. D. Braund and C. Gill, 12–40. Exeter: University of Exeter Press.

Rancière, J. 2004. *The Politics of Aesthetics: The Distribution of the Sensible*. Trans. G. Rockhill. London: Continuum.

———. 2009. *The Emancipated Spectator*. Trans. G. Elliot. London: Verso.

Rendeli, M. 1989. "Muratori, ho fretta di erigere questa casa: Concorrenza tra formazioni urbane dell'Italia centrale tirrenica nella costruzione di edifici di culto arcaici." *RIA* 12:49–68.

Reuther, O. 1957. *Der Heratempel von Samos: Der Bau seit der Zeit des Polykrates*. Berlin: Gebr. Mann.

Ridley, R. T. 2005. "Unbridgeable Gaps." *BullCom* 106:83–103.

Rodenwaldt, G. 1939. *Korkyra: Archaische Bauten und Bildwerke*. Berlin: Gebr. Mann.

Roth, L. M. 1979. *A Concise History of American Architecture*. New York: Harper and Row.

Sassatelli, G., and E. Govi. 2005. *Culti, forma urbana e artigianato a Marzabotto: Nuove prospet-*

tive di ricerca. Atti del convegno di studi, Bologna, S. Giovanni in Monte, 3–4 giugno 2003. Bologna: Ante quem.

Sear, F. 1989. *Roman Architecture.* London: Batsford.

Sherratt, S., and A. Sherratt. 1993. "The Growth of the Mediterranean Economy in the Early First Millennium B.C." *World Archaeology* 24:361–378.

Stamper, J. W. 2005. *The Architecture of Roman Temples: The Republic to the Middle Empire.* Cambridge: Cambridge University Press.

Stefani, E. 1944. "Scavi archeologici a Veio in contrada Piazza d'Armi." *MonAnt* 40:178–290.

———. 1953. "Veio—Tempio detto dell'Apollo: Esplorazione e sistemazione del santuario." *NSc* 7:29–112.

———. 1954. "Ardea (Contrada Casalinaccio): Resti di un antico tempio scoperto nell'area della città." *NSc* 8:6–30.

Tucci, P. L. 2006. "Il Tempio di Giove Capitolino e la sua influenza sui templi di età imperiale." *JRA* 19:386–392.

Turfa, J. M., and A. G. Steinmayer Jr. 1996. "The Comparative Structure of Greek and Etruscan Monumental Buildings." *PBSR* 64:1–40.

Vitali, D., A. M. Brizzolara, and E. Lippolis. 2001. *L'acropoli della città etrusca di Marzabotto.* Bologna: University Press.

Il viver quotidiano in Roma arcaica: Materiali degli scavi del Tempio Arcaico nell'area sacra di S. Omobono. 1989. Rome: Procom.

Waarsenburg, D. J. 1995. "Nuove ricerche sulla necropolis nord-ovest di Satricum." *ArchLaz* 12:583–590.

———. 2001. "Living Like a Prince: The Habitation Counterpart of the *tombe principesche,* as Represented at Satricum." In *From Huts to Houses: Transformations of Ancient Societies. Proceedings of an International Seminar Organized by the Norwegian and Swedish Institutes in Rome, 21–24 September 1997,* ed. J. R. Brandt and L. Karlsson, 179–188. Stockholm: Paul Åströms Förlag.

Welch, K. E. 2007. *The Roman Amphitheatre: From Its Origins to the Colosseum.* New York: Cambridge University Press.

Whiffen, M., and F. Koeper. 1981. *American Architecture, 1607–1976.* Cambridge, Mass.: MIT Press.

Wikander, C. 1986. *Sicilian Architectural Terracottas: A Reappraisal.* Göteborg: Paul Åströms Förlag.

Winter, N. A. 1993. *Greek Architectural Terracottas: From the Prehistoric to the End of the Archaic Period.* New York: Oxford University Press.

———. 2006. "The Origin of the Recessed Gable in Etruscan Architecture." In *Deliciae Fictiles, III: Architectural Terracottas in Ancient Italy: New Discoveries and Interpretations,* ed. I. E. M. Edlund-Berry, G. Greco, and J. Kenfield, 45–49. Oxford: Oxbow Books.

———. 2009. *Symbols of Wealth and Power: Architectural Terracotta Decoration in Etruria and Central Italy, 640–510 B.C. MAAR* Suppl. 9. Ann Arbor: University of Michigan Press.

Wiseman, T. P. 1993. "Lying Historians: Seven Types of Mendacity." In *Lies and Fiction in the Ancient World,* ed. C. Gill and T. P. Wiseman, 122–146. Austin: University of Texas Press.

———. 1995. *Remus: A Roman Myth.* Cambridge: Cambridge University Press.

———. 2008. *Unwritten Rome.* Exeter: University of Exeter Press.

Zevi, F., G. Bartoloni, and M. Cataldi Dini. 1982. "Aspetti dell'ideologia funeraria nella necropoli di Castel di Decima." In *La Mort, les morts dans les sociétés anciennes,* ed. G. Gnoli and J.-P. Vernant, 257–273. Paris: Editions de la Maison des Sciences de l'Homme.

VII ON THE INTRODUCTION OF STONE ENTABLATURES IN REPUBLICAN TEMPLES IN ROME

PENELOPE J. E. DAVIES

IN REPUBLICAN ROME, AS IN IMPERIAL ROME, RADI-cal innovation in temple design was unusual. Yet during the course of the Republic there was an increasing interest in monumentality. Buildings derived grandeur from diverse sources: from sheer size (though none was as vast as the sixth-century Temple of Jupiter Optimus Maximus on the Capitoline), from impressive votive gifts, or from a highly visible location.[1] Material, too, could constitute a powerful form of monumentality. When Q. Caecilius Metellus was struggling to win a consulship after his defeat of Macedonia as praetor in 148, he imported stone from Greece and hired Hermodorus of Salamis, an architect from Greek Cyprus, to construct the first all-marble temple of Rome, dedicated to Jupiter Stator and located in the Porticus Metelli on the Circus Flaminius.[2] It was probably one of his chief rivals, L. Mummius, consul of 146 and conqueror of Corinth, who followed suit with the round temple by the Tiber (probably his Temple of Hercules Victor), built of crisp white Pentelic marble (fig. 7.1).[3] Yet well before the introduction of costly Greek marble, another modification in fabric occurred in temple design in Rome, with a similar view to achieving monumentality: the replacement of wooden entablatures with entablatures of stone. This substitution and the new aesthetic it entailed constituted a small revolution in Roman temple design. Structurally, a stone architrave enhanced durability; visually, the proximity of the columns and the solidity of the superstructure signaled unmitigated architectonic—and symbolic—power.

Fig. 7.1. Round temple by the Tiber (Temple of Hercules Victor?), second half of the second century, *detail*, with Temple of Portunus, first half of the first century (photo P. Davies).

Stone entablatures were in use for temples in Greece and in Sicily and south Italy from the Archaic period. Yet on the question of when architects introduced stone entablatures to temples in Rome, scholars mostly shrug their shoulders, and for good reason: archaeological evidence is scanty at best, and literature provides no assistance. Vitruvius is surprisingly silent on the matter, Livy is concerned with the fact of buildings rather than their materials, and despite Pliny's interest in the latter, Italic temples appear with relative infrequency in his text. Tenney Frank deduces from the presence of peperino *caementa* in the composition of restored temple foundations that earlier phases of these buildings had peperino entablatures. His method yields stone entablatures, *inter alia*, for the initial phase of the Temple of Magna Mater on the Palatine, begun in 204 and dedicated in 191, as well as for a restoration of ca. 102; L. Opimius's Temple of Concord, vowed in 121 after the death of C. Gracchus; and the Temple of Castor in the extensive reconstruction phase attributed to L. Caecilius Metellus Delmaticus in ca. 117.[4] Most estimates on the date of the earliest stone entablatures mesh with Gabriele Cifani's:

> The use of wooden trabeation would remain widespread in Rome until the advent of concrete (end of the third, be-

ginning of the second century BCE), and with it the use of
wooden shingles, attested until the end of the third century
in a passage of Cornelius Nepos reported in Pliny the Elder's *Natural History*, who records the widespread use of
wooden roof revetments in Rome until the end of the war
with Pyrrhus.[5]

For Cairoli Giuliani, Romans continued to use wood even when stone was available to them because of "a particular attachment to tradition, especially evident in
cult spaces, but above all because of an objective difficulty in construction, deriving
from the custom of having very wide intercolumniations, more easily spanned by
wooden structures."[6] This verges on circular reasoning. Using archaeological evidence, I hypothesize that the design change took root almost a century earlier than
scholars have supposed, with the construction of the Temple of Victoria on the
Palatine, and I explore a possible sociopolitical context for the development.

Approximately a dozen temples constructed in Rome in the first two centuries
of the Republic are documented by archaeological and literary evidence.[7] In the
rare cases where details of their forms are preserved, these temples seem to have
shared some essential features—albeit on a reduced scale—of the Temple of Jupiter
Optimus Maximus (see fig. 7.4). They stood high above ground level on a podium
built of *opera quadrata* of locally quarried cappellaccio (tufo di Palatino), Mon-
teverde, or Grotta Oscura tufo filled with rubble, accessed by a frontal staircase.
Such podia survive for the Temples of Saturn and Castor, dating to the first decades
of the Republic;[8] the Temples of Fortuna and Mater Matuta in the *area sacra* of
Sant' Omobono in their early fifth-century phase;[9] the Temple of Apollo Medicus,
of ca. 433;[10] and the first phase of the Temple of Portunus, dating to the late fourth
or early third century.[11] The podium lifted the temple and its contents above the
constant floodwaters and elevated visitors into a sacred space above the quotidian
fray. Traces of early walls suggest that in the Temple of Apollo Medicus the cella
block sat toward the rear of its podium, leaving room in front for a monumental
raised forecourt, where archaeologists posit an altar and a basin for lustral water
for the purification rites intrinsic to the cult.[12] By contrast, the Temple of Castor
occupied its entire podium, and thus its monumentality resided partly in its size.
Two rows of columns (as compared to one, perhaps, in the Temple of Apollo Medicus) made for a deep porch, where visitors could mill about in a quasi-autonomous
space. A pair of columns *in antis* (as in the Temples of Fortuna and Mater Matuta)
or a row of prostyle columns (as in the Temple of Castor) defined the façade.[13] The
columns were probably stone.[14] Unlike the Temple of Jupiter Optimus Maximus,
most temples had solid lateral walls rather than colonnades, reaching as far as the
frontal *antae* to create wings, or *alae*; the exception is the Temple of Castor, where
the lateral walls extended only as far as the front of the cella.

In the rare passages where Vitruvius mentions early temples in Rome he describes them as tetrastyle, which also sets them apart from the Capitoline temple, with its hexastyle façade. Regarding column spacing, he specifies that they were diastyle or aeraeostyle, which is consistent with the scanty archaeological evidence:

> The diastyle temple is composed that we may put the breadth of three columns in the intercolumnar space, just as occurs in the temple of Apollo and Diana [probably the Temple of Apollo Medicus]. . . . It is not possible to make an aeraeostyle temple with epistyles in stone or marble; instead, above the columns wooden beams must be placed all around. . . . Their roofs are decorated with terracotta ornaments or gilded bronze in Etruscan style, as in the temple of Ceres near the Circus Maximus . . . and also the Capitoline Temple.[15]

The façade columns screened a porch and a triple cella (the Temple of Castor) or a single cella (the Temples of Saturn, Apollo Medicus, Fortuna, and Mater Matuta). Outer walls must have been tufo to support the weight of the roof structure, and inner walls of tufo or *opus craticium*.[16] According to Varro the Temple of Semo Sancus Dius Fidius of ca. 466 was hypaethral so as to allow the god to bear witness to the oaths he guaranteed, but this was an exception; most had gabled roofs

Fig. 7.2. Temple of Victoria: actual state, from north (photo P. Davies).

with wide overhanging eaves to shield the walls, since tufo—particularly cappellac-cio—loses a great deal of weight-bearing capacity and strength when exposed to moisture.[17] Painted terracotta revetments such as those discovered in the vicinity of the Temples of Castor and Apollo Medicus protected the timbers;[18] since the tympanum wall was recessed far back from the front of the pediment, and the bottom of the pediment was tiled and decorated with antefixes like a roof, there were no pedimental sculptures.[19]

Beneath an early first-century *opus caementicium* podium on the southwest side of the Palatine, facing the Circus Maximus and adjacent to the later Temple of Magna Mater, lies evidence for a Republican temple of a different sort (fig. 7.2). On an imposing system of Grotta Oscura substructures, walls of Grotta Oscura *opera quadrata* framed the east and south sides of a foundation for an earlier temple podium, while robber trenches indicate its full extent on the west and north sides (fig. 7.3).[20] Additional foundations within these walls, along with imprints from blocks in the later cement foundations, reveal the form of a single cella. The foundations lead excavator Patrizio Pensabene to reconstruct an early temple that was

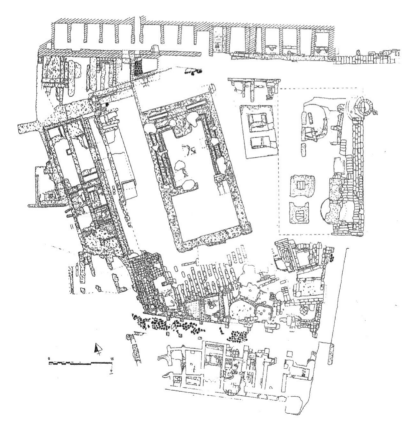

Fig. 7.3. Excavation plan, Temple of Victoria (from Pensabene 1988).

peripteral on three sides with eight lateral columns and rear corner pilasters.[21] A single staircase at the center of the façade provided access to a dipteral porch and, judging from the temple's proportions, Pensabene gives the temple a hexastyle façade.[22] The position of the cella wall foundations supports this conclusion, since a temple's cella walls typically align with two of its inner façade columns. The temple probably underwent substantial modifications to the front of the podium during construction of the sanctuary of Magna Mater in 204–191 and was heavily restored at the beginning of the first century after a fire in 111.[23]

If Pensabene's reconstruction is correct, the Palatine temple is the first known temple with colonnades on three sides since the Temple of Jupiter Optimus Maximus.[24] More significantly, perhaps, it is also the first hexastyle temple since the Capitoline temple. What is more remarkable still is that at 19.35 m by 33.40 m the temple was no broader than earlier tetrastyle temples, and similar or slightly narrower in width: the Temple of Castor was approximately 27.50 m wide, the Temple of Apollo Medicus approximately 21.45 m, and the Temple of Saturn in the range of 15–20 m. The columns of the Palatine temple must have been much more narrowly spaced. In the absence of a full set of column positions and dimensions, it is only possible to construct crude comparative interaxials for these early temples, but even these are telling (fig. 7.4). For the Temple of Capitoline Jupiter scholars calculate interaxials of approximately 7.30 m for the outer pair, and 8.65 and 12 m for the central columns;[25] for the Temple of Castor and the Temples of Fortuna and Mater Matuta around 7.50 m, and for the Temple of Apollo Medicus about 6.50 m.[26] The Palatine temple, by contrast, must have had interaxials measuring around 3.20 m (calculated by centering the lateral colonnades on the foundation walls, as Pensabene does). These set it closest to the earliest phases of the Temple of Portunus in the Forum Boarium with its interaxials of about 3.6 m and the slightly later Temple A in Largo Argentina (possibly the Temple of Juturna of ca. 241) at roughly 3.20 m. These last two temples were tetrastyle like earlier Republican temples but narrow, with façades of approximately 11 and 9.50 m respectively.[27] A very conservative estimate (calculated by combining the interaxials with slender lower column diameters of approximately the size of the early column fragment discovered at Temple C in Largo Argentina, 0.75 m)[28] would give the Palatine temple intercolumniations about two and one-half times its lower column diameters, just above Vitruvius's eustyle design (two and one-fourth column diameters)—but with thicker columns they could have been narrower, possibly systyle (two column diameters).

This abrupt swing away from broad, squat proportions toward a more slender, vertically accented appearance marks a radical shift in temple aesthetics, from the far end of the later Vitruvian spectrum to at least the center. Vitruvius noted the aesthetic and functional effects of the different façade styles and judged them in strong terms: in aeraeostyle temples "the columns stand further apart than is desirable" and "the appearance of [diastyle and aeraeostyle] temples is splayed,

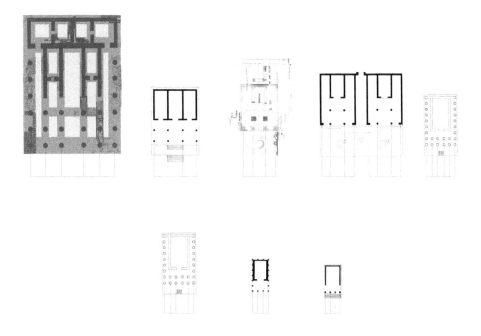

Fig. 7.4. Scale comparison of temple plans, with interaxials. *Top row, from left*: Temple of Jupiter Optimus Maximus, ca. 509: approximately 9.5–12 m; Temple of Castor, ca. 484: 8 m; Temple of Apollo Medicus, ca. 435: 6.5 m; Temples of Fortuna and Mater Matuta, early fourth century: 7.5 m; Temple of Victoria, ca. 294: 3.2 m. *Bottom row, from left*: Temple of Victoria, 294: 3.2 m; Temple of Portunus, late fourth/early third century: 3.6 m; Temple A, Area Sacra di Largo Argentina (Temple of Juturna?), ca. 241: 3.2 m.

top heavy, low, and sprawling." The diastyle design "has the following difficulty: because of the wide intercolumnar space the epistyle has a tendency to break." Eustyle, by contrast, "is the most laudable, and has principles developed with an eye to usefulness, attractiveness, and soundness. . . . The building's design will have an attractive appearance, its unimpeded entrance, utility, and the walkway around the cella, authority."[29]

I suggest that this striking aesthetic shift occurred because of the introduction of a stone entablature, which necessitated narrower intercolumniations than its wooden precursors. Pensabene reconstructs the temple with a wooden trabeation because of the discovery of architectural terracottas near the temple. These finds include fragments of openwork sima cresting, a strigillated sima, an architrave revetment with a vegetal frieze, and a *cortina pendula* (the terracotta sheathing hanging below the edge of an exposed beam). There is, however, no reason why a temple with a stone entablature could not have terracotta revetments, especially at the start of a transitional phase between construction materials. At Temple C at Selinunte, terracotta decorations appear to have coexisted with a stone superstructure,[30] and

Arvid Andrén notes that in Rome the practice of terracotta revetment lingered long after the use of stone entablatures should have rendered it obsolete.[31]

Terracotta sculptural fragments also came to light at the site, and Pensabene identifies them as a figure of Rhea Silvia holding a vessel, a bearded head of Jupiter, and an unbearded head of Dionysos (figs. 7.5 and 7.6). He assigns them to the pediment, characterizing the scene as a representation of the life of Romulus.[32] If so, they are the first known pedimental sculptures from a temple in Rome, and they indicate another striking change: the architect had shifted the rear wall of the pediment forward, in harmony with Greek temple design.

Fig. 7.5. Fragment of a terracotta pedimental figure of Jupiter from southwest Palatine. Palatine Antiquarium (photo P. Davies).

Peperino makes the likeliest choice for the entablature of the Palatine temple. Quarried in the Alban hills, it had become easily available to Roman architects from ca. 312 with the construction of the Via Appia, and Marie Jackson and Fabrizio Marra describe it as one of the most durable tufi—strongly grain-supported and well cemented, with good weight-bearing capacity.[33] There was probably a stucco coating on exposed parts of the podium and columns, with the dual objective of protecting the stone from moisture and giving it a decorative appearance.[34]

Ferdinando Castagnoli and Peter Wiseman propose that this Palatine podium should be recognized as the base for the Temple of Victoria. According to Livy, in his second consulship in 294, "after issuing a proclamation calling upon his soldiers to assemble at Sora, [L. Postumius Megellus] dedicated a temple to Victory, which he had built, as curule aedile, with money received from fines."[35] Castagnoli's and Wiseman's argument rests on a number of points. Dionysius of Halicarnassus claims that in the time of Evander a shrine of Victoria stood near the Lupercal—in other words, on the Palatine.[36] Livy relates that the aniconic black stone representing Magna Mater was stored in the Temple of Victoria between its arrival in Rome from Asia Minor and the completion of the Temple of Magna Mater, suggesting that the two buildings stood close to one another.[37] Two inscriptions naming Victoria—one on a fragment of Augustan marble architrave, the other on a Republican cippus—were discovered south of the church of S. Theodorus beneath the western corner of the Orti Farnesiani, having presum-

Fig. 7.6. Fragment of a terracotta pedimental figure of Dionysos from southwest Palatine. Palatine Antiquarium (photo P. Davies).

ably fallen from the temple terrace above.[38] Moreover, a temple depicted in a wall-painting of Rhea Silvia and her sons from the house of Fabius Secundus at Pompeii probably represents the Temple of Victoria. Livy also places M. Porcius Cato's *aedicula* to Victoria Virgo of 195 *prope aedem Victoriae* (near the Temple of Victoria), and a small podium next to the podium in question is sometimes thought to have accommodated this shrine.[39]

Claudia Cecamore prefers to identify the Palatine podium as the Temple of Jupiter Victor that Q. Fabius Maximus Rullianus vowed as consul during the final stages of battle at Sentinum in 295, and she would place Postumius Megellus's aedilician Temple of Victoria on the smaller podium alongside it. For her, this neatly solves two problems: the location of the Temple of Jupiter Victor, which the Regionary Catalogs place on the Palatine, and the question of whether an aedile could raise sufficient funds for a full-scale temple (see below).[40] As attractive as Cecamore's argument is, literary sources are consistent in calling the Temple of Victoria an *aedes* rather than an *aedicula*, implying that it was a full-scale temple, not a shrine.

A Sociopolitical Context

AS SPARSE AS INFORMATION IS ON THE EARLIEST TEM-ples of Republican Rome, they appear to demonstrate relative uniformity in form and material. This consistency can be explained by either of the prevailing views of Rome at that time. According to one model, the recently impoverished city, struggling to keep aggressive neighbors at bay, could no longer maintain the opulent lifestyle of regal times. According to the other, material austerity was a deliberate choice of the elite in the interests of *isonomia*; individual politicians held back from conspicuous display out of respect for constitutional principles.[41] Temple vows in these years apparently responded to state concerns, such as famine (the temple of the agrarian gods Ceres, Liber, and Libera on the Aventine, purportedly vowed by the dictator A. Postumius Albus just before the Battle of Lake Regillus), plague (Apollo Medicus, to whom Cn. Iulius, a consul of 433, vowed the temple when the city was gripped by prolonged illness),[42] and war (the Temple of Juno Regina, supposedly dedicated by M. Furius Camillus in ca. 392 as a measure of Rome's new supremacy over the Etruscans and heightened stature among the cities of Latium after the conquest of Veii, and the Temple of Semo Sancus Dius Fidius on the Quirinal, dedicated by Sp. Postumius Albinus in 466 after a victory over the Hernici, who had betrayed their alliance with Rome).[43] Some temples represented specific constituencies: the Temple of Ceres, Liber, and Libera may have been a stronghold of the plebeians, whereas the Temple of Castor, purportedly vowed immediately after the Battle of Lake Regillus by Postumius Albus and dedicated in 493 by his son, A. Postumius Albus Regillensis, was a patrician center;[44] the former temple and the Aventine Temple of Mercury of ca. 495 may have been responses to the debt-bondage crisis.[45] In a few cases, the political elite used temple commissions to shore up its collective power and, at times, to coax the masses into collaboration with its goals. For instance, recognizing that social inequities weakened the city and kept it from pursuing a more aggressive military policy, Postumius Albus may have hoped to persuade the masses to join battle by vowing the Temple of Ceres, Liber, and Libera.[46] Still, the political motivations behind these temple vows appear to represent group—not individual—agendas.

By contrast, circumstances conspired to make the end of the fourth century and the start of the third brutally competitive between members of the governing elite. One factor was the emancipation of the plebeians, who had gradually gained access to upper magistracies beginning with the Licinian-Sextian Law of 367. The *lex Genucia* of 342 reserved at least one consulship for a plebeian every year, and the *lex Publilia* of 339 established that at least one censor should be plebeian.[47] The last major obstacle crumbled with the *lex Ogulnia* of 300, which allowed plebeians into the colleges of the pontiffs and the augurs. Other laws aimed at relieving indebtedness, guaranteeing the right of popular appeal against magistrates' decisions, and making plebiscites binding helped to ease the plebeian path into politics.[48] With these changes the pool of candidates eligible for office increased dramatically, and a new political elite known as the *nobiles* emerged, determined not by inherited status or specialized religious knowledge as before but by personal merit and achievements in war.[49]

Secondly, during the course of the fourth century ongoing conflict on the edges of a growing territory exposed inadequacies in the command structure. With the consuls increasingly overextended in the field and in Rome, in 367 the electorate voted to establish the praetorship to assist them.[50] Though the *lex Genucia* of 342 banned politicians from holding the same magistracy more than once in ten years (in order to curb competition), in quasi-contradiction of the law and to allow Q. Publilius Philo to complete the capture of Naples in 326, the senate inaugurated the practice of prorogation (extension of authority in the role of proconsul or propraetor), to which it resorted repeatedly in ensuing decades.[51] Despite the apparent accessibility of the curule magistracies, prorogation led to a concentration of power in a small group of individuals whose extraordinary qualities it acknowledged and highlighted; it also kept consuls in a state of rivalry since they could hope for continued command after the end of a one-year term of office.

Finally, on the wider international stage this was the age of Alexander the Great and the struggle for succession between his generals after his death. To minimize their impact on Roman politicians would be to imagine an improbably isolated Italy. Word of Alexander's prowess appears to have echoed throughout the Mediterranean, transmitted especially through Sicily and south Italy, where Lysippos, the general's one-time portraitist, who had been instrumental in constructing the cult of his personality, had settled in 314.[52] In south Italy, for instance, Alexander's equestrian image was well known by the end of the fourth century; in Sicily the tyrant Agathocles chose to construct his defeat of the Carthaginians as a western analogy to Alexander's victory over the Persians.[53] In Rome at precisely this time, larger-than-life personalities began to dominate politics; they were ready to trust in their own charisma, flout instructions, and confound the senate. Fabius Maximus Rullianus was one such man: son of M. Fabius Ambustus (three times consul, *princeps senatus*, and active in Roman politics from 360 to 322), he was consul in 310, proconsul in 309, consul in 308, and proconsul in 307. During these terms he returned stunning Etruscan and Samnite victories. His administration of the grain supply in 299 delivered Rome from imminent famine. In 297, 296, and 295 he was elected consul without even standing, and he triumphed in 295 for a landmark victory at Sentinum over a vast Samnite, Etruscan, Umbrian, and Gallic coalition.[54] Thanks largely to the prejudices of his later relative Fabius Pictor, his fame survives;[55] but even allowing for the historian's embellishments to his life, Fabius Maximus Rullianus emerges as an over-life-size figure whose powerful confidence in his own abilities antagonized other members of the elite. A handful of other men, among them L. Papirius Cursor, M. Valerius Maximus Corvus, P. Decius Mus, and Postumius Megellus, strove to compete on similar terms, but their memories have faded.

The intense rivalry among politicians resulting from these combined circumstances played itself out in Rome's visual landscape, stimulating a marked phase of urban monumentalization.[56] Lacking a client base, ambitious plebeians and new men deployed innovative, aggressive tactics to emphasize their possession of the virtues of the new *nobilitas* in order to break into politics, as did patricians with weak lineage.

In the semi-private realm of funerary commemoration, where individuals had most latitude, architecture took a great leap forward in monumentality. The modest hypogea of earlier decades, cut horizontally into tufo embankments outside the city walls, gained external accentuation with large stone doors, as seen on Via San Stefano Rotondo on the Caelian and on the Esquiline.[57] More dramatic was the Tomb of the Scipios, probably commissioned at the end of the fourth century or the beginning of the third by L. Cornelius Scipio Barbatus (fig. 7.7).[58] Scion of an established family, he achieved some measure of political success as consul and victor over the Samnites in 298; yet in an age when generals triumphed three times (Fabius Maximus Rullianus or Papirius Cursor and M'. Curius Dentatus) or even four (Valerius Corvus), he was all but eclipsed for being unable to secure the honor even once. The design of his hypogeum tomb suggested otherwise, however. The embankment facade was cut and finished over an area of approximately 8 m in length and 2 m in height, and narrative frescoes covered the entire surface, probably extolling his role in subordinating enemy cities.[59] Within the tomb was a quad-

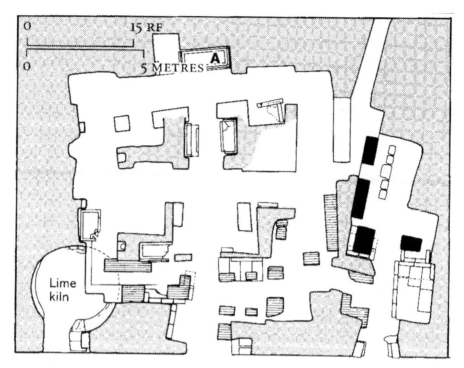

Fig. 7.7. Plan of the Tomb of the Scipios. Early phase: quadrangular chamber to the left (adapted from Claridge 1998).

Fig. 7.8. Sarcophagus of Scipio Barbatus. Vatican Museums (photo P. Davies).

rangular network of corridors, with intersecting galleries at the center. At the end of the central corridor on axis with the entrance stood his monumental peperino sarcophagus, identified by inscriptions (fig. 7.8).[60] Its axial placement and altarlike design—with Ionic volutes at the ends of the lid and a Doric frieze with rosettes on the chest—evoked a Hellenistic kingly *heroön*.[61]

Meanwhile, other members of the elite began to construct tombs above ground. A series of single-cella rectangular tombs built of peperino *opera quadrata* was conspicuously sited just outside the Porta Esquilina in the recent fortifications and alongside the consular roads (the Via Praenestina and Via Labicana).[62] Like the Tomb of the Scipios, some were painted. A fragment of painting preserves scenes of parlay and battle in four superposed registers; labels identifying two of the protagonists suggest that the tomb belonged either to the Fabii (Fabius Maximus Rullianus or his son Fabius Maximus Gurgetes) or to the Fannii, a less illustrious family known from later records.[63]

In the public realm of civic building, it was at this time that censors began to exploit the responsibilities of the magistracy to advance their political careers. As well as counting the citizenry, the censor controlled contracts for the expenditure of public money collected through taxes and rent on the *ager publicus*, and when both increased with the conquest of Latium in 338, the censorship grew commensurately in stature.[64] By 312 Ap. Claudius (later Caecus), a patrician from a relatively lackluster family, had served as military tribune and curule aedile but found himself unable to land a consulship.[65] Instead he stood for and won the censorship. His censorial measures were unusually aggressive and proved highly provocative to the elite. Among them were two ground-breaking contracts: Rome's first major road and Rome's first aqueduct.[66] Extending 132 miles from the Porta Capena to Capua, the Via Appia served Rome's growing hegemony; a fast route for military deployment to the south, it linked recently acquired territories in southern Latium and Campania to ensure Rome's dominance in previously Hellenized regions. Yet since these territories were valuable centers of voting power, it also served the interests of a man with little inherited political capital and no time to waste in developing a clientele. The thoroughfare enhanced economic development for those regions and for Rome—and opened an easy path to Roman elections for his new clients.[67] The Aqua Appia, for its part, conveyed an astounding 75,000 m^2 of water a day from a source over 16 km away along the Via Praenestina. There is no indication that a shortage of water prompted this project; rather, judging from the aqueduct's distribution point near the Porta Trigemina at the Clivus Publicius on the northwest side of the Aventine, its principal purpose was to benefit plebeians and merchants in this bustling commercial zone.[68]

Taken together, Ap. Claudius's measures seem to have been innovative strategies for rewarding and earning the gratitude of politically useful groups in order to win election to the consulship. Often his tactics pushed against the limits of legality; often they infuriated his opponents, plebeian and patrician alike. In terms of building, his censorship broke new ground, not just by introducing new architectural forms but also in the extent to which he recognized the enormous power in granting contracts and his skillful exploitation of his magisterial mandate to amass political capital.[69] Through utilitarian building projects he also raised standards of living in order to win favor; without even seeking senatorial approval, he used state funds to approximate the euergetism of Hellenistic dynasts.[70] Diodorus Siculus insists that Romans understood that the Via Appia would be an "immortal" monument to the censor, because instead of naming it for function, location, or destination, he named it—and the aqueduct—for himself.[71] The choice of his *praenomen* completed the analogy with Philip of Macedon or Alexander, who gave their first names to cities they founded. Though patrician, Ap. Claudius played directly to the electoral strength of the plebeian masses.[72] His strategy would become a favorite recourse for those who lacked the support of, or had alienated, the senatorial elite.

At the same time triumphing generals began to explore ways to translate the fleeting fame of their triumphs into permanent memorials.[73] As consul during the Samnite War in 311, C. Iunius Bubulcus became the first consular general and the first plebeian to vow a temple.[74] Fabius Pictor then decorated the cella walls of his Temple of Salus with paintings, probably representing his triumph.[75] Both commissions inaugurated new trends. Generals also began to convert their spoils into lasting monuments rather than simply depositing them or their value in the state treasury. Papirius Cursor probably led the charge as consul in 308, when he distributed enemy shields around the *tabernae* in the Forum to celebrate his third victory over the Samnites, but others were close behind: in 293 his son of the same name displayed Samnite spoils around the city and particularly at his father's Temple of Quirinus.[76] In the same year Sp. Carvilius melted down his spoils to supply bronze for a colossal statue of Jupiter in the *area Capitolina* along with a smaller statue of himself.[77]

Postumius Megellus

LIKE AP. CLAUDIUS, POSTUMIUS MEGELLUS WAS A patrician but lacked an illustrious pedigree. He was the first member of the *gens* Postumia to hold political office since the humiliating defeat and abdication of the consul Sp. Postumius Albinus at the Battle of the Caudine Forks in 321, when the Samnites forced the army to pass under the yoke in submission.[78] Presumably he intended his grand Temple of Victoria to put him on the political map. Hexastyle, peripteral on three sides and all stone, it conveyed the majesty and monumentality of the Hellenistic world to the heart of Rome. It also seems to have been the first temple of Rome after the Temple of Jupiter Optimus Maximus to be sited for spectacular visibility (fig. 7.9): with its prospect over the Circus Maximus and the Forum Boarium, it was the Palatine mirror of the Capitoline temple. This topographical relationship underscored a common symbolic value of cultural expansionism: in their respective forms, both temples pushed beyond Roman boundaries, reaching out to the wider Mediterranean world. Also built into the vast *platea* on which it stood was an ancient *fossa* that must have come to light during embankment work. This was set off and monumentalized as Romulus's mythical hut, the *casa Romuli*. Pensabene draws an analogy between this phase of monumentalization on the Palatine and the Athenian Acropolis, where the Parthenon honored Athena as a victory goddess and the Erechtheion celebrated Athens' foundation myth.[79]

The very choice of Victoria bespeaks Postumius Megellus's engagement in the competitive fray of the age. From classical times in Greece, victory had served as the justification of authority that was essentially illegal—that is, authority assumed without the consent of the governed. Once it was construed as a divine gift from the goddess Victoria or from Jupiter, victory in and of itself justified a victor's supremacy. Fourth-century kings subsequently adopted what scholars have termed a "theology of victory" to justify individual rule lacking any constitutional basis.[80] This concept was paramount to Alexander's success: he encouraged a notion that

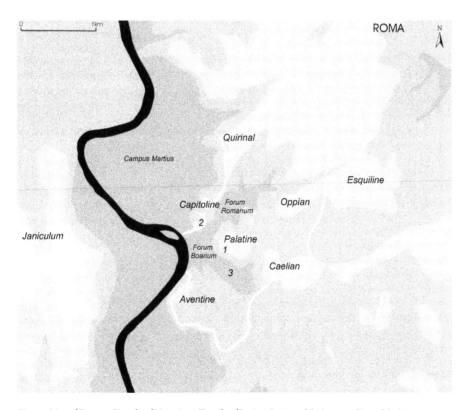

Fig. 7.9. Map of Rome. 1: Temple of Victoria; 2: Temple of Jupiter Optimus Maximus; 3: Circus Maximus

it was not just his personal capabilities or *arête* that guided him, but a divine gift, *eutychia*, which gave him a special charisma. The concept quickly migrated west. Only upon declaring victory against the Carthaginians in 304 did Agathocles assume the royal title, and he issued coins depicting a Nike crowning a trophy.[81] As the Samnite Wars drew to an end, victory and the theme of invincibility grew prevalent in Rome, where they neatly justified imperial expansion through military force. In theory victory belonged to the state, but like Alexander, Roman generals began to construct their successes as the outcome of their personal qualities combined with the personalized favor of the gods.

A sudden burst of temple vows associated with victory followed closely on the construction of Postumius Megellus's temple and reflects this trend. In 296, Ap. Claudius vowed a temple to Bellona Victrix while battling Samnites and Etruscans (and the temple became a primary location for debates over granting triumphs).[82] Fabius Maximus Rullianus next vowed a temple to Jupiter Victor for his victory at Sentinum in 295.[83] In 294, the year Postumius Megellus dedicated his temple, Fabius Maximus Rullianus's son-in-law Atilius Regulus vowed a temple to Jupiter Stator, who promised victory in dangerous circumstances.[84] In concept these buildings clearly responded to Postumius Megellus's building. Whether they responded in form is up for conjecture; but it might be worth noting that on fragments 31d–e of the *Forma Urbis Romae*, Ap. Claudius's Temple of Bellona Victrix— the only one for which there is any evidence at all for form—is hexastyle, on a podium of about the same width as the Temple of Apollo Medicus.[85]

At no point does Livy indicate when Postumius Megellus was aedile. Although it is likely that he took the post before his first consulship in 305—in 306 or 307 perhaps—the progression of the *cursus honorum* was not established until the *lex annalis* of 180. Finding the ten-year interval between his first consulship and his propraetorship of 295 problematic, J. Seidel suggested that his aedileship followed his first consulship.[86] Adam Ziolkowski is skeptical that an aedile could raise sufficient funds through fines to finance a large temple, and believes that he vowed it as consul in 305 in connection with his conquest of Bovianum; Livy's claim reflects an ancient attempt to discredit him.[87] In this case the temple would probably celebrate the charisma that led him to victory. From the edge of the Palatine, it looked out proudly over the path of the triumphal procession as it widened into the Circus Maximus.

Yet as Cecamore stresses, Livy's source for Postumius Megellus's accomplishments is generally favorable, according him a triumph in 305 that does not survive in the *Fasti Triumphales* and describing his successes in 294 as a glorious antithesis to the difficulties that beset his colleague.[88] Moreover, hostility between Postumius Megellus and the two dominant factions in Rome—the Claudii and the Fabii—may go some way to explaining the interval between his curule offices. Assessments of the amounts of money aediles could raise in fines and use for public projects must take into account the novelty of the practice in these years; Postumius Megellus may even have initiated it. If Livy's account is to be trusted and Postumius Megellus made the vow as aedile, it presumably honored the goddess in return for the state's divinely inspired military success. Yet in this case too there may have been an additional self-promotional motive. Livy does not specify the source of the fines Postumius Megellus collected. In the years immediately following his aedileship, Livy records, most of the fines used by the aediles to create artworks or monuments were levied against the landed and moneyed elite in enforcement of fourth-century laws banning usury (particularly the *lex Genucia* of 342, which abolished interest on usury) and illegal grazing on the *ager publicus* (such as a law of 356 that limited individual holdings of public land to 500 *iugera*).[89] More than that, it was fairly transparent that the artworks or monuments themselves celebrated plebeian advances into the political structure. Thus as curule aedile in 304 Cn. Flavius used income from fines on usurers to dedicate a bronze shrine to Concordia at the Comitium. Close by he publicized the calendrical *fasti*, previously reserved by the pontiffs. Ostensibly the shrine celebrated the conciliation between plebeians and patricians, yet in doing so it inevitably rejoiced in the headway made by plebeians like himself, and Livy reports that the shrine provoked *summa invidia nobilium*.[90]

Similarly, as curule aediles in 296 Cn. and Q. Ogulnius

> brought a number of usurers to trial, and, confiscating their possessions, employed the share which came to the public treasury to put brazen thresholds in the Capitol, and silver vessels for the three tables in the shrine of Jupiter, and a statue of the god in a four-horse chariot on the roof, and at the fig-tree Ruminalis a representation of the infant Founders of the City being suckled by the wolf. They also made a paved walk of squared stone from the Porta Capena to the temple of Mars.[91]

As tribune of the plebs in 300 Q. Ogulnius had championed the *lex Ogulnia*, and so his political status and leanings were no secret. The brothers' dedications at Rome's principal temple, honoring the god who bestowed victory, served as a commentary on this triumph: bronze thresholds symbolized access to the realm of religion, while the silver vessels suggested a stake in ritual affairs. The paved road for its part was a tract of the Via Appia, which at its start and its destination favored the plebeian voting bloc.[92] Perhaps the most aggressive of their commissions was the sculpture of the she-wolf suckling Romulus and Remus; the first known appearance of Remus as a brother to Romulus in Rome's foundation myth, it emphasized the new parity between plebeians and patricians.[93] Meanwhile the plebeian aediles of 296, "Lucius Paetus and Gaius Fulvius Curvus, likewise with the money from fines, which they exacted from convicted graziers, held games and provided golden bowls for the temple of Ceres,"[94] and in doing so inaugurated a long-standing tradition of plebeian aediles using fines to make dedications of vessels and sculptures at the plebeian stronghold.

Given these patterns it is likely that Postumius Megellus also used fines against the elite; taking his cue from Ap. Claudius, in other words, he used his magistracy to garner political support from the plebeian ranks. The temple's location suggests as much: looking out over the east end of the Circus Maximus, it stood in topographical dialogue with the Aventine; moreover, incorporated within the southern extension of its massive substructures was a monumentalized version of the Archaic rocky path leading to the Velabrum and the Forum Boarium, Rome's commercial district and port. The new road even took its name from the temple, the *Clivus Victoriae*.[95] It is tempting to understand Victoria as a goddess with two aspects, addressing not only victory abroad but also—implicitly—victory at home, as she would do in the late 120s.[96]

Whether or not it celebrated a plebeian cause, Postumius Megellus's temple was his bid for visibility. His career advanced: after his consulship of 305, the capture of Bovianum and his magnificent Samnite victory, he was appointed propraetor against Etruscan forces in 295.[97] His failure to align himself with either of Rome's dominant factions left him vulnerable to elite hostility, and indeed the senate denied him a triumph in his second consulship of 294 despite spectacular successes against the Samnites and the Etruscans, possibly claiming excessive losses.[98] Citing cases when consuls triumphed by vote of the people, but recognizing that certain tribunes of the plebs would impose their veto if he put the matter to a popular vote, Postumius Megellus proclaimed that his triumph was the people's will. In the face of seven tribunes and the whole senate, with three tribunes at the ready to block any opposition, he triumphed the next day.[99] His defiance did not go unrewarded: at the end of his third consulship in 291, during which he drove the proconsul Fabius Maximus Gurges from his army as it besieged Cominium in Samnium, he was convicted of using military labor on his estate and fined 50,000 silver pieces.[100] Still, in 282 he was selected to head an embassy to Tarentum to demand restitution for the Thurines and the Romans, perhaps because he was one of the oldest living exconsuls.[101] F. Cassola saw him as one of the most influential men of his generation;[102] yet unlike his primary competitors, the Fabii, the Claudiii, the Fulvii, and the Atilii, whose families prospered in the third century, he failed to produce a large and illustrious family, and this probably cost him his place in history. His only son, also L. Postumius Megellus, was consul in 262 and praetor in 253 but did not win a triumph despite his capture of Agrigento.[103] Postumius Megellus may even have lost credit for a triumph or two in the *Fasti Triumphales* as a result of later falsification and captation (after-the-fact expropriation of a triumph actually celebrated by a colleague in office), which became a common practice when subsequent genera- tions of other families exalted their own ancestors in funerary orations.[104]

I have suggested that, if Pensabene's reconstruction of the Temple of Victoria as a hexastyle building is accurate, it may be the first temple in Rome with a stone entablature. Given the paucity of archaeological and literary evidence for this early period, I offer this proposal in the spirit of speculation. However, it might go some small way toward explaining why, after defeating the Carthaginians decisively with a spectacular naval victory in 241 and effectively ending the First Punic War, the consul C. Lutatius Catulus may have raised such a diminutive temple to the wa- ter goddess Juturna in Largo Argentina (fig. 7.4) next to a substantially larger pre- existing temple (possibly to Feronia). Perhaps his building derived a compensatory monumentality from a stone entablature.

Notes

I dedicate this essay to Ingrid Edlund-Berry, a generous col- league and a valued friend. The research for this paper was supported by a Hugh Last Fellow- ship at the British School at Rome, funded by the British Academy. I owe thanks to Matt Cat- terall, Michael Davies, Janet DeLaine, Mario Erasmo, John Hopkins, James Packer, and Mark Wilson Jones for their input at various stages, and, most of all, to Gretchen Meyers and Michael Thomas for inspiring and developing this book project.

1. At an astounding 54 × 72 m, the Temple of Jupiter on the Capitoline dwarfed other tem- ples on the Italian peninsula; its dimensions set it alongside the great Archaic temples in the Greek cities of Ionia and Sicily. Mura Sommella 2001; Davies 2006; Hopkins 2010. For comparanda, see Dinsmoor 1975, 99, 101, 124, 127, 134; Lawrence 1983, 146.
2. Vitr. *De arch.* 3.2.5; Gros 1973.
3. Ziolkowski 1988; *contra* Coarelli 1988, 180–204.
4. Frank 1924, 23–24.
5. Plin. *HN* 16.36; Cifani 2001, 55–61: "L'impiego di trabeazioni lignee rimarrà infatti diffuso a Roma fino all'avvento del calcestruzzo (fine III, inizi II sec. a.C.), ed insieme ad esso l'uso di scandole lignee, attestato fino al III a.C. in base ad un passo di Cornelio Nepote, riportato nella *Naturalis Historia* di Plinio il Vecchio che ricorda l'impiego diffuso di rivestimenti lignei dei tetti a Roma fino alla guerra con Pirro."
6. Cairoli Giuliani 1982, 34: "Questo motivo si puó ricercare sì in un attaccamento partico- lare alla tradizione, evidente soprattutto per i luoghi di culto, ma soprattutto in un'oggettiva difficoltà di costruzione, derivante dall'uso di avere intercolumni molto ampi, più facil- mente superabili con strutture di legno."
7. See Ziolkowski 1992; Orlin 1997.

8. Pensabene 1982; Nielsen and Poulsen 1992; Coarelli 1999a.

9. For the extensive bibliography, see Pisani Sartorio 1995. On the date, see Hopkins 2010, ch. 3.

10. Viscogliosi 1993; 1996, 15–43.

11. Buzzetti 1999.

12. The podium measured at least 38.20 × 21.45 m, of which the cella block occupied only approximately 25 × 21.45 m; Ciancio Rossetti 1997–1998, 189. There was a similar definition of space at the Sanctuary of Fortuna and Mater Matuta, where the twin temples stood at the rear of a large peperino *opera quadrata* platform measuring approximately 47 × 47 m.

13. The evidence at the Temple of Apollo Medicus is inconclusive, and could support either a prostyle arrangement or a pair of columns *in antis*.

14. Nielsen and Poulsen 1992, 78.

15. Vitr. *De arch.* 3.3.4–5 (trans. Rowland and Howe).

16. La Rocca 1990, 295; Nielsen and Poulsen 1992, 78.

17. Varro *Ling.* 5.66; Non. 793; Coarelli 1999c; Jackson and Marra 2006, 425.

18. The Temple of Castor and Pollux had revetment plaques with a cream, red, and black strigil pattern, sima plaques with a cream and reddish-brown guilloche pattern, and openwork cresting with spiral bands and palmettes in cream, red, and black, all perhaps from the pediment area. The pediment antefixes depict diademed maenads and *silenoi*, and heads of Juno Sospita and a *silenos* may have alternated along the eaves; see Grønne 1992. Fragments of terracotta revetment with a painted meander pattern survive from the Temple of Apollo Medicus; see Ciancio Rossetto 1997–1998, 193–195; 1999. A terracotta head from the Aracoeli gardens may be part of an acroterial sculpture, dated stylistically to the first half of the fifth century; see Giannelli 1982; Cifani 2008, 77.

19. Andrén 1940, ccxii.

20. Pensabene 1988; 1991, 11; 1998, 26–34, 1999; Pensabene and D'Alessio 2006.

21. Pensabene 1991, 11.

22. Pensabene 1988; 1991, 11: "Un doppio colonnato sul fronte ricostruibile come esastilo per le dimensione." Pensabene divides the entire platform into 28 squares of 16 × 16 ft., of which the cella occupies eight (two wide, four long), the pronaos eight (four wide, two long), and the podium's avancorpo four (four wide, one long). The resulting dimensions for the podium are 64 × 118 ft, supporting a temple of 32 × 64 ft, with a cella : *alae* ratio of 2 : 1 and a cella : pronaos : avancorpo ratio of 4 : 2 : 1. These proportions make it analogous to the north temple in the Forum Holitorium, Temple C in Largo Argentina, the Italic Temple at Paestum, and the Temple of Juno at Gabii; see Pensabene 1991, 11.

23. Pensabene and D'Alessio 2006.

24. Other examples of early peripteral temples are known at Pyrgi (Temple B), Satricum (Temple II), and Vulci (peripteral temple); see Hopkins 2010, 272.

25. Hopkins 2010.

26. See calculations in Rowe 1989 and plans in Nielsen and Poulsen 1992; Viscogliosi 1996.

27. Coarelli 1981, 16; Ruggiero 1991–1992.

28. Coarelli 1981, 14.

29. Vitr. *De arch.* 3.3.1, 3.3.5, 3.3.6 (trans. Rowland and Howe).

30. I am grateful to John N. Hopkins for drawing my attention to this parallel.

31. Andrén 1940, ccxlii: "Even in Rome terracotta decoration in the form of crestings, figured antefixes, etc., lingered on the roofs of stone temples of Greek order, as is shown by the Republican temples in the Largo Argentina." According to Pensabene (1991, 14), peperino column fragments among the *caementa* in the first-century BCE foundations may

argue for a stone colonnade resting on the early Grotta Oscura podium. He notes that the peperino *caementa* were fluted, which could support an additional hypothesis that the temple was Ionic. All the same, as he notes, they may well come from a restoration phase during the construction of the Temple of Magna Mater, especially since he also finds peperino Corintho-Italic capitals.

32. Pensabene and d'Alessio 2006, 32 and n. 5.

33. Jackson and Marra 2006, 428; also Vitr. *De arch.* 2.7.1. As Temple C in Largo Argentina (possibly the Temple of Feronia of ca. 290) indicates, architects could use different types of stone in different parts of a building. See also Frank (1924, 23–24), who judged that "though ugly," peperino was the only stone available at the time that could bear the weight of the roof and tolerate carving.

34. Jackson and Marra 2006, 429.

35. Livy 10.33 (adapted from the Loeb translation); Castagnoli 1964, 185–186.

36. Dion. Hal. 1.32.5.

37. Livy 29.14.13.

38. *CIL* 6 31060, 1² 805 = 6 3733; 6 31060; Wiseman 1981, 36–40. See also Pensabene 1980, 73; Ziolkowski 1992, 173.

39. Livy 35.9.6; Wiseman 1981; Pensabene 1985, 200–201; Ziolkowski 1992, 173. The podium measures approximately 7 × 12 m. But see Pensabene 1998.

40. Cecamore 2002, 122–126. She also identifies the temple of Victoria on a series of Campana plaques. She finds the eleven or so years taken to complete the temple between an early aedileship and the consecration of 194 to be "eccessivamente dilatati," though the size of the enterprise (the large podium, on top of a substantial platea) adequately justifies the time frame.

41. See Flower 2010, 37; Smith 2006, 316. See also Torelli 2006, 85–86; 2007, 113.

42. Livy 4.25.3, 4.29.7, 40.51.6; Orlin 1997, 22; Torelli 2007, 113.

43. Juno Regina: Livy 5.21.3, 22.6–7, 23.7, 31.3, 52.10; La Rocca 1990, 313; Andreussi 1996a. Semo Sancus Dius Fidius: Tert. *Ad nat.* 2.9.28; Dion. Hal. 9.60.8; Varro *Ling.* 5.66; Non. 793; Coarelli 1999c. Livy (6.5.8) offers little historical context for a Temple of Mars that T. Quinctius dedicated as *duumvir sacris faciendis* in 388.

44. Livy 2.20.12.

45. Livy 2.27.6–7; Val. Max. 9.3.6; Andreussi 1996c; Oakley 2004, 16. See also Torelli 2007, 112. La Rocca (1990, 325) suggests that the presence of two myrtle trees at L. Papirius Cursor's Temple of Quirinus—one patrician and one plebeian—also symbolizes pride in easing social tensions.

46. La Rocca 1990, 295; Orlin 1997, 24, 111. See also the temple to Concordia, which according to literary tradition represented the combined interests of plebeians and patricians in ca. 367. Ov. *Fast.* 1.641-4; Plut. *Cam.* 42.4-6; La Rocca 1990, 313–314; Ferroni 1993; Torelli 2007, 116–117.

47. Lintott 1999, 37.

48. Oakley 2004, 18–19. The last plebeian secession, still on account of indebtedness, was in 287, after which plebiscites were reaffirmed.

49. Oakley 2004, 19–21; Flower 2010, 51–52.

50. Brennan 2000, 58–75.

51. Lintott 1999, 113.

52. Bastien 2007, 168.

53. Ferrary 1988, 578–588; Bastien 2007, 167.

54. Livy 10.11.9, 10.13, 10.15, 10.22.

55. Bastien 2007, 13.

56. See Torelli 2006, 90–98; 2007, 118–123.

57. Santa Maria Scrinari 1968; La Rocca 1973; 1990, 321; Albertoni 1983.

58. Or, less probably, his son L. Cornelius Scipio, consul in 259.

59. La Rocca 1977; 1990, 354ff.; Coarelli 1988, 8–9; Talamo 2008a, 119.

60. See also the Tomb of the Cornelii for fledgling signs of personalized commemoration (Pisani Sartorio and Quilici Gigli 1987–1988).

61. The closest parallels for the sarcophagus are a series of small altars produced in Sicily and a monumental altar to Hieron II in Syracuse; see Zevi 1973, 238; Humm 1996, 742.

62. Lanciani 1875, 190–191; Lissi Carona 1969, 85–87.

63. Lanciani 1875, 191; Pinza 1914. For the Fabii: Coarelli 1976. For the Fannii: La Rocca 1984. See also Oriolo 1996; Talamo 2008b.

64. Lintott 1999, 115–120. The first to exploit it was probably C. Maenius, one of the first generation of plebeian consuls and only the third plebeian censor in Rome's history. He probably used state funds to modify the northwest side of the Forum, close to the Comitium, relocating the butchers' shops further northeast to a zone beyond the Forum, leaving bankers and moneychangers to take over the shops on the northeast side of the piazza. Above these redesigned *tabernae argentariae* were erected wooden balconies, from which crowds could view spectacles in the center of the Forum as well as the rostra of enemy ships and the equestrian statues that the people had erected on the Comitium to honor the consuls of 338. Taking his name, these balconies were known as *maeniana*. Varro fr. 72; Torelli 2006, 90–91; 2007, 119–124.

65. His grandfather, Appius Claudius Crassus Inregilensis, was tribune (403) and dictator (362) before assuming an undistinguished consulship in 349; his father, C. Claudius Inregilensis, was no sooner appointed dictator in 337 than he abdicated. MacBain 1980, 360–361.

66. He reorganized the city's voting tribes to benefit landless urban dwellers; drew up a revised list of senators that the consuls refused to recognize in 311; established the *duumviri navales* to oversee the equipping and refitting of warships; arrogated the cult of the Ara Maxima from the extinct *gens* Potitia to the state; and may even have introduced silver coinage. He was the first censor to prolong his term (without his colleague) beyond the customary eighteen months to accomplish his goals. Stuart Staveley 1959; MacBain 1980; Cornell 1995, 373–377; Humm 1996, 732; Humm 2005; Torelli 2006, 92.

67. Stuart Staveley 1959, 418–419; MacBain 1980, 364; Humm 1996, 744–746. Though the majority of the Campanian citizenry lacked suffrage, they could use their wealth and contacts to enhance the censor's prestige.

68. Torelli 2007, 127–128.

69. As Polybius did over 150 years later: 6.17. Torelli 2007, 119.

70. La Rocca 1990, 324; Humm 1996, 733.

71. MacBain 1980, 361.

72. It propelled him on his way to a stellar career. An inscription from the Forum at Arretium (Arezzo) records his offices: after his censorship he was twice consul, dictator, quaestor, curule aedile, and three times interrex: *CIL* 1²: 10 = *ILS* 54.

73. On the process see Hölscher 2006.

74. Livy 10.1.9. Ziolkowski 1992, 242.

75. Plin. *HN* 35.19; Val. Max. 8.14.6; Dion. Hal. 16.3.6; Holliday 1980.

76. Livy 10.46.2–8; La Rocca 1990, 346. The passage is problematic because it closely mirrors the account of his son's behavior in 293 and some scholars therefore discredit it. See Hölscher 1978, 320; Bastien 2007, 158–159.

77. Plin. *HN* 34.43; Sehlmeyer 1999, 113–116.

78. See sources in Broughton 1951, 150–151; Cecamore 2002, 146.

79. Pensabene and D'Alessio 2006, 33.

80. Gagé 1933; Fears 1981.

81. Fears 1981; Bastien 2007, 154.

82. Bastien 2007, 154.

83. Livy 10.29.14; Bastien 2007, 154. On its location see summary of views in Cecamore 2002, 99–114.

84. Livy 10.37.15; Coarelli 1996; Bastien 2007, 154. By 300 a statue of Victoria had also been dedicated in the Forum.

85. Viscogliosi 1993, 192.

86. Seidel 1908, 12–13.

87. Ziolkowski 1992, 174.

88. Cecamore 2002, 122–123.

89. A Licinian-Sextian law of 366 relieved plebeian indebtedness; and the *lex Poetelia* of 326 outlawed debt bondage. Fabius Maximus Gurges' vow of a temple to Venus Obsequens when he was curule aedile in 295 may be an exception. According to Livy (10.31.9) he funded it using fines on adulterous women, though Servius describes it as an ex-voto after the end of the Samnite War (*Aen.* 1.720). La Rocca 1990, 325; Papi 1999; Bastien 2007, 182–183.

90. Son of a freedman, he had served as scribe to Ap. Claudius, who helped to raise him to curule status. Livy 9.46.6; Plin. *NH* 33.19; Ferroni 1993; Torelli 2007, 122.

91. Livy 10.23.13 (Loeb translation).

92. In 238 the plebeian aediles L. and M. Publicius would use fines levied on illegal lessors of public grazing lands to extend the road within the walls; the first paved street inside the city, their *Clivus Publicius* traversed the mercantile district and climbed the Aventine. Varro *Ling.* 5.158; Ov. *Fast.* 5.275; Festus 276L; Coarelli 1993; Staccioli 2003, 17–19.

93. Dulière 1979, 55–56; Holleman 1987; DeRose Evans 1992, 59–86; Wiseman 1995, 73, 107–128; Torelli 2007, 122.

94. Livy 10.23.13. Ti. Sempronius Gracchus's later Temple of Jupiter Libertas of 238 also stood on the Aventine; see Ziolkowski 1992, 85–87; Andreussi 1996b.

95. Pensabene and D'Alessio 2006, 33.

96. On the reverse of denarii of M. Porcius Laeca, Victoria crowns Libertas in a quadriga, in response to the *leges Porciae de provocatione*. See Fears 1981, 786.

97. Livy 10.32–34, 37.1–12; Zon. 8.1.

98. Livy 10.36.19, but also 10.37.13–14, and Dion. Hal. 17[18].5.3, who places his triumph in 291. See summary of ancient accounts in Cecamore 2002, 146–147.

99. Livy 10.37.11–12; Bastien 2007, 102–108; Pelikan Pittenger 2008, 42–44.

100. Livy *Per.* 11; Vell. 1.14.16; Dion. Hal. 17–18.5.4; Càssola 1963, 194–198; Bastien 2007, 107.

101. Dion. Hal. 19.5, 6.3; App. *Sam.* 7.2; Dio fr. 39.6–8; Zon. 8.2. See other sources in Broughton 1951, 189–190.

102. Càssola 1963, who posits that he may have tended toward the interests of small farmers. See refutal in Cecamore 2002, 149.

103. Bastien 2007, 112.

104. Bastien 2007, 85–118, 163; Gagé 1957, 16. These orations served the purpose of focusing attention on pedigree, and implicit in the practice were two notions: that ability was hereditary, and that an ancestor who had served Rome well deserved a gratitude that the electorate could repay to his progeny.

Bibliography

Albertoni, M. 1983. "La necropolis esquilina arcaica e repubblicana." In *L'archeologia in Roma capitale tra sterro e scavo*, 140–155. Venice: Marsilio.

Alexander, M. C. 2006. "Law in the Roman Republic." In *A Companion to the Roman Republic*, ed. N. Rosenstein and R. Morstein-Marx, 236–255. Oxford: Blackwell.

Andrén, A. 1940. *Architectural Terracottas from Etrusco-Italic Temples*. Lund: C. W. K. Gleerup.

Andreussi, M. 1996a. "Iuno Regina." *LTUR* 3:125–126.

———. 1996b. "Iuppiter Libertas, aedes." *LTUR* 3:144.

———. 1996c. "Mercurius, aedes." *LTUR* 3:245–247.

Bastien, J.-L. 2007. *Le triomphe romain et son utilisation politique à Rome aux trois derniers siècles de la république*. Rome: École française de Rome.

Brennan, T. C. 2000. *The Praetorship in the Roman Republic*, vol. 1. Oxford: Oxford University Press.

Broughton, T. R. S. 1951. *Magistrates of the Roman Republic*, vol. 1. New York: American Philological Association.

Buzzetti, C. 1999. "Portunus, aedes." *LTUR* 4:153–154.

Cairoli Giuliani, F. 1982. "Architettura e tecnica edilizia." In *Roma repubblicana fra il 509 e il 270 a.C.*, ed. I. Dondero and P. Pensabene, 29–36. Rome: Quasar.

Càssola, F. 1963. *I gruppi politici romani nel III sec. a.C.* Rome: L'Erma di Bretschneider.

Castagnoli, F. 1964. "Note sulla topografia del Palatino e del Foro Boario." *ArchCl* 16:173–199.

Cecamore, C. 2002. *Palatium: Topografia storica del Palatino tra III sec. a.C. e I sec. d.C.* Rome: L'Erma di Bretschneider.

Ciancio Rossetto, P. 1997–1998. "Tempio di Apollo: Nuove indagini sulla fase repubblicana." *RendPontAc* 70:177–195.

———. 1999. "Apollo, aedes in circo." *LTUR* 5:224–225.

Cifani, G. 2001. "Le origini dell'architettura in pietra a Roma." In *From Huts to Houses: Transformations of Ancient Societies. Proceedings of an International Seminar Organized by the Norwegian and Swedish Institutes in Rome, 21–24 September 1997*, 55–61. Stockholm: Svenska institutet in Rom.

———. 2008. *Architettura romana arcaica: Edilizia e società tra monarchia e repubblica*. Rome: L'Erma di Bretschneider.

Claridge, A. 1998. *Rome: An Oxford Archaeological Guide*. Oxford: Oxford University Press.

Coarelli, F. 1976. "Cinque frammenti di una tomba dipinta dall'Esquilino." In *Affreschi romani dalle raccolte dell'Antiquarium Comunale*, 22–28. Rome: Assessorato antichità, belle arti e problemi della cultura.

———. 1981. "L'area sacra di Largo Argentina: Topografia e storia." In *L'Area sacra di Largo Argentina*, by F. Coarelli, I. Kajanto, U. Nyberg, and M. Steinby, 11–51. Rome: Studi e materiali dei Musei e monumenti comunali di Roma.

———. 1988. *Il Foro Boario dalle origini alla fine della repubblica*. Rome: Quasar.

———. 1993. "Clivus Publicius." *LTUR* 1:284.

———. 1996. "Iuppiter Stator, aedes, fanum, templum." *LTUR* 3:155–157.

———. 1999a. "Saturnus, aedes." *LTUR* 4:234–236.

———. 1999b. "Quirinus, sacellum." *LTUR* 4:185–187.

———. 1999c. "Semo Sancus in colle, aedes, fanum, sacellum, templum." *LTUR* 4:263–264.

Cornell, T. J. 1995. *The Beginnings of Rome: Italy and Rome from the Bronze Age to the Punic Wars (c. 1000–264 B.C.).* London: Routledge.

Davies, P. J. E. 2006. "Exploring the International Arena: The Tarquins' Aspirations for the Temple of Jupiter Optimus Maximus." In *Proceedings of the XVIth International Congress of Classical Archaeology, Boston 2003*, ed. C. Mattusch and A. Donohue, 186–189. Oxford: Oxbow.

DeRose Evans, J. *The Art of Persuasion: Political Propaganda from Aeneas to Brutus.* Ann Arbor: University of Michigan Press.

Dinsmoor, W. B. 1975. *The Architecture of Ancient Greece.* New York: Norton.

Dulière, C. 1979. *Lupa Romana: Recherches d'iconographie et essai d'interpretation.* Brussels-Rome: Études de philologie, d'archéologie et d'histoire anciennes publiées par l'Institut historique belge de Rome.

Fears, J. Rufus. 1981. "The Theology of Victory at Rome: Approaches and Problems." *ANRW* 2.17.2:736–826.

Ferrary, J.-L. 1988. *Philhellénisme et impérialisme: Aspects idéologiques de la conquête romaine du monde hellénistique, de la seconde guerre de Macédoine à la guerre contre Mithridate.* Rome: BEFAR.

Ferroni, A. M. 1993. "Concordia, aedes." *LTUR* 1:316–320.

Flower, H. I. 2010. *Roman Republics.* Princeton: Princeton University Press.

Frank, T. 1924. *Roman Buildings of the Republic: An Attempt to Date Them from Their Materials.* Rome: American Academy in Rome.

Gagé, J. 1933. "La théologie de la victoire impériale." *RevHist* 171:1–43.

———. 1957. "Les clientèles triomphales de la République romaine." *RevHist* 218:1–31.

Giannelli, G. 1982. "Il tempio di Giunone Moneta e la casa di Marco Manlio Capitolino." *BullComm* 87:7–36.

Grønne, C. 1992. "The Architectural Terracottas." In *The Temple of Castor and Pollux I*, ed. I. Nielsen and B. Poulsen, 157–176. Rome: de Luca.

Gros, P. 1973. "Hermodoros et Vitruve." *MEFRA* 85:137–161.

Holleman, A. W. J. 1987. "The Ogulnii Monument at Rome." *Mnemosyne* 40:427–429.

Holliday, P. J. 1980. "'Ad Triumphum Excolendum': The Political Significance of Roman Historical Painting." *Oxford Art Journal* 3:3–10.

Hölscher, T. 1978. "Die Anfänge römischer Repräsentationskunst." *MDAI* 85:351–357.

———. 2006. "The Transformation of Victory into Power: From Event to Structure." In *Representations of War in Ancient Rome*, ed. S. Dillon and K. E. Welch, 27–48. Cambridge: Cambridge University Press.

Hopkins, J. N. 2010. "The Topographical Transformation of Archaic Rome: A New Interpretation of Architecture and Geography in the Early City." PhD diss., University of Texas at Austin.

Humm, M. 1996. "Appius Claudius Caecus et la construction de la via Appia." *MEFRA* 108:693–749.

———. 2005. *Appius Claudius Caecus: La République accomplie.* Rome: École française de Rome.

Jackson, M., and F. Marra. 2006. "Roman Stone Masonry: Volcanic Foundations of the Ancient City." *AJA* 110:403–436.

Lanciani, R. 1875. "Decreto edilizio intorno il sepolcreto esquilino." *BullComm* 3:190–203.

La Rocca, E. 1973. In *Roma medio repubblicana: Aspetti culturali di Roma e del Lazio nei secoli IV e III a.C.,* 241–246. Rome: Assessorato Antichità, Belle Arti e Problemi della Cultura.

———. 1977. "Cicli pittorici al sepolcro degli Scipioni." In *Roma Comune I.* Suppl. to No. 6–7, 14ff.

———. 1984. "Fabio o Fannio: L'affresco medio-repubblicano dell'Esquilino come riflesso dell'arte 'rappresentativa' e come espresione di mobilità sociale." *DialArch* 2:31–45.

———. 1990. "Linguaggio artistico e ideologia politica a Roma in età repubblicana." In *Roma e l'Italia: Radices imperii,* 289–498. Milan: Libri Schweiwiller.

Lawrence, A. W. 1983. *Greek Architecture.* Harmondsworth: Penguin.

Levick, B. 1978. "Concordia at Rome." *Scripta Nummaria Romana: Essays Presented to Humphrey Sutherland,* 217–233. London: Spink and Son.

Lintott, A. 1999. *The Constitution of the Roman Republic.* Oxford: Clarendon Press.

Lissi Caronna, E. 1969. "Rinvenimento di un tratto del diverticulum a via Salaria vetere ad portam Collinam e di tombe della necropoli tra via Aniene e via S. Teresa." *NSc* 23:72–113.

MacBain, Bruce 1980. "Appius Claudius Caecus and the Via Appia." *CQ* 30:356–372.

Mura Sommella, A. 2001. "Primi risultati dale indagini archeologiche in Campidoglio nell'area del Giardino Romano e del Palazzo Caffarelli: Giornata di studio presso l'Istituto Archeologico Germanico di Roma. 3 maggio 2001." *BullComm* 102:261–364.

Nielsen, I. 1993. "Castor, aedes, templum." *LTUR* 1:242–245.

Nielsen, I., and B. Poulsen, eds. 1992. *The Temple of Castor and Pollux.* Rome: de Luca.

Oakley, S. P. 2004. "The Early Republic." In *The Cambridge Companion to the Roman Republic,* ed. H. I. Flower, 15–30. Cambridge: Cambridge University Press.

Oriolo, F. 1996. "Sepulcrum: Fabii/Fannii." *LTUR* 4:288.

Orlin, E. M. 1997. *Temples, Religion, and Politics in the Roman Republic.* Leiden: Brill.

Papi, E. 1999. "Venus Obsequens, aedes ad Circum Maximum." *LTUR* 5:118.

Pelikan Pittenger, M. 2008. *Contested Triumphs: Politics, Pageantry, and Performance in Livy's Republican Rome.* Berkeley: University of California Press.

Pensabene, P. 1980. "La zona sud-occidentale del Palatino." *ArchLaz* 3:65–81.

———. 1982. *Tempio di Saturno: Architettura e decorazione.* Rome: de Luca.

———. 1988. "Scavi nell'area del tempio della Vittoria e del santuario della Magna Mater sul Palatino." *ArchLaz* 9:54–67.

———. 1991. "Il Tempio della Vittoria sul Palatino." *Bollettino di archeologia* 11–12:11 51.

———. 1998. "Vent'anni di studi e scavi dell'Università di Roma 'La Sapienza' nell'area Sud Ovest del Palatino." In *Il Palatino: Area sacra sud-ovest e Domus Tiberiana,* ed. C. Giavarini, 1–154. Rome: L'Erma di Bretschneider.

———. 1999. "Victoria, aedes." *LTUR* 5:149–150.

Pensabene, P., and A. D'Alessio, eds. 2006. "L'immaginario urbano: Spazio sacro sul Palatino tardo-repubblicano." In *Imaging Ancient Rome: Documentation, Visualization, Imagination. Proceedings of the Third Williams Symposium on Classical Architecture Held at the American Academy in Rome, the British School at Rome, and the Deutsches Archäologisches Institut, Rome, on May 20–23, 2004,* ed. L. Haselberger, J. Humphrey, and D. Abernathy, 30–49. Portsmouth, R.I.: Journal of Roman Archaeology.

Pinza, G. 1914. "Le vicende della zona esquilina fino ai tempi di Augusto." *BullComm* 42:117–176.

Pisani Sartorio, G. 1995. "Fortuna et Mater Matuta, Aedes." *LTUR* 2:281–285.

Pisani Sartorio, G., and S. Quilici Gigli. 1987–1988. "A proposito della Tomba dei Cornelii." *BullComm* 92:247–264.

Rawson, E. 1990. "The Antiquarian Tradition: Spoils and Representations of Foreign Armour." In *Staat und Staatlichkeit in der frühen römischen Republik*, ed. W. Eder, 539–589. Stuttgart: Freie Universität Berlin.

Rowe, P. M. 1989. "Etruscan Temples: A Study of the Structural Remains, Origins, and Development." PhD diss., Florida State University.

Rowland, I. D., T. N. Howe, and M. Dewar. 1999. *Vitruvius: Ten Books on Architecture*. New York: Cambridge University Press.

Ruggiero, I. 1991–1992. "Ricerche sul tempio di Portuno nel Foro Boario: Per una rilettura del monumento." *BullComm* 94:253–286.

Santa Maria Scrinari, V. 1968 [1972]. "Tombe a camera sotto via S. Stefano Rotondo presso l'Ospedale di S. Giovanni in Laterano." *BullComm* 81:17–23.

Sehlmeyer, M. 1999. *Stadtrömische Ehrenstatuen der republikanischen Zeit*. Stuttgart: Steiner.

Seidel, J. 1908. *Fasti aedilicii von der Einrichtung der plebejischen Aedilität zum Tode Caesars*. Breslau: Breslauer Genossenschafts-Buchdruckerei.

Smith, C. J. 2006. *The Roman Clan: The Gens from Ancient Ideology to Modern Anthropology*. Cambridge: Cambridge University Press.

Staccioli, R. A. 2003. *The Roads of the Romans*. Los Angeles: Getty Museum.

Stuart Staveley, E. 1959. "The Political Aims of Appius Claudius Caecus." *Historia* 8:410–433.

Talamo, E. 2008a. "La fronte depinta del sepolcro degli Scipioni." In *Trionfi romani*, ed. E. La Rocca and S. Tortorella, 119. Milan: Electa.

———. 2008b. "Frammento di affresco con scena storica." In *Trionfi romani*, ed. E. La Rocca and S. Tortorella, 169. Milan: Electa.

Torelli, M. 2006. "The Topography and Archaeology of Republican Rome." In *A Companion to the Roman Republic*, ed. N. Rosenstein and R. Morstein-Marx, 81–101. Oxford: Blackwell.

———. 2007. "L'urbanistica di Roma regia e repubblicana." In *Storia dell'urbanistica: Il mondo romano*, ed. P. Gros and M. Torelli, 81–157. Rome-Bari: Gius. Laterza & Figli.

Turfa, J. M., and A. G. Steinmayer. 1996. "The Comparative Structure of Greek and Etruscan Monumental Buildings." *PBSR* 64:1–39.

Viscogliosi, A. 1993. "Bellona, aedes in circo." *LTUR* 1:190–192.

———. 1996. *Il Tempio di Apollo in Circo e la formazione del linguaggio architettonico augusteo*. Rome: L'Erma di Bretschneider.

Wiseman, T. P. 1981. "The Temple of Victoria on the Palatine." *AntJ* 61:35–52.

Zevi, F. 1973. In *Roma Medio repubblicana: Aspetti culturali di Roma e del Lazio nei secoli IV e III a.C.*, 238. Rome: Assessorato antichità, belle arti e problemi della cultura.

Ziolkowski, A. 1988. "Mummius' Temple of Hercules Victor and the Round Temple on the Tiber." *Phoenix* 42:309–333.

———. 1992. *The Temples of Mid-Republican Rome and Their Historical and Topographical Context*. Rome: L'Erma di Bretschneider.

AFTERWORD   REFLECTIONS

INGRID E. M. EDLUND-BERRY

NOT SO LONG AGO THE CITYSCAPE OF AUSTIN WAS dominated by two tall buildings, the State Capitol and the Tower of the main campus of the University of Texas at Austin. Each is characterized by a distinct building style, and each is visible from any location throughout the city (fig. A.1). The Capitol, completed in 1888, was at the time considered the Seventh Largest Building in the World,[1] whereas the Tower, completed in 1937, replaced the original Main Building of the campus as part of an effort to expand the library facilities.[2]

Today, downtown Austin is dotted with skyscrapers, of which the tallest building, the Austonian, a condominium with 56 stories, 206 m tall, is considered the tallest residential building west of the Mississippi.[3] Other notable profiles include the 360 Condominiums, with 43 stories, 172 m tall, and the Frost Bank Tower, with 33 stories, 157 m tall.[4] In terms of height, all of these dwarf both the Capitol and the Tower, which are 95 m and 94 m tall respectively.

As we evaluate these individual structures and their part in creating the distinctive appearance of downtown Austin, it seems that the Capitol and the University Tower separately and together once provided the city with a sense of visual focus that it may have lost with the creation of the new skyscrapers. Yet it was not the individual size or proportions of these two buildings that made them stand out; rather, it was the setting and their relationship to each other (fig. A.2). The Capitol still dominates Congress Avenue and the grid of downtown streets as part of the original layout of the city, bounded by the Colorado River and confluent streams.[5]

The University campus was created on the forty acres of land set aside to the immediate north of the original city, in a location originally named College Hill.[6]

For buildings such as these in today's Austin, the monumentality of the structures and their relation to each other is easy to appreciate, regardless of their architectural style, building material, and function. For ancient buildings, however, key information, such as the original height or the arrangement of interior spaces, is often missing, and we must piece together the criteria of ancient monumentality based on a number of factors, of which size may be the most obvious to modern viewers.

To be sure, monumentality is more than sheer size, as Greg Warden has shown in his article on Poggio Colla.[7] The Capitoline temple in Rome, however, discussed by John Hopkins in this volume, may serve as a good test case for evaluating the monumental quality of a building.[8] In many ways it is a perfect example of ancient architecture in central Italy, because of its continuous history from the end of the monarchy into the Empire. Its building history and many restorations are outlined in ancient texts, and the temple is illustrated on coins and reliefs. As a center for the cults of Jupiter Optimus Maximus, Juno, and Minerva it represented the epitome of Roman religion, placed in a structure that reflects strong Etruscan traditions—for example, in the use of Etruscan round mouldings, as discussed by Nancy Winter[9]—but also Roman innovations. Penelope Davies emphasizes that this temple was so huge that it belongs in the category of Greek monumental temples at Samos, at Ephesos, and on Sicily, rather than in the group of temples from central Italy, whether Etruscan or Latial.[10] Although it has been debated whether

Fig. A.1. View of Austin with the State Capitol (*right*) and Tower of the University of Texas at Austin (*left*) (photo I. Edlund-Berry).

Fig. A.2. View of the State Capitol from the doorway of the original Main Building at the University of Texas at Austin (Photo Professor William J. Battle Collection, Department of Classics, University of Texas at Austin, B-Ph003).

the measurements for the podium also reflect the size of the actual temple, all the preserved features, including the architectural terracottas, suggest that this was a truly monumental structure.[11] Yet the ancient authors do not seem to elaborate on the importance of the size of the building, and one wonders what criteria besides size were used in considering the significance of the building. Was it the location, the plan, the size, or the function, or a combination of all of these?

Although the plan and elevation of the Capitoline temple in Rome can only be estimated, the size of the podium, its location on a major hill (fig. A.3), and its importance as a religious center throughout the history of Rome would seem to warrant its recognition as a truly monumental structure. Whether conceived within the Etruscan, Roman, or Mediterranean tradition, its dimensions, 54 × 74 m,[12] correspond well with a building, also located on a hill but with a very different plan and much disputed function, at the Etruscan site of Poggio Civitate (Murlo) (fig. A.4).

During the early years of excavations at Poggio Civitate, the dimensions of the foundation walls that were excavated gradually revealed that they belonged to a large building complex.[13] As discussed by Gretchen Meyers,[14] the plan (see figs. 1.1, 1.3) shows remains of a structure, ca. 60 × 61 m, consisting of a courtyard surrounded on all four sides by rooms of different sizes, some connected to each other, and some entered directly from the courtyard.[15] The width of the foundation walls may indicate that the building originally had two stories. Because of finds of decorative painted terracotta plaques and architectural elements such as simas, antefixes, and ridgepole statues, the building has been interpreted as having had an important function within Etruscan society in the sixth century BCE, and it has been referred to by many different names, of which the purely descriptive include "Archaic Building Complex"[16] and "monumental courtyard building."[17] Efforts to interpret the function of the complex have resulted in additional terms such as "Sanctuary," "Political Sanctuary," and "Archaic Meeting Hall,"[18] all based on the assumption that the size, decoration, and location of the building suggest that it was a gathering point for groups of people from neighboring areas, and that in antiquity (Etruscan or other) any such gathering was under divine protection. Through a twist of language, however, the building is often referred to as a *palazzo* in Italian, a word which ranges in meaning from large building or apartment complex to a dwelling for an aristocrat, or prince, or "palace" in English usage.[19] And, in the understandable quest for an interpretation of the function of the monumental complex at Poggio Civitate, the excavator, Kyle Phillips, first applied the term "sanctuary," but later preferred "Archaic Meeting Hall" to emphasize the many functions of the structure as a central gathering place for neighboring Etruscan cities.[20] Others have connected the plan of the building with the wealth of the material found there (including precious metals and ivories) and the architectural decoration—in particular the ridgepole statues—and regard the building as an important political center and domicile for a ruling family whose ancestors were portrayed in seated and standing statues on the roof.[21]

Even after so many years of continued discussions of the identification of the building and its decoration, I believe that we still have not found the "correct" interpretation of the site within the Etruscan

Fig. A.3. View of the Capitoline Hill in Rome (photo I. Edlund-Berry).

culture of its time. Since the Etruscans seemed to have relied to a large extent on visual iconography rather than the written word to illustrate people and events, the appearance of a large, monumental, richly decorated building would in all likelihood have spoken directly to the Etruscans, whereas we tend to be influenced by the terminology and values of later history and our own times.

Fig. A.4. View toward Poggio Civitate (Murlo) (photo I. Edlund-Berry).

If then the remains of Etruscan buildings alone may not be sufficient to enable us to appreciate their perceived monumentality and allow for a clear-cut interpretation, I believe that by viewing the location of a building complex and evaluating its setting in the landscape, we can gain a different, and perhaps better, understanding of its purpose. Granted that the landscape and vegetation have changed since antiquity, the basic configuration of lines of vision and sense of distance and proximity have remained, and ultimately it is not the measured height of a tower or square meters of a courtyard that would have provided a sense of monumentality and importance for ancient visitors or inhabitants.

Regardless of the size of an Etruscan building, its monumentality was accentuated by its setting in the landscape, appreciated even today by the location of cities and towns perched on hilltops and visible from afar. Even when surrounded by city walls, with tall cathedrals rising over the houses as in Siena (fig. A.5), the Tuscan hills provided a platform for connecting human-made structures with the valleys, slopes, and hilltops. And it is perhaps because of this age-old part of the Tuscan tradition of placing settlements on hills that the Etruscans seem to have paid less attention to the kind of linear monumental setting that was popular with the Romans, as for example in the Imperial fora, and has continued into modern city planning.

Fig. A.5. View toward the Duomo in Siena (photo I. Edlund-Berry).

In taking account of the varying levels of hills, Etruscan architects seem to have used criteria other than direct visibility and a linear approach for the spectators or visitors. Instead, they planted the buildings in such a way that they conformed with the configuration of the hill, as for example Phase II of the complex at Poggio Colla, discussed by Greg Warden[22]—regardless of the means of access, whether this be from a winding road or through a city gate.[23] At other times, the direction may have been determined by the cult, in the case of temples,[24] or intentionally oriented, as at Pyrgi, in a way that suggests that visibility from the sea was more important than the view from the entrance to the temenos proper.[25] Likewise, the layout of sanctuary complexes, with temples, altars, and other structures set within a sacred space, seems to have focused on the individual elements rather than on an architectural master plan.[26] In a similar fashion, as outlined by Tony Tuck, funerary altars were highly visible, reflecting the importance of the rituals conducted there.[27]

The subject of identifying and evaluating monumentality in Etruscan architecture will no doubt continue to create much scholarly interest, coupled with the frustration of not being able to securely identify the function of some building types, a debate which ultimately must remain a theoretical issue separate from archaeological reality. Therefore, acknowledging Nancy Winter's use of the term "courtyard building" for the Archaic structure at Poggio Civitate,[28] I believe that it is wise to observe a degree of respect and humility in superimposing historical and political values onto monuments built by Etruscans and others for whom features such as monumentality and significance were to a large extent determined by factors unknown to us.

In spite of having to rely on less than ideal building materials (tuff, wood, clay) for creating monumental buildings, the Etruscans did remarkably well (as did their neighbors in Latium, as illustrated by Elizabeth Colantoni[29],) and their technology and innovative spirit were inherited and even augmented by their neighbors in Rome. During the Roman Republic, the most massive constructions ranged from the Capitoline temple to the Servian wall and the aqueducts, and with the advent of new building materials (such as the use of concrete), the door was opened to the large-scale buildings of the Roman Empire. Building bigger certainly seems to have been a goal of Imperial Rome, but is that simply the result of the mastery of building techniques such as those discussed by Penelope Davies,[30] or is there a hidden message that size also reflects on the political and cultural excellence of the Romans? And, if so, how much of this did the Romans owe their neighbors, the Etruscans and others, whose landscape and buildings conveyed monumentality by interlacing location, plan, decoration, and, perhaps, function?

Notes

I am honored to contribute to this volume dedicated to a subject to which I have devoted much of my research and teaching. I thank Gretchen Meyers and Michael Thomas for organizing the session of the Annual Meeting of the Archaeological Institute of America in 2009, and I am truly grateful to all the authors for their contributions to this volume and for their friendship.

In planning the illustrations I am indebted to Shelley Rubin and Kimberly Morgan, Austin, Texas, who facilitated access to the building in downtown Austin from which fig. A.1 was taken, and I thank Beth Chichester, senior media support technician, Department of Classics, University of Texas at Austin, for preparing the illustrations for publication. My appreciation of Etruscan architecture was always encouraged by my mentors, Arvid Andrén, Kyle M. Phillips, Jr., and Lucy T. Shoe Meritt, and I dedicate these Reflections to their memory.

1. http://en.wikipedia.org/wiki/Texas_State_Capitol (accessed July 10, 2011).
2. http://en.wikipedia.org/wiki/Main_Building_of_The_University_of_Texas_at_Austin (accessed July 10, 2011).
3. http://en.wikipedia.org/wiki/The_Austonian (accessed July 7, 2011).
4. http://en.wikipedia.org/wiki/List_of_tallest_buildings_in_Austin (accessed July 10, 2011).
5. Barkley 1963, 37–51; http://www.tshaonline.org/handbook/online/articles/hvw13 (accessed July 21, 2011).
6. Berry 1980, 4–5.
7. Warden, supra 82–110.
8. Hopkins, supra 111–138.
9. Winter, supra 61–81.
10. Davies 2006.
11. Hopkins, supra 111–138; Winter, supra 71–73.
12. Mura Sommella 2001 and 2009; Davies 2006; Hopkins 2010.
13. It is easy to forget that the plan of the building that now appears in all books and articles on Etruscan architecture was the result of many years of excavation and study. Thanks to the careful drawings of the poorly preserved foundation walls by the excavation architect, Hans Lindén, SAR, and the meticulous evaluation of the architecture and the related finds by the director, Kyle M. Phillips Jr., the different phases of the plan were published in the preliminary reports and have resulted in the plans of today.
14. Meyers, supra 2–4.
15. Meyers 2003.
16. Phillips 1993, 7. To distinguish between this building and its predecessor at the site, the term "Upper Building" is also used.
17. Winter 2009, 552.
18. Nielsen and Phillips 1985, 64–69; Phillips 1993, 7–12; Edlund-Berry 2011, 9.
19. Torelli 1985, 21–32; Sassatelli 2000, 143–153; Torelli 2000, 67–78; Rowland 2004, 138–139.
20. Phillips 1993, 7–12.
21. The discussion is well summarized by Rowland 2004, 138–139.
22. Warden, supra 83–84.

23. For example, the Portonaccio temple at Veii is placed alongside the foot of the city hill (Colonna 2006, 157, fig. VIII.37), whereas the Sanctuary at Poggio Colla covers the length of the hill (Warden 2011) and the Belvedere temple at Orvieto has its back to the edge of the city hill (Colonna 2006, 161, fig. VIII.43). The contrast between the imposing hill of Orvieto and its surrounding countryside, mentioned by Michael Thomas, supra IX, is further accentuated by the important finds from the Campo della Fiera excavations, very likely to be identified with the site of the pan-Etruscan sanctuary, the fanum Voltumnae, for which see Stopponi 2011. At Castiglion Fiorentino, the Etruscan temple is oriented north–south and would thus have been seen from the side by visitors entering through the gate from the Chiana valley (Edlund-Berry 2010).

24. Edlund-Berry 2006, 119.

25. Colonna 2006, 133, fig. VIII.1. It is worth noting that while the frontality of the Tuscan temple, often marked with a flight of steps, seems to leave no doubt as to how it was accessed, the approach could as easily have been from the side or back of the building.

26. For example, at the sanctuary of Pyrgi, Colonna 2006, 133–134, figs. VIII.1–2.

27. Tuck, supra 41–60.

28. Winter 2009, 552.

29. Colantoni, supra 21–40.

30. Davies, supra 139–165.

Bibliography

Barkley, M. S. 1963. *History of Travis County and Austin, 1839–1899*. Waco: Texian Press.

Berry, M. C. 1980. *The University of Texas: A Pictorial Account of Its First Century*. Austin: University of Texas Press.

Colonna, G. 2006. "Sacred Architecture and the Religion of the Etruscans." In *The Religion of the Etruscans*, ed. N. T. de Grummond and E. Simon, 132–168. Austin: University of Texas Press.

Davies, P. J. E. 2006. "Exploring the International Arena: The Tarquins' Aspirations for the Temple of Jupiter Optimus Maximus." In *Common Ground: Archaeology, Art, Science, and Humanities. Proceedings of the XVIth International Congress of Classical Archaeology, Boston, August 23–26, 2003*, ed. C. C. Mattusch, A. A. Donohue, and A. Brauer, 186–189. Oxford: Oxbow.

Edlund-Berry, I. E. M. 2006. "Ritual Space and Boundaries in Etruscan Religion." In *The Religion of the Etruscans*, ed. N. T. de Grummond and E. Simon, 116–131. Austin: University of Texas Press.

———. 2010. "Öppen eller stängd? Den etruskiska stadsporten som kontaktpunkt och gränsmarkör för stad och landsbygd." In *Tankemönster*, ed. F. Faegersten, J. Wallensten, and I. Östenberg, 45–52. Kristianstad: Kristianstads Boktryckeri.

———. 2011. "Introduction." In *The Archaeology of Sanctuaries and Ritual in Etruria*, ed. N. T. de Grummond and I. Edlund-Berry, 7–15. *JRA* Suppl. 81. Portsmouth, R.I.: Journal of Roman Archaeology.

Hopkins, J. N. 2010. "The Topographical Transformation of Archaic Rome: A New Interpretation of Architecture and Geography in the Early City." PhD diss., University of Texas at Austin.

Meyers, G. E. 2003. "Etrusco-Italic Monumental Architectural Space from the Iron Age to the Archaic Period: An Examination of Approach and Access." PhD diss., University of Texas at Austin.

Mura Sommella, A., et al. 2001. "Primi risultati delle indagini archeologiche in Campidoglio nell'area del Giardino Romano e del Palazzo Caffarelli." *BullCom* 102:261–364.

———. 2009. "Il tempio di Giove Capitolino: Una nuova proposta di lettura." In *Gli Etruschi e Roma, AnnFaina* 16:333–372.

Nielsen, E. O., and K. M. Phillips, Jr. 1985. "3. Poggio Civitate (Murlo)." In *Case e palazzi d'Etruria*, ed. S. Stopponi, 64–69. Milan: Electa.

Phillips, K. M., Jr. 1993. *In the Hills of Tuscany: Recent Excavations at the Etruscan Site of Poggio Civitate (Murlo, Siena)*. Philadelphia: University Museum, University of Pennsylvania.

Rowland, I. D. 2004. *The Scarith of Scornello*. Chicago: University of Chicago Press.

Sassatelli, G. 2000. "Il palazzo." In *Principi etruschi tra Mediterraneo ed Europa*, ed. G. Bartoloni et al., 143–153. Venice: Marsilio.

Stopponi, S. 2011. "Campo della Fiera at Orvieto: New Discoveries." In *The Archaeology of Sanctuaries and Ritual in Etruria*, ed. N. T. de Grummond and I. Edlund-Berry, 16–44. *JRA* Suppl. 81. Portsmouth, R.I.: Journal of Roman Archaeology.

Torelli, M. 1985. "Introduzione." In *Case e palazzi d'Etruria*, ed. S. Stopponi, 21–32. Milan: Electa.

———. 2000. "Le *regiae* etrusche e laziali tra Orientalizzante e Arcaismo." In *Principi etruschi tra Mediterraneo ed Europa*, ed. G. Bartoloni et al., 67–78. Venice: Marsilio.

Warden, P. G. 2011. "The Temple Is a Living Thing: Fragmentation, Enchainment, and Reversal of Ritual at the Acropolis Sanctuary of Poggio Colla." In *The Archaeology of Sanctuaries and Ritual in Etruria*, ed. N. T. de Grummond and I. Edlund-Berry, 55–67. *JRA* Suppl. 81. Portsmouth, R.I.: Journal of Roman Archaeology.

Winter, N. A. 2009. *Symbols of Wealth and Power: Architectural Decoration in Etruria and Central Italy, 640–510 B.C. MAAR* Suppl. 9. Ann Arbor: University of Michigan Press.

Electronic Sources

http://en.wikipedia.org/wiki/List_of_tallest_buildings_in_Austin (accessed July 10, 2011).

http://en.wikipedia.org/wiki/Main_Building_of_The_University_of_Texas_at_Austin (accessed July 10, 2011).

http://en.wikipedia.org/wiki/Texas_State_Capitol (accessed July 10, 2011).

http://en.wikipedia.org/wiki/The_Austonian (accessed July 7, 2011).

http://www.tshaonline.org/handbook/online/articles/hvw13 (accessed July 21, 2010).

Elizabeth Colantoni received her PhD from the Interdepartmental Program in Classical Art and Archaeology at the University of Michigan, where she wrote a dissertation on sacred sites and religion in earliest Rome. She is an assistant professor of Classics in the Department of Religion and Classics and a member of the steering committee for the Program in Archaeology, Technology, and Historical Structures at the University of Rochester. She currently directs excavations at the pre-Roman and Roman-period San Martino site in Torano, Italy, in the territory of the ancient Aequi. Her primary areas of scholarly interest are Roman religion, archaic Rome, and early Italy. She has published articles on Etruscan architectural sculpture; Bacchic cult groups in ancient Italy; and the role of sex and gender in Roman religion. She is currently at work on a book about the archaeology of early Roman religion.

Penelope J. E. Davies is an associate professor in the Department of Art and Art History at the University of Texas at Austin. She earned her PhD in Classical Archaeology from Yale University. Her work focuses primarily on public monuments of Rome and their propagandistic functions. She is author of *Death and the Emperor: Roman Imperial Funerary Monuments from Augustus to Marcus Aurelius* and co-author of *Janson's History of Art*, 7th ed. She is currently working on a book on architecture and politics in Republican Rome, to be published by Cambridge University Press. She is the recipient of fellowships from the American Philosophical Society, the American Council of Learned Societies, and the British School at Rome.

Ingrid E. M. Edlund-Berry is professor emerita in the Department of Classics at the University of Texas at Austin. She received her FK, FM, and FL degrees from the University of Lund, Sweden, and her MA and PhD from Bryn Mawr College. She has excavated at Poggio Civitate (Murlo), Metaponto, and Morgantina. Her publications include *The Gods and the Place: Location and Function of Sanctuaries in the Countryside of Etruria and Magna Graecia (700–400 B.C.)* (1987); *The Seated and Standing Statue Akroteria from Poggio Civitate (Murlo)* (1992); with Lucy Shoe Meritt, *Etruscan and Republican Roman Mouldings. A Reissue* (2000); *Deliciae Fictiles III: Architectural Terracottas in Ancient Italy: New Discoveries and Interpretations* (2006). Her current research focuses on the history and development of architectural mouldings in central Italy and the interaction of non-Romans and Romans during the Roman Republic.

John N. Hopkins is ACLS New Faculty Fellow in the Department of Art History at Rice University. He received his PhD in art history from the University of Texas at Austin in 2010. He has published articles on the construction and reception of the Cloaca Maxima in Rome; his article in *Arqueología de la construcción* II (2010) addresses the colossal scale of the Capitoline Temple and sets the stage for his contribution to this volume. He is currently completing a book on the genesis of Roman architecture and is in collaboration with the UCLA Experiential Technologies Center on a virtual, interactive model of early Rome, to be released by the ACLS Humanities E-Book series. He has been a fellow of the American Academy in Rome, the American Council of Learned Societies, and the Getty Research Institute.

Gretchen E. Meyers received her PhD in classical archaeology from the University of Texas at Austin in 2003 with a dissertation on Etrusco-Italic monumental architecture. She is currently an assistant professor in the Classics Department at Franklin and Marshall College. Her teaching and research interests focus on Etruscan architecture and society, particularly in relation to the development of early Rome. Since 2004, she has served as the director of materials at the Etruscan excavations at Poggio Colla, and she has recently published a study of the site's roof tiles (*JRA* 23). Thanks to funding from the Etruscan Foundation, she is also examining evidence for textile production at Poggio Colla, and is completing a project on the production and significance of ceremonial cloth in Etruria. Her previous publications include articles on Vitruvius and Etruscan architecture and the iconography of Tiberinus, the deified form of the Tiber River.

Michael L. Thomas received his PhD in 2001 from the University of Texas at Austin, where he currently serves as director of the Center for the Study of Ancient Italy. He has taught at UT Austin, Southern Methodist University, and the University of Michigan, and has held a Mellon Postdoctoral Fellowship at Tufts University. His teaching and research center on Etruscan and Roman art, architecture, and archaeology. He has excavated in Italy for eighteen years and he currently co-directs two archaeological projects: at the Roman villa at Oplontis and at the Etruscan site of Poggio Colla in Tuscany. The Oplontis Project received a National Endowment for the Humanities Collaborative Research Grant for 2009 and 2010. His publications include articles in the *Journal of Roman Archaeology*, the *American Journal of Numismatics*, *Etruscan Studies*, and the *Memoirs of the American Academy in Rome*. Thomas currently serves on the advisory council for the Meadows Museum of Art in Dallas.

Anthony Tuck is associate professor of classical archaeology in the Department of Classics at the University of Massachusetts Amherst. He received his PhD from Brown University, studying issues related to Etruscan burial practices. Today, Tuck is the co-director of excavations at the site of Poggio Civitate. He publishes on a range of issues related to the social development and burial practices of the Iron Age and early Etruscan periods and recently completed a volume examining the tombs of the necropolis of Poggio Civitate, Poggio Aguzzo. He also supervised the construction of a comprehensive, publicly available digital archive of all materials related to the history of excavations at Poggio Civitate. In addition to his work in early Italy, he studies the ancient phenomenon of songs that encode information related to patterns in textile production of Central Asia and Western Europe. He is a co-founder of the University of Massachusetts Amherst's Center for Etruscan Studies and is the co-editor of the center's online journal, *Rasenna*. He also serves on the advisory board of the Etruscan Foundation and on the editorial board of the foundation's journal, *Etruscan Studies*.

P. Gregory Warden is a University Distinguished Professor of Art History and associate dean for Research and Academic Affairs at SMU. He received a BA in anthropology from the University of Pennsylvania and MA and PhD degrees in classical and Near Eastern archaeology from Bryn Mawr College. Warden was appointed the 1995–1996 Meadows Foundation Distinguished Teaching Professor and taught at Bowdoin College and the University of Pennsylvania before coming to SMU in 1982. He has authored or co-authored five books and over fifty articles and reviews in journals such as the *American Journal of Archaeology*, *Art History*, *Etruscan Studies*, *Studi Etruschi*, *Römische Mitteilungen*, *Journal of the Society of Architectural Historians*, and the *International Foundation for Art Research Journal*. His research interests have included Greek archaeology (the Demeter sanctuary at Cyrene, Libya); Etruscan archaeology, archaeometallurgy, and ritual; and Roman architecture (the Villa of the Papyri and Nero's Domus Aurea). Warden served as interim director of the Meadows Museum, where he helped organize the exhibit "Greek Vase Painting: Form, Figure, and Narrative. Treasures of the National Archaeological Museum in Madrid" (2003). He coordinated, edited, and contributed to the catalogue of *From the Temple and the Tomb: Etruscan Treasures from Tuscany*. Warden is also the former editor of *Etruscan Studies*, and has been elected to the Istituto di Studi Etruschi e Italici.

Nancy A. Winter received her PhD in classical archaeology from Bryn Mawr College and was librarian of the Blegen Library at the American School of Classical Studies at Athens. While in Athens, she organized and edited the proceedings of two conferences on Greek architectural terracottas, and published *Greek Architectural Terracottas from the Prehistoric to the End of the Archaic Period* (1993). She has recently completed another book, *Symbols of Wealth and Power: Architectural Terracotta Decoration in Etruria and Central Italy, 640–510 B.C.* (2009). Some of her recent authored or co-authored articles include "New Light on the Production of Decorated Roofs of the 6th century B.C. at Sites in and around Rome," *JRA* 22 (2009); "Sistemi decorativi di tetti ceretani fino al 510 a.C.," *Munera caeretana in ricordo di Mauro Cristofani, in Mediterranea* 5 (2009); "The Caprifico Roof in Its Wider Context," in *Il tempio arcaico di Caprifico di Torrecchia (Cisterna di Latina): I materiali e il contesto* (2010); "Solving the Riddle of the Sphinx on the Roof," in *Etruscan by Definition: Papers in Honour of Sybille Haynes* (2009); and *Etruria I: Architectural Terracottas and Painted Wall Plaques, Pinakes c. 625–200 BC* (2010).

Note: Numbers in italics refer to figures.